WELFARE AND EFFICIENCY

Their Interactions in Western Europe
and Implications for
International Economic Relations

BY THEODORE GEIGER
Assisted by FRANCES M. GEIGER

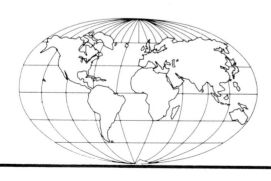

NPA Committee on
Changing International Realities

**Welfare and Efficiency: Their Interactions
in Western Europe and Implications
for International Economic Relations**

CIR Report #4
NPA Report #160

Price $7.00

ISBN 0-89068-045-0
Library of Congress
Catalog Card Number 78-63434

Copyright October 1978
by the
NATIONAL PLANNING ASSOCIATION
A voluntary association incorporated under the laws of
the District of Columbia
1606 New Hampshire Avenue, N.W.   78-8799
Washington, D.C. 20009

C 439

Contents

Welfare and Efficiency:
Their Interactions in Western Europe and Implications for International Economic Relations ·

by Theodore Geiger
assisted by Frances M. Geiger

A Statement by the Committee on Changing International Realities

In accordance with its name, the Committee on Changing International Realities is primarily concerned with current and prospective developments in the international system that are likely to affect the economic well-being of the United States. This study by Dr. Theodore Geiger, NPA's Director of International Studies, assisted by Frances M. Geiger, deals with one such set of new developments abroad: the effects on economic efficiency of the growth of national welfare systems[1] in a number of West European countries and the consequences for the international competitiveness of their economies. In turn, the policies they adopt for coping with the resulting problems have important implications for the nature of international economic relations and hence for the United States. These developments within Western Europe—as well as the possibility that similar welfare/efficiency interactions may manifest themselves in the United States[2]—have not yet received the attention they deserve from Americans.

The reasons for undertaking this study are more fully explained in the author's "Introduction." We wish to stress the importance of the subject with which this study deals. Regardless of whether or not we agree with all of the author's interpretations, we believe that the data and analysis presented in this study merit serious consideration by private-sector groups, government policy makers and opinion leaders generally in the United States. For this reason, we have sponsored the preparation of this study and, without necessarily concurring in its conclusions, we recommend that it be published by the National Planning Association as a report signed by its author.

---

1   These include the full range of governmentally mandated individual benefit payments and services, mandated requirements for worker and/or trade-union participation in corporate decision making, and proposed worker asset-formation and profit-sharing schemes to be managed by the trade unions.— **Robert G. Brown**

2   In recommending publication of this important, path-breaking study, we are concerned that certain of its findings may be misinterpreted or overlooked by those in the United States who are opposed to welfare programs or who argue that the level of government expenditures in this country is already too high for the good of the economy as a whole. Accordingly, we wish to stress certain of the conclusions and implications of this study that refute such contentions.

(1) The study shows that, contrary to the views of the opponents of welfare programs and even of many who favor them, the relationship between welfare and efficiency does not have to be nor has it generally been a tradeoff between the two. Instead, the study concludes that welfare improvements can and often do raise productivity, thereby providing the additional resources needed for further welfare increases in the future. We regret that time did not permit the author to document in greater detail this positive-sum relationship between welfare and efficiency and urge that NPA undertake a follow-up study to do so.

(2) We do not believe that a high level of government expenditures necessarily has an adverse effect on the economy, as do many who argue against desirable increases in U.S. government programs. However, even assuming that there were such a connection between a high level of government expenditures and unfavorable economic consequences for the economy as a whole, the study shows (see table on p. 17) that total government expenditures in the United States (33 percent of GDP in 1977) are still much below the percentages at which such adverse effects may have occurred in Europe. Thus, using their own line of argumentation, those who oppose increases in worthwhile government programs have no empirical grounds for asserting that total government expenditures in the United States are at or near levels that may have caused problems in other countries.

(3) The study provides more information than has yet been available on the extent to which European governments have been resorting to production subsidies and other measures that give their manufactured products unfair advantages in their own markets and in the U.S. and third-country markets, thereby having a harmful impact on employment and income in the United States. We wish to underline the conclusion in the study that the United States needs to take the steps necessary to protect its own workers from the adverse effects of subsidies and other measures in Europe.—**Edward J. Carlough, Murray H. Finley, John H. Lyons, and Glenn E. Watts**

Members of the Committee on Changing International Realities Signing the Statement

G.A. COSTANZO
Chairman; Vice Chairman, Citibank

*GLENN E. WATTS
Vice Chairman;* President, Communications Workers of America, AFL-CIO

OMER G. VOSS
Chairman of the Executive Committee; Vice Chairman, International Harvester Company

JOHN MILLER
Secretary; Vice Chairman and President, National Planning Association

ROBERT B. AMES
Regional Vice President-East, Allis Chalmers Corporation

WILLIAM S. ANDERSON
Chairman of the Board, NCR Corporation

RICHARD C. ASHLEY
Group Vice President, Allied Chemical Corporation

ROBERT A. BELANGER
Senior Vice President, North America Division, Bank of America

HOWARD W. BELL
Director and Financial Vice President, Standard Oil Company of California

RICHARD M. BISSELL, JR.
Consultant

RAYMOND L. BRITTENHAM
Senior Vice President, International Telephone & Telegraph Corporation

* ROBERT G. BROWN
Executive Vice President, Corporate Development, Eaton Corporation

* EDWARD J. CARLOUGH
General President, Sheet Metal Workers' International Association

J.G. CLARKE
Director and Senior Vice President, Exxon Corporation

HAROLD van B. CLEVELAND
Vice President, Citibank

LEROY CULBERTSON
Senior Vice President, Corporate Planning and Budgeting, Phillips Petroleum Company

DONALD J. DONAHUE
Vice Chairman, The Continental Group, Inc.

JAMES L. DUTT
President and Chief Operating Officer, Beatrice Foods Company

GEORGE T. FARRELL
Senior Vice President, Mellon Bank, N.A.

* MURRAY H. FINLEY
President, Amalgamated Clothing and Textile Workers' Union

RAYMOND G. FISHER
Business Consultant

*See footnotes to the Statement.

ROBERT R. FREDERICK
Senior Vice President, Corporate Planning and
Development, General Electric Company

CHARLES S. GANOE
Senior Executive Vice President, The Fidelity Bank of
Philadelphia

RICHARD J. GOODMAN
Vice President, Continental Grain Company

ALLEN GRANT
President, American Farm Bureau Federation

ROGER W. GRAY
Professor, Food Research Institute, Stanford
University

ROGER D. HANSEN
Professor of International Organization, Johns
Hopkins University, School of Advanced
International Studies

G. GRIFFITH JOHNSON
Executive Vice President, Motion Picture Association
of America, Inc.

LEONARD KAMSKY
Corporate Vice President, Business Planning and
Economics Group, W.R. Grace & Company

TOM KILLEFER
Chairman and President, United States Trust
Company of New York

LAWRENCE B. KRAUSE
Senior Fellow, The Brookings Institution

PETER F. KROGH
Dean, Edmund A. Walsh School of Foreign Service,
Georgetown University

JAMES E. LEE
President, Gulf Oil Corporation

LEWIS E. LEHRMAN
President, Rite Aid Corporation

EDWARD LITTLEJOHN
Vice President–Public Affairs, Pfizer, Inc.

* JOHN H. LYONS
General President, International Association of
Bridge, Structural and Ornamental Iron Workers

BARRY J. MASON
Executive Vice President, Republic National Bank of
Dallas

WILLIAM J. McDONOUGH
Executive Vice President, International Banking
Department, The First National Bank of Chicago

WILLIAM R. MILLER
Executive Vice President, Bristol-Myers Company

ALFRED F. MIOSSI
Executive Vice President, Continental Illinois
National Bank and Trust Company of Chicago

WILLIAM S. OGDEN
Executive Vice President, The Chase Manhattan
Bank, N.A.

WILLIAM R. PEARCE
Corporate Vice President, Cargill Incorporated

KEITH R. POTTER
Executive Vice President and Chief Financial Officer,
International Harvester Company

THOMAS A. REED
Group Vice President, International Control Systems,
Honeywell Incorporated

JERRY REES
Executive Vice President, National Association of
Wheat Growers

NATHANIEL SAMUELS
Chairman, Louis Dreyfus Corporation;
Limited Partner, Kuhn, Loeb & Company

DANIEL I. SARGENT
General Partner, Salomon Brothers

WILLIAM F. SPENGLER
President and Chief Operating Officer, International
Operations, Owens-Illinois

HENRY KING STANFORD
President, University of Miami

WALTER STERLING SURREY
Senior Partner, Surrey, Karasik and Morse

THOMAS N. URBAN
Executive Vice President, Pioneer Hi-Bred
International

JOHN A. WAAGE
Vice Chairman of the Board, Manufacturers Hanover
Trust Company

MARINA v. N. WHITMAN
Professor of Economics, University of Pittsburgh

MARK H. WILLIS
President, Federal Reserve Bank of Minneapolis

WILLIAM S. WOODSIDE
President, American Can Company

RALPH S. YOHE
Editor, *Wisconsin Agriculturist*

*See footnotes to the Statement.

The opinions expressed and the recommendations presented in the policy statement are solely those of the individual members of the Committee on Changing International Realities whose signatures are offered hereto and do not represent the views of the National Planning Association or its staff. Committee member's agreement or disagreement with specific points of this statement is expressed in signed footnotes.

Introduction:
The Reasons for This Study

One of the most important developments of the post-World War II period has been the increasing economic interdependence among the nations comprising the international system. From the early 1950s to the early 1970s, world trade grew faster than gross world product. This difference was particularly marked during the period from 1963 to 1970, when world trade increased by 50 percent while gross world product rose by only 44 percent, and from 1970 to 1973, when the rate of growth of world trade was 44 percent and that of gross world product was 33 percent. The United States, too, has experienced an increasing dependence on the world economy: U.S. imports and exports of goods and services totaled only 10.2 percent of gross national product (GNP) in 1965 but rose to 15 percent in 1973 and to 19.1 percent in 1977. In certain commodities, the increase has been even greater: U.S. petroleum imports were only 21.4 percent of U.S. petroleum consumption in 1965 but amounted to 48 percent in 1977.

That increasing international economic interdependence involves both benefits and costs is a generally accepted proposition. The benefits are the long-familiar gains in employment, income and living standards that result from the flows of goods, capital and technology among nations. One type of cost is the adverse effect on the national security and economic well-being of importing countries that would result from restriction of their access to adequate or reasonably priced supplies of needed food, raw materials, fuel, and manufactured products. This kind of cost had to be paid by the oil-importing countries after 1973, when the Organization of Petroleum Exporting Countries (OPEC) tripled the real price of its petroleum exports. Also, the threat to form additional commodity cartels has been used by the developing countries in their efforts to pressure the developed nations into acceding to their demands for a "new international economic order."

Although the possibility of such additional producers' cartels should not be discounted, restricted access to supplies of needed imports—except for the OPEC price rise—has not been the major kind of cost that has been paid for the benefits of greater international economic interdependence. Since the 1974–75 recession, another type of cost has become increasingly important, especially for the industrialized nations comprising the Organization for Economic Cooperation and Development (OECD). This is the adverse impact on a country when its producers are losing their ability to compete with exports from other nations not only in foreign markets but also in their own domestic market. For, unless the labor and capital employed in producing noncompetitive goods and services can readily be shifted to more efficient activities, the country concerned will suffer rising unemployment and stagnant or falling income.

Economic theory postulates that, so long as such adjustments can freely occur, the benefits to employment and income of the new, more efficient activities will sooner or later exceed the short-term costs of shifting out of the noncompetitive lines of production. In reality, however, the condition that adjustments could take place unimpeded has never been wholly met due to the lack of mobility of some of the capital and labor employed in the noncompetitive industries. In recent years, such impediments to shifting resources to more efficient activities have become markedly greater in the OECD nations as economic and social changes—some of the most important of which are analyzed in this study—have reduced the willing-ness and the ability of the affected employers, workers and farmers to make the requisite adjustments or have blocked them completely. In these circumstances, the costs of greater international economic interdependence are not temporary but are persistent and may become cumulative.

One result is that political pressures build up for government actions to prevent further employment and income losses or to reverse those already in-curred. The adversely affected employers, workers and farmers usually demand relief in the forms of tariffs, quotas or other barriers against competing imports and of subsidies to make their exports more price competitive in foreign markets. Palliatives of these kinds are naturally preferred because they do not require employers and workers to change their modes of production or ways of living—remedies that are usually difficult or expensive to adopt and, in some cases, are not feasible for economic or social reasons. In addition, governments are inclined on their own initiative to resort to palliatives, rather than to politically unpopular remedies, to cope with the adverse macroeconomic effects, especially on the balance of payments, of the declining international competitiveness of their producers.

Since the 1974–75 recession, OECD governments have been impelled to adopt a variety of such protectionist measures as political pressures and macromanage-ment constraints have become stronger. Their increased urgency is usually attrib-uted to the lagging recovery from the recession, especially the slower growth of demand for exports compared with the pre-1973 period; to the effects of the OPEC price rise on costs; and to the competition in certain industries (textiles and clothing, steel, shipbuilding, consumer electronics, and so forth) from lower-cost producers in the more advanced developing countries (such as Korea, Taiwan, Hong Kong, Singapore, and Brazil) as well as in Japan. However, there is also a fourth set of developments contributing to the current neomercantilist trend that is not generally recognized, especially in the United States, and that could become much more important in the future.

The study deals with this fourth set of factors in a number of West European countries, where their impact has become particularly significant in recent years. These developments consist of the interrelationships between the growth of national welfare systems, on the one hand, and the efficiency—and hence the international competitiveness—of market-sector enterprises, on the other. In the European members of the OECD under study here, the definition of *national welfare system* is much broader than in the United States. It covers not only the income in cash and kind provided to retired persons and to disadvantaged groups in the United States (e.g., the unemployed, the indigent and the disabled) but also those benefits available to all citizens in European countries regardless of need (e.g., medical care, family allowances and student allowances in addition to free tuition). The definition also includes employee benefits that market-sector enterprises are legally required to provide, such as sick pay, paid vacations and special holiday bonuses, and disability payments, as well as the mandated requirements for worker and/or trade-union participation in corporate decision making through works councils and board representation, and for stock-issuance schemes aimed at eventual trade-union control of these enterprises.

The interrelationships between welfare and efficiency can be positive (i.e., mutually reinforcing) or negative (i.e., mutually diminishing). The study endeavors to distinguish those kinds of, and methods of financing, welfare benefits that raise—or at least do not reduce—efficiency and those that adversely affect the productivity and growth of the market sector, thereby limiting the increase of resources required for further improvements in the welfare system or even compelling its eventual curtailment.

As negative welfare/efficiency interactions accumulate, they strengthen the pressures for neomercantilist policies in countries, such as those studied here, that are highly dependent on foreign trade and investment. This effect occurs in a variety of ways, among the most important of which are the rise in unemployment due to increasing production costs, declining market-sector profits, and in-adequate productive investment; the frustration of popular expectations for continuing improvements in living standards resulting from the combination of inflation with slow or no market-sector growth; and the difficulties of mac-roeconomic management under severe balance-of-payments and budgetary con-straints. These and other developments can be partly or wholly caused by negative welfare/efficiency interactions. They impel governments not only to control im-ports directly but, more important, to provide wage, investment, inventory, and other kinds of subsidies to producers that have the effect of enabling them to export and to compete with imports in the domestic market. These subsidies are not prohibited by the General Agreement on Tariffs and Trade (GATT)—since they are available to all enterprises and not solely to those producing for export—and, in the course of the 1970s, they have become the most significant new manifesta-tion of neomercantilism. Because of the role played in these developments by negative welfare/efficiency interactions, the study is mainly concerned with these adverse effects and devotes much less attention to the beneficial consequences of positive welfare/efficiency interrelationships.

Insofar as negative welfare/efficiency interactions contribute to the neomer-cantilist trend currently and in the future, their effect on the international economic system could be different from that of the three other factors noted earlier. The latter are likely to reduce the degree of international economic interdependence but not to change fundamentally the nature of the international economic system. That is, given the requisite will on the part of the OECD countries, their impact could be limited so that market forces would be preserved as the major determinants of international trade and investment. In contrast, the accumulation of negative welfare/efficiency interactions combined with the politi-cal and economic changes implicit in certain features of the related movement for industrial democracy (analyzed in Chapter 3) could so reduce the role of market forces within the national economies concerned as to necessitate the management of their external relations by government decisions. In turn, this development would make unilateral and joint government actions the effective determinants of international trade and investment. Such a possible long-term outcome would be foreshadowed by policy changes under which export prices would be increasingly divorced from real domestic production costs, trade and payments would more and more be balanced bilaterally or through multilateral intergovernmental clearing arrangements, officially sponsored market-sharing and price-fixing agreements would become more numerous, and exporting and importing companies would be constrained to operate as if they were state-trading organizations even though they were not nationalized. In these and other ways, a truly neomercantilist international economic system could gradually come into existence.

This possible outcome seems far-fetched at the moment. Nonetheless, if its probability is to remain low over the foreseeable future, it is important to recognize that the existing form of international system is by its nature conducive to such a development unless deliberate efforts are made to prevent it. Since the mid-1960s, a genuine *international* system has emerged for the first time in human history. All regions of the planet now contain independent nation-states of varying degrees of military power, economic strength and political effectiveness, and their interactions are characterized by the dynamic tensions between two conflicting sets of motivations. On the one hand, none is willing to sacrifice much, if any, of the economic, security and other benefits of the high degree of international interdependence developed during the 1950s and '60s. On the other hand, each strives to minimize the costs of this integration and to preserve the widest possible freedom of action in both its internal and its external affairs. This ambivalence, inherent in a system of independent nation-states, underlies the current manifestations of neomercantilism in the OECD countries, as well as the stagnation of the movement for greater economic integration within the European Community (EC).

The neomercantilist propensities of the existing international system are stronger than those of the 1950s and early 1960s. True, the system was then, too, composed of nation-states. But, leaving aside the communist countries, they were either recovering from the devastation of World War II, as in Western Europe and Japan, or were newly independent, as in Asia and Africa, or were still accustomed to playing very subordinate roles in world affairs, as in Latin America. In those circumstances, the relative power of the United States to influence the behavior of other nations was much greater than it is today, and so also was their dependence on the United States for protection, reconstruction and development aid, and trade and investment. As the hegemonic leader of the system, the United States had the will and the capacity to persuade or constrain the others to join in the substantial lowering of trade, monetary and investment barriers undertaken during the 1950s and '60s as part of the U.S. design for a reconstructed world order. Both the security of such a system and the maintenance of its unprecedentedly high degree of international economic integration depended in part on the willingness and ability of its hegemonic leader either to assume a substantial portion of the resulting costs or to compel the other members to bear them—as the Soviet Union has largely done within its own hegemonic grouping.

Although the United States continued to protect certain parts of its economy, it nevertheless bore the largest share of the costs of international security and economic integration during the 1950s and '60s. It did so essentially in three ways: (a) by providing massive reconstruction and development aid; (b) by paying most of the human and economic costs of defending the system; and (c) by opening the bulk of its domestic market—by far the biggest and most dynamic on the planet—

to other countries without in many cases requiring equivalent treatment for its own exports. Thus, for the sake of its design for world order, the United States encouraged the formation of customs unions, such as the European Community, and other free-trade arrangements which involved discrimination against its exports; it acquiesced in the continued maintenance of other restrictions, such as Japan's very effective nontariff barriers; and it gave one-way import preferences to Asian, African and Latin American nations.

In the course of the 1960s, the very success of these U.S. policies contributed to important changes in the international system. On the one hand, due in part to the substantial costs borne by the United States, the economic capabilities of the West European states, Japan and the more dynamic developing countries rapidly increased, while most other developing nations sought greater freedom of action as a means of improving the benefits and reducing the costs of participating in the international system. On the other hand, the willingness and ability of the United States to bear so large a portion of the costs of international integration weakened. These two converging trends were manifested during the 1970s in various U.S. actions that reflected the *relative* decline of U.S. economic power—the balance-of-payments deficits, the abandonment of gold convertibility, the falling exchange rate of the dollar, the growing import restrictions. In effect if not in intent, these and other developments are means by which the United States has been trying to shift more of the costs of the integrated system to other countries. At the same time, however, the latter have been experiencing the internal pressures and external changes that have impelled them to resist or offset the imposition of greater costs on their own economies. Thus, the question today is whether the high degree of international integration achieved during the 1960s can be maintained in a system of independent nation-states that no longer has a hegemonic leader with the disproportionately great economic capabilities possessed by the United States during the two postwar decades.

Negative welfare/efficiency interactions have been among the most important domestic developments that, in the course of the 1970s, have been reducing the willingness and ability of the OECD nations, including the United States, to incur the adjustment costs necessary to maintain the high degree of international economic interdependence attained under the U.S. hegemony of the postwar period. The social forces expressed in the expectations for rising living standards, improved quality of life, better welfare benefits, greater equality of income, more paid leisure, and the other related movements analyzed in this study are among the most deeply rooted in modern Western societies and exert powerful influences on the actions of governments. Accordingly, the problem of minimizing their negative effects and fostering their positive effects on economic efficiency is one of the most difficult issues confronting policy makers in the OECD countries. And, to the extent to which they fail to resolve it constructively in the coming years, the prospects for the emergence of a neomercantilist international economic system will increase.

The study does not analyze these complex processes in detail but only to the extent necessary to sketch the origins and nature of the social and economic trends involved and their existing and probable future consequences for the international economic system. Nor, because it is primarily concerned with economic developments, does the study do more than indicate briefly their potentially serious political implications within Western Europe. Also, it does not deal with all of the European members of the OECD but only with the six nations in Northern Europe—Denmark, Germany, the Netherlands, Norway, Sweden, and the United Kingdom—in which national welfare systems provide the most comprehensive and liberal benefits and political or other factors do not complicate or obscure welfare/efficiency interactions. The latter reason accounts for the omission of Italy, in which current or prospective political developments strongly affect economic conditions. Nonetheless, the analysis and conclusions are generally relevant to that nation and to Belgium, Canada, France, and other OECD members—including the United States—that could not be specifically studied due to limitations of funds and time.

The data and analyses in this study are derived not only from published materials but also from extensive interviews in the countries involved with government officials and politicians, business and trade-union leaders, university scholars and students, journalists, and others, as well as with members of the secretariats of the OECD and the EC.

The main purpose of the study is to bring to the attention of government and private-sector policy makers important developments which, particularly in the United States, have tended to be overlooked. Also, it is hoped that the study will stimulate others to test the hypotheses and expand the analyses offered in it through the more comprehensive and detailed empirical research suggested in the concluding chapter and in Appendix A.

* * *

This study is part of the research program sponsored by NPA's Committee on Changing International Realities and Their Implications for U.S. Policy. It was funded jointly by the National Planning Association and the U.S. Department of State (under Contract 1722–620185). The analyses and conclusions contained herein are not to be interpreted as representing the official opinions or policies of the Department of State or the views of the National Planning Association and its Committee on Changing International Realities.

The author is grateful to the members of the Committee on Changing International Realities for the opportunity to undertake this study and for their helpful comments on the preliminary draft. His special thanks are due to Edward Littlejohn, chairman of the subcommittee for this study, whose personal interest and encouragement and many constructive suggestions have been invaluable.

This project could not have been completed without the assistance of Frances M. Geiger, whose participation in the interviews, help in finding relevant data, sound advice in interpreting them, and editorial skills made essential contributions to such merit as the study may possess.

Neil J. McMullen, NPA's Deputy Director of International Studies, participated in formulating the conceptual approach used in the study, developed the theoretical analysis presented in Appendix A, and provided valuable comments on the draft. Harold van B. Cleveland, Vice President of the Citibank, very kindly wrote the appendix on the meaning of efficiency. Peter Morici and Gordon Donald, international economists at NPA, carefully reviewed the entire text and made helpful suggestions. Finally, the author's deep appreciation must be expressed to the many people in Europe who were willing to answer questions, provide data and react to his ideas.

The author takes full responsibility for the information, analyses and interpretations in this study.

Washington, D.C.   Theodore Geiger
July 1978

ABOUT THE AUTHOR

Theodore Geiger is Vice President and Director of International Studies of the National Planning Association and also Adjunct Professor of International Relations in the School of Foreign Service, Georgetown University. His previous books include *Tales of Two City-States: The Development Progress of Hong Kong and Singapore* (London: The Macmillan Press, Ltd., revised hardcover edition 1975; Washington, D.C.: National Planning Association, original paperback edition 1973), with Frances M. Geiger; *The Fortunes of the West: The Future of the Atlantic Nations* (Bloomington: Indiana University Press, 1973); *The Conflicted Relationship: The West and the Transformation of Asia, Africa and Latin America* (New York: McGraw-Hill for the Council on Foreign Relations, 1967); and *The Economy of the American People* (Washington, D.C.: National Planning Association, 1958; 3rd edition revised, 1967), with Gerhard Colm. Dr. Geiger has also written numerous monographs and journal articles on international trade and monetary problems; European economic and political integration; economic development and sociocultural change in Asia, Africa and Latin America; interrelations of world politics and world economics; and other subjects.

NOTE ON EXCHANGE RATES

All current conversions of foreign currencies into U.S. dollars are at the rates prevailing on June 30, 1978 as published in the *New York Times* and for past years at the average annual rate prevailing in that year.

The Problem
of Welfare and Efficiency

1

Rarely are even the most beneficial developments in human societies accomplished without either unexpected costs or unanticipated adverse consequences.

During the 1960s and early 1970s, most West European countries instituted unprecedented increases in health services, retirement pensions, educational benefits, family allowances, rent and house-owning subsidies, child-care facilities, unemployment compensation, and other forms of welfare in cash and in kind, as well as in the other services provided by governments and required of private enterprises. By redistributing income, these measures substantially raised the living standards of many people in the OECD nations; and, by improving the skills, health and morale of their workers, as well as by helping to sustain aggregate demand, they also contributed to the increasing productiveness of their economies as a whole. At the same time, however, the cost of such gains had to be met by higher taxes, which reduced the earned disposable income of most households, or by greater government borrowing, which had similar effects through inflation on real income. In addition, the big increases in the size and variety of welfare and other government services and of those that private enterprises must provide, although in many cases desirable in themselves, began to weaken the incentives to work, save, invest, and innovate, thereby threatening to impair the very economic productiveness that makes high and rising living standards possible.

This relationship between desired gains and unanticipated costs and adverse consequences is the essence of the problem of welfare and efficiency as it has arisen in the OECD countries in recent years. In this chapter, the historical background of the problem is sketched, and its nature and present and prospective significance are viewed in a variety of analytical perspectives that will be explored in greater detail in subsequent chapters.

HISTORICAL BACKGROUND OF THE PROBLEM

The welfare/efficiency problem has its roots in some of the most basic social and cultural trends in Western civilization going back to the 11th century. Of central importance has been the gradually growing conviction that human beings are capable of understanding and controlling the processes of nature and society so as to obtain continually rising material and psychic satisfactions. This conviction played a major role in motivating the technical advances and institutional changes that culminated in the industrial revolution in the 19th century—that is, in the development and application of new production and management techniques yielding massive continuing increases in economic output on a scale previously unknown in human history. In turn, this unprecedented expansion of resources made it possible for the first time in human experience to realize the aspirations for progressive improvements in the conditions of life that had hitherto seemed attainable, if ever in this world, only in some distant utopian future.

During the first half of the 19th century when laissez-faire economic theory and utilitarian political theory predominated, it was generally expected that the "invisible hand" of untrammeled market forces would not only produce continuing increases in resources but would also distribute them in ways that would bring "the greatest good to the greatest number." During the second half of the century, however, there was a gradual recognition that inherent "market imperfections" and disproportionate political power and economic capabilities were preventing certain groups of people from sharing adequately in the benefits of economic productiveness and would continue to do so unless remedial measures were adopted. Bismarck's pioneering social legislation in Germany was the first major step for assuring that the old, the sick and the disabled could maintain a minimum necessary level of consumption despite their inability to work.

In the course of the 20th century, further important changes have occurred in the productiveness of Western economic systems, in the size and variety of the gains expected by their people in consumption and welfare benefits, in the rationale governing the distribution of income, and in the agencies by which it is effected. Except for intervals of depression, the Western economies enjoyed continuing growth of output as successive technological and organizational advances raised productivity at compounded rates not only in industry but also in agriculture. These developments were particularly pronounced after World War II when the gross national products of OECD countries rose at unprecedented rates for nearly three decades—that is, until the great inflation and severe recession of the mid-1970s. The resulting abundance of resources during the postwar period both stimulated and made possible the satisfaction of expectations for increasing earned income and for expanding the volume and variety of welfare benefits and other government services.

At the same time, the conceptions of distributive justice that validated the division of the fruits of mounting productivity were also changing. Historically, these principles have both reflected and helped to maintain the institutional characteristics of the societies in which they prevailed. Thus, in the largely nonmarket agrarian economy and authoritarian social structure of Western society in the early middle ages, income distribution was conceived to be a function of inherited social status, with lord and serf each entitled to the share appropriate to his position in the social hierarchy. With the expansion of the market economy that began in the 11th century, the distributional principle was broadened to include the conception of income as a justified return for investment and risk-taking and as a merited reward for personal achievement, skill and effort. Also, the Judaeo-Christian ethic encouraged with greater or lesser effectiveness the distribution—or rather redistribution by religiously motivated individuals—of income for the relief of need. During the past 100 years, this personalistic concept of charity as a form of income redistribution has been progressively secularized and stripped of its voluntary element, eventuating in the contemporary welfare principle of the large-scale redistribution of income by impersonal government agencies in response to need.

A new principle of distributive justice emerged during the 1960s to join—perhaps eventually to supersede—the others. As yet influential only in Northern Europe, it is the notion that every human being is entitled to an adequate income by natural right—by legal right, too, when embodied in legislation—regardless of status, investment, risk-taking, merit, or need.[1] In Scandinavia and the Netherlands particularly, this natural-right conception is increasingly expressed in combination with the principle of equality—that is, every person is entitled to a reasonably *equal share* of the national income as a matter of right.

As will be explained in subsequent chapters, the implementation of the egalitarian natural-right distributional principle currently takes two forms. One involves reducing the wage differentials among the various grades of unskilled and skilled workers by raising the incomes of the former at much faster rates than those of the latter. The second aims to provide the nonworking portion of the population with incomes equal to, or at least not much below, those earned by the economically active portion. The idea is that people who cannot work—and some Europeans believe even those who do not wish to work—should not *ipso facto* be penalized relative to those who are able and willing to work. Accordingly, welfare benefits for the nonworking portion of the population in most North European nations have been raised closer to the earnings of the employed portion in recent years, and they are also now indexed to inflation and, in some countries, to the average annual increase in wages. The ultimate implication of the egalitarian natural-right principle is that, insofar as work continues to be regarded as a good, it—like virtue—becomes its own reward.

WELFARE CRITERIA AND EFFICIENCY CRITERIA

These current developments in the value systems of Western societies involve major changes in the distribution of income and the rewards for work effort and productive investment. They may be viewed in economic terms as representing the culmination of a trend that has been under way in Western societies for the past 100 years—the increasing substitution of welfare criteria for efficiency criteria in economic decision making. This substitution has been taking place in decisions affecting the national economy as a whole (macro level) and in those made within the individual enterprises (micro level) comprising the economy.

The paramountcy of efficiency criteria is a comparatively recent phenomenon in the history of Western society. It reflects the particular development from the 16th to the 19th centuries of what Max Weber called "the specific and peculiar rationalism of Western culture."[2] Until the Protestant Reformation—specifically

---

1   A natural-right justification for distributive justice has been implicit or explicit in the various forms of 19th- and 20th-century socialism. But, it has provided the rationale for political action and legislation in the West European nations only since World War II and especially since the mid-1960s in Northern Europe.

2   The very summary historical account given here is derived from the fuller analysis in Theodore Geiger, *The Fortunes of the West: The Future of the Atlantic Nations* (Bloomington: Indiana University Press, 1973), Chapter II.

until the spread of Calvinistic ways of thinking and acting—there was no doubt that an economy and its individual enterprises should serve a wide variety of social values, many of which took priority over the maximization of economic returns. In the rising European dynastic states of the early modern period, patrimonial values—as Weber characterized them—prevailed at both macro and micro levels. For the monarch and his officials, the national economy was expected to operate in ways that advanced dynastic and territorial ambitions and family and individual status, and provided resources for luxurious living, ceremonial display, indiscriminate or compassionate charity, sports and amusements, and the support of art and science. To produce and allocate the resources needed for these purposes, the national economy was regulated and controlled, both internally and externally, in accordance with government policies that came to be collectively designated as *mercantilism*. Similarly, at the level of the firm, financiers and merchants sought not only the efficient increase of their wealth but also various personalistic goals unrelated to their business activities per se—the preservation and advancement of their families' social status, the achievement of noble rank and political power, conspicuous consumption and leisure, patronage of art and learning, support of religious institutions and charities, and civic contributions.

However, to the new Calvinist entrepreneurs who emerged in the 16th century, these pursuits of the kings and officials of the patrimonial state and of the older and then-dominant type of businessmen

> were deemed sinful because wasteful, and frivolous because functionally irrelevant.
>
> The Calvinists' sense of righteous mission to labor in their occupations with rational self-control and single-minded efficiency, no less than the specific interests inherent in the economic activities to which they believed God called them, predisposed the members of these sects in England and on the continent to become the most stubborn enemies of the patrimonial state [and of its economic policies no less than of its political absolutism and religious uniformity]. . . . They condemned personal absolutism and royal centralization; official supervision and detailed regulations, monopolies and trade restrictions; . . . [and demanded] religious independence, communal autonomy and freedom of enterprise. . . .
>
> [During the 18th and 19th centuries], the gospel of work, the morality of conscientious performance of occupational responsibilities, the logic of impersonal rational calculation, and decision making by strict efficiency criteria gradually spread far beyond the professing membership of the sects that had developed and nurtured [these values and behavioral norms]. Inculcated by innumerable practical moralists and popular rule books, these increasingly secularized norms of behavior . . . contribute[d] powerfully to the development of industrialism, a unique economic system destined to be decisively more productive than any previously evolved on the planet.[3]

Nor was it an accident that, in the 19th century, the laissez-faire concept of the liberal state reached its fullest realization in those countries, especially the English-speaking nations, most heavily influenced by Calvinism. For, in essence,

---

3   Geiger, *The Fortunes of the West*, p. 28.

the liberal state represented a secularized manifestation of the Protestant ethic— no longer expressed only in the life-style and business activity of Calvinist entre- preneurs but now also in the purposes and system of order of the national society as a whole. In effect, the principle of strict functional relevance was applied to the political regime: both the goals and the functions of government in liberal states were drastically pruned in accordance with the laissez-faire ideal that administra- tion should be limited to preserving national security and domestic order, dispens- ing justice, and collecting the minimum revenues necessary for these activities. Accordingly, the liberal states abolished virtually all domestic restrictions on pri- vate economic activity, and—although Great Britain alone adopted free trade— many nontariff controls on foreign trade and monetary movements were also eased or eliminated.

In the liberal-state ideal, the steady progress of society and the improvement of social welfare were expected to result from the rigorous and voluntary applica- tion of the principle of functional relevance by self-instigating and self-responsible individuals operating more or less freely in a decentralized social order. But, as explained above, during the second half of the 19th century, it gradually became evident that efficiency criteria alone were not going to enable all social groups to share more equitably in the benefits of the rapidly increasing productivity. Hence, over the past 100 years and especially since World War II, Western societies have been seeking to realize these social goals by reversing the liberal state's earlier substitution of efficiency criteria for the noneconomic values of the former pat- rimonial order. In essence, the determinative power of efficiency criteria has been steadily eroded by the increasing importance of welfare criteria in economic decision making at both macro and micro levels. And, to ensure that resources would in fact be allocated in accordance with such decisions, Western govern- ments have greatly increased the proportion of gross national product they control directly through taxation and borrowing and have expanded once again their regulation of the activities of private enterprises within the domestic economy and in external trade and monetary relationships.

POSITIVE-SUM AND NEGATIVE-SUM OUTCOMES

It is essential to emphasize that there is *no necessary conflict* between welfare criteria and efficiency criteria. The substitution of the former for the latter can and often does improve both welfare and efficiency. In other words, the two sets of decision criteria can be mutually reinforcing—in effect producing a positive-sum outcome, i.e., more of both. Thus, during the past 100 years, improvements in the nutrition, health, housing, education, and other kinds of welfare of the people as a whole certainly contributed to increases in the productive efficiency of the labor force both directly and by raising workers' morale. Although initially in the 19th century these improvements were resisted as wasteful and inefficient expendi- tures, they were eventually recognized as necessary and effective investments in the development of the human resources needed to increase economic productivity.

Nonetheless, the substitution of welfare criteria for efficiency criteria can also be a negative-sum game (more fully defined in the next section), that is, one in which not only efficiency but, sooner or later, welfare too would be reduced. For, if the resources needed to finance research and development and capital investment are diverted to welfare expenditures or if the incentives to work, save, invest, and innovate are impaired by the provision of excessive welfare benefits, the goods and services required to meet the consumption demands generated by the rising expectations of families and individuals will soon not be forthcoming in sufficient volume, in the desired variety and quality, and at reasonably stable prices. In these circumstances, not only will living standards stagnate or even deteriorate but also the ability of the government and of private enterprises to finance welfare benefits and other services will eventually decline. *Thus, too much or the wrong kinds of welfare can, by undermining efficiency, lead in time to a reduction of welfare as well.*

Some advocates of increasing welfare insist that such a negative-sum outcome is impossible because market-sector goods and public "goods" are mutually substitutable and can be "traded off" for one another. That is, they maintain that, because the marketed goods and services purchased by families and individuals with their aftertax earnings and the welfare and other benefits they receive in cash or kind from the government and private enterprises together comprise their total income, an increase in either component is an equally acceptable way of improving their level of living. The conclusion drawn is that, as the economy grows, living standards can—and should—be raised by increasing the supply of public goods while limiting or reducing the consumption of marketed goods. However, the assumption is mistaken in two related respects.

First, most welfare benefits and other government services in fact require resources drawn from the market sector both for the necessary capital investments and for operating purposes—that is, to provide welfare benefits in cash and kind and to pay the salaries (and hence meet the consumption demands) of the government employees administering the welfare programs. Second, experience to date in the OECD countries shows that earned disposable income and the welfare and other benefits provided by the government and private enterprise are not generally regarded as substitutes for one another. Most people seek increases in both. Given the power of the government to preempt the resources it requires by command decisions, the resources available to the market sector and the returns to investment in it may be insufficient to provide the levels of production, investment and exports needed to maintain adequate rates of economic growth and job creation, reasonably stable prices, international competitiveness and balance-of-payments equilibrium. Such adverse effects can be induced even when an economy is operating below its effective capacity by the disincentives to work, save, innovate, and invest that can result from certain kinds of welfare and other government policies, as will be explained in subsequent chapters.

The expectation of continuing increases in the consumption of both marketed goods and public goods that has become widespread in Western Europe since the mid-1960s is unfamiliar to many Americans because of the differences between European welfare systems and that of the United States. When Americans think of their welfare system, they usually have in mind the federal, state and local government programs designed to help or to support not the entire population but only those families and individuals with incomes below the defined poverty level. And, even when all Americans are eligible to participate in a welfare program—e.g., social security retirement, unemployment compensation, accident and disability benefits—they do so only during certain limited periods of their lives, notably when they are unemployed or in old age. Thus, the welfare system is not perceived as contributing on a day-to-day basis to the living standards of most Americans. It is otherwise in Western Europe. Although the coverage and composition of welfare systems vary among the West European countries, it is a fair generalization to state that welfare benefits play an important role in the daily lives of virtually all Europeans. Health care and sick pay, family and child allowances, educational subsidies in addition to free public schooling, rent subsidies or subsidized home ownership, maternity and even paternity benefits, child-care centers, vacation bonuses in addition to paid leave, and other welfare benefits are available to most Europeans. True, some welfare services (e.g., education supplements, housing subsidies, free child-care centers) may be income-related, declining and eventually terminating as incomes rise. But, the great majority of Europeans are continually in receipt of some kinds of welfare benefits. Hence, they tend to expect both improved welfare services and increased earned income, and they are opposed to the higher taxes needed to finance the former because direct taxes reduce the latter and indirect taxes lower its purchasing power.

There is, however, an American equivalent of this European dilemma. Although most Americans react negatively to any government activity labeled as "welfare," they tend to favor such a program when called by a functionally descriptive title—for example, better health care for the poor and the aged, assistance for indigent families in which none of the adults are able to work, and providing food to the hungry. Also, many Americans believe that the government should substantially expand its provision of the public goods that are not ordinarily regarded as part of the "welfare" system, such as environmental protection and improvement, urban redevelopment and regional development, mass transportation, parks and wildlife refuges, and other types of recreational facilities. At the same time, they are increasingly objecting to the higher taxes needed to finance many government programs, as recently demonstrated in California and perhaps soon in other states. As in Europe, this opposition reflects their desire to maintain or raise their aftertax earned incomes. Thus, Americans, too, want both improved welfare—under other names—and greater earned income.

DEFINITIONS

Before proceeding further with the analysis, it would be desirable to define more precisely the key terms and concepts introduced in the foregoing pages.

Welfare is used in this study in a very broad sense. As noted earlier, it includes not only the social security and other transfer payments with which Americans are familiar (e.g., unemployment compensation, retirement pensions and supplementary assistance, accident and disability payments, aid to poor families with dependent children, and food stamps) but also European-type health services and sick pay, family and child allowances, student stipends, housing subsidies, maternity and paternity benefits, child-care centers, and so forth. The term covers public education at all levels, environmental protection, agricultural and industrial subsidies, and other forms of income maintenance, supplementation and redistribution provided by government agencies. It also includes the welfare-type benefits that private enterprises are legally required to provide directly—redundancy (severance) pay, vacation bonuses in addition to paid leave for a required number of weeks, high disability payments, and others. Thus, welfare involves (a) action by government authorities that is primarily intended (b) to change the pattern of resource allocation to production, consumption and investment and/or (c) to redistribute income between market and nonmarket sectors (defined below) and among social groups. By definition, therefore, employee benefits that are not legally required but are granted voluntarily by private enterprises or under collective-bargaining agreements are excluded from this study.

Efficiency is used in the conventional sense as maximization of current output of goods and services with the available factors of production and with adequate provision of resources for future growth.[4]

Positive-sum interactions occur when both welfare and efficiency are increased or when welfare is improved without significant loss of efficiency. A welfare improvement affects efficiency in these ways by (a) increasing the supply of marketed goods and services through improving the quality of the factors of production at the same time as, or soon after, it increases aggregate demand or (b) increasing aggregate demand in conditions of general underutilization of the factors of production.

Negative-sum interactions involve significant losses of efficiency and eventually of welfare as well. They usually occur when a welfare improvement adversely affects efficiency by reducing the supply and increasing the real costs of the factors of production in the short or medium term (a) by lowering the incentives to work and/or (b) by lowering the incentives to innovate and invest.

Market sector comprises the individuals and organizations producing goods and services for sale at prices intended to cover factor costs and yield a return on the investment involved. In national income accounting terms, *market-sector income* refers to the payments for the services of land, capital and labor, minus taxes and government borrowing, in those activities where goods and services are produced for sale at prices intended to cover factor costs and yield a return on investment. These aftertax income payments are equal to the value of goods and services produced in the market sector less taxes and government borrowing and also are equal to market-sector factor payments less taxes and government borrowing. *Nonmarket-sector income* refers to payments for the services of land, labor and capital employed in government activities, all government transfers and subsidies, and government purchases of final goods and services from the market sector. This income is financed through taxation and government borrowing. The government disperses this income by producing government services (national defense, justice, roads, and so forth), by providing transfers (welfare benefits, debt service, and so forth), and by subsidizing public and private enterprises.

The distinction between market-sector income and nonmarket-sector income does not coincide with that between the private sector and the public sector as conventionally defined in national income accounting. The main differences are that all transfer payments in cash, all services provided in kind by government

---

4   For a more philosophical discussion of the economic meaning of efficiency and its relation to the market economy, see Appendix B.

agencies, and the directly or indirectly subsidized deficits of public and private enterprises are included in nonmarket-sector income. However, government-owned enterprises that are able to cover their factor costs without subsidies or other government preferences are included in the market sector. Because of these differences, public-sector data in the conventional national accounts give only a partial indication of the magnitude and composition of nonmarket-sector income, and the statistics needed to quantify it more accurately are not yet available in OECD countries.

INDICATORS OF POSSIBLE ADVERSE WELFARE/EFFICIENCY RELATIONSHIPS

Subsequent chapters will analyze the specific beneficial and adverse effects of welfare/efficiency relationships, the experiences of selected OECD countries in these respects, and the implications of present and prospective welfare/efficiency developments for U.S. policy. Before turning to these subjects, however, it would be helpful to present a set of indicators that could signal when negative-sum outcomes of welfare/efficiency interactions were already under way at macro and micro levels or would be the likely consequences of existing policies and trends.

There are several ways of conceptualizing the kinds of interactions involved in welfare/efficiency relationships at the macro level. That presented in the next two paragraphs is derived from the formulation developed by Robert Bacon and Walter Eltis in their recent study of the British economy.[5] A different approach—but consistent with that of Bacon and Eltis—has been worked out by Neil J. McMullen for this study and is explained in considerable detail in Appendix A. The difficulty does not lie in conceptualizing welfare/efficiency relationships but in the scarcity of the data needed to quantify many of the specific indicators of negative-sum interactions.

The starting point of a conceptual framework derived from the Bacon and Eltis formulation is the relationship between the market and nonmarket sectors of the economy of an OECD country. The question of their relative sizes, or shares of GNP, can be of critical importance. It involves two crucial issues: (1) whether the market sector retains enough of its own output to maintain adequate rates of growth of productivity and of job creation to satisfy the consumption, investment and export requirements it has to meet in the future; and (2) whether welfare and other government policies and wage and tax rates are conducive to the requisite attitudes toward and incentives for work, saving, innovation, and productive investment.

The trends relevant to these two crucial questions can be manifested in several different ways. If the government for its own use, the people employed by the government and by other nonmarket institutions, and the nonworking recipients of welfare benefits absorb too much marketed goods and services, then insufficient resources will remain in the market sector to provide for the consumption claims of its workers and of the owners of capital; for the research and develop-

---

5   Robert Bacon and Walter Eltis, *Britain's Economic Problem: Too Few Producers*, 2nd edition (London: The Macmillan Press, Ltd., 1978).

ment and the investment needed for productivity growth, job creation, and the maintenance of international competitiveness; and for the exports necessary to help finance the required imports. If the aftertax earned income of market-sector workers and salaried employees is too small relative to their consumption expectations for marketed goods and services or if the welfare payments they receive when not working are sufficiently close to their aftertax earned income, then market-sector workers are likely to press for a larger share of market-sector resources through wage increases in excess of productivity growth or to reduce their productivity through greater *paid* leisure (e.g., high absenteeism rates, more frequent use of sick leave, shorter working hours, longer vacations, and earlier retirements). If the aftertax return on capital invested in the production of marketed goods and services is too small, then the owners and managers of productive enterprises in the market sector will have neither the resources nor the incentives to maintain adequate levels of research and development and of investment.

Using total expenditures of central and local governments as a very crude indicator of the size of the nonmarket-sector, Table 1–1 below has been compiled to show the growth of nonmarket sectors as percentages of the gross domestic products (GDP) of the six countries surveyed in Chapter 4 for selected years from 1965 to 1977. Intercountry comparisons should not be made because a government-expenditures series prepared on a common statistical basis is not available, and national statistics with different definitions and coverage have had to be used. However, the table does indicate the growth of each country's nonmarket sector over the period.

Table 1–1. Total Public Expenditures as Percent of Gross Domestic Product at Market Prices

	1965	1970	1975	1977
Denmark	31	40	46	46
Germany	37	38	48	47
Netherlands	38	44	55	55 (1976)
Norway	34	43	50	51
Sweden	35	43	52	62
United Kingdom	37	41	50	44
United States	27	32	35	33

Sources: Various national statistics and estimates.

The regression analysis undertaken by Neil J. McMullen, explained in Appendix A, shows that, over the period 1965–75, increased productivity was positively correlated with investment as a proportion of GNP and negatively correlated with high levels of government expenditures and high rates of inflation. Statistical correlations per se do not constitute proof of a causal connection, but they do indicate a reasonable probability that such a relationship may exist, particularly if the variables involved are parts of the same operational system—in this case, the economy. Hence, statistical correlations are valuable tools for formulating hypotheses regarding causal relationships that can then be verified by more or less direct empirical means.

Based on both the empirical work done for this study and the theoretical analysis in Appendix A, it may tentatively be concluded that the growth of the relative size of the nonmarket sector is a necessary but not a sufficient condition for the adverse market-sector/nonmarket-sector interactions sketched above. Institutional capabilities and social values, attitudes and norms of behavior also play essential roles in these interactions. A country—e.g., Germany—whose institutions and behavioral norms remain conducive to innovation, managerial dynamism and conscientious work effort may be able to sustain a bigger income share for its nonmarket sector relative to that of its market sector without adverse consequences than another country—e.g., the United Kingdom—in which sociocultural conditions are significantly less favorable to these prerequisites for productivity increases and efficiency. But, at some point in the relative growth of the nonmarket sector's income share, the former nation, too, would begin to experience negative-sum welfare/efficiency interactions. More empirical research than funds and time permitted for this study will be needed to determine with reasonable certainty for any country the approximate percentage of GDP at which the growth of the nonmarket sector generates significant adverse effects.

Specific indicators at the macro level that negative-sum welfare/efficiency interactions may be occurring include changes in:

▶ the size and components of the nonmarket sector's income;

▶ the percentage of marketed goods and services acquired by the nonmarket sector;

▶ the number of people employed in the nonmarket sector and of nonworking welfare recipients relative to the number of people working in the market sector;

▶ the size of the disposable income for purchasing marketed goods and services of the people employed in the nonmarket sector and of the nonworking welfare recipients relative to the total output of the market sector;

▶ the rate of growth of productivity in the market sector;

▶ the relative returns to labor and capital in the market sector;

▶ the preference for leisure as manifested in participation rates, absenteeism rates, the length of the work week and of vacation time, retirement age, etc., relative to changes in productivity and wage incomes;

▶ the basic and marginal rates of income tax, the rates of payroll taxes and social security contributions, the rates of indirect taxes affecting consumption (such as value-added tax and excise taxes), and the proportions of the total tax revenue that are paid by those employed in the nonmarket sector and by the various kinds of wage and other income earners in the market sector;

▶ the subsidies provided to local governments, public enterprises and market-sector enterprises;

▶ the amounts of research and development undertaken by the market sector and available to it from the nonmarket sector;

▶ the rate of productive investment in the market sector;

▶ the level of employment and the rate of new job creation in the market sector;

▶ the rate of inflation;

▶ the shares of domestic and export markets obtained by a country's industrial producers;

▶ the deficit on goods and services in the balance of payments.

It is readily apparent that many of these variables can serve as indicators of changes
not only in welfare/efficiency relationships but also in other important relationships in the economy—such as cyclical trends, demographic developments and
international shifts in technological capabilities.

Unfortunately, the existing data for most West European countries are not
now adequate for quantifying many of these indicators and, therefore, do not
permit at this time a systematic quantitative analysis of welfare/efficiency interactions. For example, the statistics available for the six countries covered in Chapter 4
are insufficient for separating and specifying the components of the market and
nonmarket sectors. Comparable series for the OECD countries on the amount and
the composition of government expenditures, including transfer payments to
individuals and institutions, do not exist, and the information available from
national sources is difficult to obtain and interpret. There are no breakdowns of the
tax revenues between the amounts paid by nonmarket-sector employees and
those paid by people employed in or deriving other types of income from the
market sector. Series are not available for measures of net rates of return on capital
investment, except in the United Kingdom. Data on absenteeism are very spotty.
Studies of basic and marginal tax rates exist for some countries for some years, but
no time series or intercountry comparisons can be prepared except for those
presented for 1972–76 in a recent OECD study.[6] Series on the shares of domestic
and export markets obtained by a country's industries are lacking. In short, the
data base needed to conduct a systematic statistical analysis of these important
economic issues is not available. True, governments and international institutions
have developed a more or less uniform range of quantitative information suitable
for applying the conventional Keynesian-type of demand-management policies in
the OECD nations. However, those kinds of data do not provide enough of the
statistics needed for dealing with the new economic policy problems arising from
supply constraints, welfare/efficiency interactions and the impact of large external
price shocks, such as that experienced in energy.

Statistical data on adverse welfare/efficiency interactions at the micro level—
that is, for individual productive enterprises—are even more difficult to obtain.
Such indicators would reflect the extent to which the taxation of, and the legally
required welfare benefits provided by, market-sector enterprises lowered their
efficiency by raising their real costs faster than their productivity growth; or by
reducing the latter through disincentives to work, save, innovate, and invest; or by
slowing down their decision-making processes, thereby resulting in missed opportunities. True, negative effects on individual market-sector enterprises are often
produced by other causes, for example, by shifts in comparative advantages,
changes in consumer preferences, and the inefficiency or inertia of management.
Nevertheless, in recent years, taxation and mandated welfare benefits have been

---

6   *The Tax/Benefit Position of Selected Income Groups in OECD Member Countries* (Paris: OECD,
1978).

increasing in most OECD countries and have begun to affect adversely the productivity of individual enterprises.

Among the mandated welfare benefits at the micro level, potentially the most important government actions that could have adverse consequences in the foreseeable future are the variety of measures collectively known as "industrial democracy" in Western Europe. These legally require the increasing participation of employees and trade-union officials in decision making at various levels in the enterprise and, in some countries, are aimed at eventual trade-union control over market-sector enterprises through the gradual growth of the voting stock owned by union-directed central funds. The beneficial as well as adverse effects of industrial democracy are analyzed in detail in Chapter 3.

EFFECTS OF NEGATIVE-SUM OUTCOMES ON ECONOMIC RELATIONS AMONG OECD COUNTRIES

So far, the reason given for trying to minimize negative-sum welfare/efficiency interactions is that their cumulative effect would sooner or later be to reduce welfare itself. But, there is an additional reason for preventing such consequences that is particularly important for the United States. It is that the accumulation of negative-sum outcomes is likely to impel the OECD countries involved to expand regulation and subsidization of their market sectors and, hence, of their external economic relations. In turn, the other OECD nations would be constrained to make similar changes in order to protect themselves against the adverse effects on their own employment and income of such restrictive and discriminatory measures. How might such an interacting process take place?

Leaving aside for the moment the reinforcing or offsetting effects of cyclical fluctuations and of unpreventable external developments—such as further increases in real energy costs—the cumulative negative-sum process essentially reflects the inability of the market sector to provide the necessary employment and socially desired levels of income due to inadequate growth or actual decline of its productivity. The main outlines of this vicious circle were sketched in the preceding section, which focused on the market-sector/nonmarket-sector relationship per se. But, the employment and inflation aspects also need to be taken into account. This can best be done by outlining briefly the economic history of the West European nations since World War II and the economic policy dilemmas they currently face.

Until the great inflation and world recession of the mid-1970s, virtually all West European countries enjoyed unprecedentedly high rates of economic growth and full employment. True, inflation rates tended also to be higher than during the first half of the 20th century but not so high as to preclude a substantial growth of real income, a portion of which was used for the expansion of the welfare systems. However, since the mid-1960s, when the increase in the coverage and cost of welfare systems accelerated, much of the growth of employment has been in the nonmarket sector to administer the expanding welfare benefits and other public goods provided by the government and quasi-official agencies (such as the various social insurance funds in Germany) and to offset the declining rate of job creation in the market sector, particularly in industry. Also, more market-sector enterprises were nationalized and subsidized—as well as subsidies increased to other public and private enterprises—to prevent bankruptcy and thereby to save their workers' jobs. Thus, nonmarket-sector employment and income grew more rapidly than market-sector employment and income.

In turn, the expansion of welfare systems and the growth in nonmarket-sector employment and income drained more and more resources from the market sector directly through higher taxation and indirectly through larger—often inflationary—government borrowing. Nevertheless, until the early 1970s, market-sector growth rates, although declining, were still high enough and the incentives to work, innovate and invest were still strong enough, except in the United Kingdom, to support this diversion of resources without excessively adverse consequences on market-sector consumption, investment, job creation, and exports. This is how Germany was able at the macro level to achieve positive-sum outcomes—that is, massive improvements in welfare along with continuing increases in the productivity of its market sector. In contrast, as explained in Chapter 4, the inadequate growth of employment and income in the U.K.'s market sector relative to that of its nonmarket sector and the disincentives to work, innovate and invest that were also increasing brought that country into the beginnings of a vicious circle of negative-sum interactions during the second half of the 1960s.

The great inflation, severe recession and mounting energy costs of the first half of the 1970s combined with the increasing competition from the manufactured exports of the more advanced Asian and Latin American nations and the onset of the negative-sum welfare/efficiency interactions analyzed in this study inaugurated a new period in the economic history of the West European nations, bringing their three decades of high rates of economic growth to an end. For the first time since World War II, real income stagnated or actually declined, and substantial unemployment emerged not only among the foreign workers imported to relieve the earlier labor shortages but also among native-born workers. Moreover, even after the recovery began in 1975, economic growth rates were inadequate to lower the unemployment levels in the face of the large numbers of young people entering the labor force and of the rise in the female participation rate, expressing women's new career conceptions and the pressure to maintain or increase real household income. Slow or no growth during the second half of the 1970s reflected low rates of market-sector investment and the combined effects of sluggish demand in export markets and the loss of international competitiveness, except by Germany.

One consequence of these developments of the 1970s was the inability even of the rich North European countries to continue to meet popular expectations for both improved welfare and rising real earned income. Under the conditions of simultaneous high inflation and unemployment that prevailed or threatened to prevail in the West European countries, this basic popular attitude tended to be expressed in a negative form—that is, as opposition to the reduction in real earned income entailed by high taxes and rising prices and to any cuts in the real value of welfare benefits. This reaction has been one of the major causes of the political upsets that have occurred in the elections in some North European nations in recent years, as well as of the antitax Glistrup movement in Denmark and similar political developments in other countries. It manifested itself not in an ideological shift to the right or the left but in opposition to whichever type of government was in office and hence was regarded as responsible for the halt in welfare improvements and in the growth of aftertax earned income.

In consequence of these and other developments of the 1970s, the West European nations were confronted with certain policy dilemmas involving the new relationships among welfare, productivity, employment, and inflation. These will be analyzed in greater detail in the country sections in Chapter 4. Suffice it to note here that welfare systems and nonmarket-sector employment and income could not be further expanded without adverse effects as long as market sectors were stagnant or slow-growing or in the face of widespread popular resistance to higher taxes and inflation. Yet, the unemployed had to be reabsorbed into the active labor force and additional jobs created for the continuing large numbers of new entrants. The basic popular attitude toward welfare and earned income continued to be expressed in either positive or negative form—that is, either for simultaneous increases in both or against declines in one or the other—which limited the remedial actions that could be taken by the political parties in power. Yet, the need to reserve adequate resources and to provide effective incentives for market-sector research and development, capital investment and job creation continued to be of crucial importance. Indeed, in the face of the intensifying international competition not only from Japan and the United States but also from the newly industrializing countries of Asia and Latin America, market-sector innovation and investment are likely to be even more urgent in the future than in the past if the West European nations are to maintain balance of-payments equilibrium.

In theory, it might be possible to operate a slow- or no-growth economy without economic strains or social unrest provided people were willing to accept improvements in their living standards in the forms of greater *unpaid* leisure (e.g., shorter work week with corresponding reductions in pay, additional vacation leave without pay) and of increased consumption of public goods requiring little or no market-sector resources. But, as already noted, few public goods are of this character, and, in any event, the predominant popular expectation is for increased consumption of marketed goods and services as well as of public goods and for greater paid leisure. Finally, for countries as highly dependent on foreign trade as are the members of the OECD, the more intensified competition in the international economic system makes continuing research and development and new productive investment in the market sector the only alternative to tariffs and import quotas, direct or indirect export subsidies, foreign-exchange controls, and other neomercantilist trade and monetary policies for maintaining balance-of-payments equilibrium.

The obvious resolution of these interrelated dilemmas would be to return to high rates of economic growth, especially in the market sector, like those of the 1950s and '60s. But, due both to the internal changes and to those in the international economic system noted above, achievement of this objective has become much more difficult than in the two postwar decades. And, it has been made even more so by the ill-repute into which economic growth as a policy goal has fallen among many of the younger political leaders and intellectuals in Western Europe. Finally, the political uncertainties that lie ahead—including the future role of the Communists in Italy, France, Spain, and Portugal—have had and continue to have an adverse effect on economic growth not only in those countries but also indirectly in the North European nations.

Thus, the West European countries have been struggling with difficult policy dilemmas in recent years, and it is by no means certain that they will effectively resolve them in the foreseeable future.[7] Because restless Western societies cannot stand still, persistent failure to achieve a positive-sum outcome would sooner or later precipitate them, willingly or perforce, into a negative-sum vicious circle. Their efforts to maintain employment and to preserve—let alone improve— welfare and earned income despite slow or no growth of market-sector productivity would necessitate further relative expansion of the nonmarket sector, increasing regulation and subsidization of the market sector, wage and price controls, and other forms of government allocation of resources for production, consumption and investment. To be effective, such internal measures would have to be reinforced by more and more severe external controls, such as import restrictions, export subsidies, foreign-exchange and capital controls, and eventually statetrading practices and quasi-official or intergovernmental arrangements to fix international prices and/or share foreign markets. Such developments in some OECD countries would compel others—including the United States—to resort to similar measures to protect their own employment and income levels. The outcome would be a neomercantilist international economic system analogous to that of the 16th–18th centuries.

In sum, to bring continuing real improvements in the conditions of life to the great majority of their people, the OECD countries will have to make certain that the kind, size, timing, and methods of financing of future welfare increases do not significantly impair the productivity of their market sectors and the efficiency of their enterprises. This prescription was not too difficult to follow during the 1950s and '60s when world economic conditions and internal needs and capabilities in Western Europe were conducive to the maintenance of high rates of economic growth. In the changed environment of the 1970s, this guideline was disregarded by several West European nations, with adverse consequences to both efficiency and welfare. Their efforts to conform to it once again, as well as those of other countries to continue to follow it, confront them now and for the foreseeable future with policy dilemmas that are exceedingly difficult to resolve. The problems and possibilities involved are explored in the chapters that follow.

---

7   The difficulty of resolving these complex, interrelated policy dilemmas underlay the refusal of the West European nations to respond to the rather simplistic exhortations of the U.S. government that reflating their economies was the way to solve the world economic problem.

Types of Welfare/Efficiency Interactions 2

That increases in welfare are intended to yield beneficial results is a truism. They do so in a great many cases, and the improvements that result are usually obvious and well-known. In contrast, the unexpected costs and unanticipated adverse effects of welfare increases are by their nature generally unknown or may be deliberately ignored. For this reason, greater attention is devoted in this chapter to the adverse than to the beneficial effects. It must be emphasized, however, that this disproportionate treatment does not imply that the positive results of welfare increases are in any sense unimportant.

To illustrate the scope and size of the national welfare systems in Western Europe, this chapter begins with a brief description of that currently existing in Sweden, whose system has long been regarded as a model of the coverage and benefits that a rich, socially concerned nation should provide to all of its citizens. Then, the ways in which welfare improvements beneficially affect the productivity of a national economy and the efficiency of its market-sector enterprises are briefly surveyed. Next, an assessment is made at greater length of the unanticipated adverse effects of welfare increases on the key factors of production: labor, capital and technological innovation. After briefly explaining workers' interest in productivity, the chapter concludes with an analysis of the more general macroeconomic effects of national welfare systems as a whole.

SWEDEN'S NATIONAL WELFARE SYSTEM

For many years, Sweden's national welfare system has been widely studied and praised as a model of "cradle to the grave" benefits provided to all citizens regardless of need. While the scope and size of the benefits cannot be described here in detail, the main features of the Swedish welfare system are outlined.

Hospitals and health-care centers are government-operated; in addition, some private practice continues. Health insurance pays all hospital costs for as long as two years, half of all prescription costs (with the patient's maximum cost per prescription limited to SKr 25—$5.50), half of dental costs, with full payment for dental care up to age 16, and all illness-related travel costs over the first SKr 10 ($2.20). A fee of SKr 20 ($4.40) is charged for visits to public-health doctors, while a maximum of SKr 30 ($6.60) per visit is generally paid to a doctor in private practice. Absence from work due to illness is reimbursed at the rate of 90 percent of the daily wage or salary, with the limitation not on the number of days of permitted sick leave but on the total amount that can be reimbursed in any one year.

At age 65, all Swedes are eligible for a basic pension of a fixed sum, currently SKr 14,630 ($3,199) for a single person and SKr 25,130 (5,495) for a married couple.

All persons who have worked for a minimum of five years are eligible in addition for the national supplementary pension (ATP), which provides 60 percent of the difference between the basic amount and the average income earned during the highest salaried 15 years. Beginning in 1981, the distinction between the basic and supplementary pension systems will be abolished and all will receive the ATP payment. Pension benefits are indexed monthly to inflation and also provide for annual increments to improve living standards.

Unemployment insurance is related to previous wages or salaries with the permitted amounts also indexed to inflation. Payments are made for up to 300 days for people under 55 and for 450 days for those over that age. Thereafter, welfare assistance at a lower rate is available.

For every child under 16, the mother receives a tax-free cash payment—currently SKr 2,260 ($494) a year—which is also periodically raised or supplemented in accordance with inflation. Up to eight months of "parenthood leave" paid at sick-leave rates is provided at childbirth, it may be divided between husband and wife as they choose, and a ninth month is available at a reduced daily rate. Places in day-care centers for the preschool children of working parents, as well as for after-school care, are currently limited and are allocated on the basis of need. However, when the expansion program now under way is completed, access will be available to all, with fees generally related to income.

Education is provided free at all levels, including graduate study at the universities. School meals are free at elementary and secondary levels, as are books and school supplies. Until age 20, every secondary-school student receives a monthly tax-free study grant—currently SKr 188 ($41)—as well as tax-free grants up to SKr 300 ($66) a month for travel to and from school and, if not living at home, a monthly lodging allowance of SKr 260 ($57). No means test is applied for these benefits but, if the family income of a student recipient exceeds a specified amount, a related portion of the benefits becomes taxable family income. Additional allowances and loans subject to a means test are also available. At higher-education levels, students receive combined grants and interest-free loans that can total as much as SKr 15,500 ($3,389) a year plus special allowances for their children. Of the total, about SKr 2,000 ($437) is a grant and the balance an interest-free loan generally repayable over 20 or more years. In addition, loans and grants are available for advanced university education in Sweden and abroad, for vocational training or retraining, and for continuing adult education.

While most of the foregoing benefits are provided to all regardless of need, there are certain welfare programs that are available only to specified persons or households. In addition to constructing housing for low- and medium-income families, the government gives rent supplements and subsidies for home ownership that are income-related, i.e., declining as family income rises and terminating when it reaches a certain level. Supplementary assistance is provided to those receiving only the basic pension and with too little or no additional income from their own savings or other sources. Disabled persons unable to work or capable of working only part-time are eligible for early retirement with full pension benefits or for income supplements equal to the amount of wages forgone.

Extensive special training programs have been instituted under which blue- and white-collar workers receive free tuition, travel allowances and daily payments equal to their wages or salaries for the duration of the course. Also, as a countercyclical measure, companies can obtain subsidies for providing in-house retraining to redundant workers who would otherwise be laid off.

It is difficult to compare the welfare systems of different countries because of the variations in national economic conditions and social goals and the incommensurability of the beneficial effects of different kinds of welfare programs. They can be roughly compared, however, on the basis of scope and cost. While the Swedish system is probably the most extensive and expensive, the systems of Denmark, Norway, Germany, and the Netherlands are not far behind. The scope and size of the British welfare system are smaller.

BENEFICIAL EFFECTS ON PRODUCTIVITY OF WELFARE IMPROVEMENTS

It has long been recognized that improvements in nutrition, health care, education, housing, and other conditions of life have positive physical, psychological and intellectual effects that increase the productiveness of workers and employees generally. Programs to provide more varied and higher labor skills, to retrain workers whose existing occupations are no longer in demand, and to facilitate the movement of people from declining industries and localities to those that are expanding either raise productivity or at least maintain it. Regulatory measures to assure on-the-job safety, to protect consumers from injurious products, to eliminate or prevent harmful environmental conditions, and to prohibit discriminatory or exploitative labor practices may also be conducive to greater productivity. These and other broadly defined welfare advances produce their beneficial effects not only in a material sense but also by improving the morale of workers and employees generally.

In addition, unemployment compensation, old-age pensions, paid sick leave, disability payments, family allowances, student stipends, and other kinds of cash benefits can have positive effects on productivity. Along with macroeconomic-management policies generally, these transfer payments can help to maintain or increase the aggregate level of effective demand during periods when the factors of production are significantly underutilized. By inducing greater output than would otherwise be the case, they make possible the more productive use of labor and facilities.

Welfare improvements can beneficially affect productivity in various other indirect and intangible ways. By raising the living standards of the poor and/or by bringing about a more equitable distribution of income, they may ease social tensions that often have an adverse impact on economic efficiency. And, insofar as they improve labor-management relations, welfare measures have a direct and immediate effect on both worker productivity and management efficiency.

Thus, that increased welfare can improve productivity, all other things being equal, is generally unquestioned. The trouble is that other things are not always equal. When this *ceteris paribus* qualification ceases to be valid in the real world, unanticipated adverse consequences occur as a result of well-intentioned welfare advances. These negative effects usually operate by weakening the motivations and incentives of labor and/or of the owners and managers of capital and thereby reduce the availability and productivity of these critical factors of production. The labor effects are analyzed in the next section, the capital effects in the one following it.

ADVERSE LABOR EFFECTS

Otherwise desirable welfare improvements may adversely affect labor availability and/or productivity directly as well as indirectly via the impairment of work incentives. Such welfare/efficiency interactions can be of several different types.

The main type of direct effect is a result of the growing desire for greater paid leisure. In most OECD countries, including the United States, there are rising pressures for a shorter work week,[1] longer vacations, more holidays, and newer kinds of increased leisure, such as paid sabbaticals for blue- and white-collar workers. Desirable in themselves, these ways of augmenting workers' leisure have adverse efficiency effects unless they are accompanied by corresponding improvements in the productivity of the existing labor force. Otherwise, unit labor costs rise and international competitiveness may be impaired. Moreover, such offsetting productivity improvements may require increased capital investment, as well as changes in production and management methods, and hence depend in part on the availability of and willingness to invest capital (discussed in the next section). However, if the market performance and tax rates of a particular enterprise are conducive to relatively high profit margins, its higher unit labor costs may be absorbed without immediate new investment or significant impairment of its competitiveness in domestic and foreign markets.

Welfare improvements can also operate indirectly to increase blue- and white-collar workers' preference for leisure as compared with work. This shift occurs because the welfare benefits received by a person when not working approach the level of aftertax pay when working. Either the welfare income has been increased relative to the earned disposable income or the latter has been reduced relative to the former.

The first type of effect may be produced by several otherwise desirable welfare advances. In the Scandinavian countries and the Netherlands, absenteeism rates are high due in part to the fact that sick pay has been increased to only slightly less than the daily wage and the conditions for obtaining it have been progressively liberalized. In turn, high absenteeism rates raise unit labor costs by unanticipated staffing disruptions and/or by necessitating the employment of additional workers to assure the presence of an adequate labor force at any given time. In some large Swedish companies, for example, absenteeism was reported in the mid-1970s at over 20 percent of the labor force, which led to substantial overmanning. Similar effects on the availability and productivity of labor may result from too liberal unemployment compensation, disability benefits and redundancy payments.

The second type of effect may occur as a result of measures that reduce aftertax earned income sufficiently to increase the leisure preference. The most important are the high direct taxes needed to help finance national welfare sys-

---

1   In some cases, a reduction in the regular work week does not increase leisure but is a means of augmenting workers' earnings through additional overtime paid at higher hourly wage rates.

tems. Details of the personal income tax and social security contributions for each country are given in Chapter 4. The following figures show for 1976 the percentages of gross earnings paid in central- and local-government income taxes and social security contributions by the average production worker—defined as receiving the average earnings in the manufacturing sector—married and with two children, and the marginal rates levied on the next 10 percent of additional gross earnings.[2]

	Percent of Gross Earnings	Marginal Rate
Denmark	33	55
Germany	27	34
Netherlands	31	42
Norway	27	42
Sweden	35	63
United Kingdom	26	41
United States	17	32

The reason for the high direct taxes paid by blue- and white-collar workers is simple: neither the number nor the incomes of families in the middle- and top-income brackets are large enough, despite steeply progressive—indeed, in some countries, confiscatory—rates of personal income tax, to yield more than a small fraction of the revenues required to pay for the national welfare system and other government expenditures. In the United Kingdom, for example, the top marginal rate for upper-income families is 83 percent for earned income, and all unearned (investment) income above £2,000 is taxed an additional 15 percent, bringing its combined top rate to 98 percent. The rates in other North European countries, although lower, are still very high. Thus, blue- and white-collar workers—the great bulk of the population—must be heavily taxed in order to generate sufficient revenues to support the national welfare systems which, in these countries, re-quire roughly two-thirds of total government expenditures. Indeed, to help pro-vide the necessary revenues, indirect taxes, too, must be very high. For example, the ubiquitous value-added tax ranges from 8 percent to over 20 percent in Northern Europe, thereby raising most retail prices, as do also the very high excise taxes on tobacco products, alcoholic beverages, gasoline, electricity, and other consumer purchases.

The result is a doubly anomalous situation in the countries that have achieved the highest levels of welfare. One anomaly is that, as their welfare systems have improved, their tax systems have perforce become more regressive due to the heavy burden of indirect taxes on the blue- and white-collar workers—and in some countries also to the fact that local income taxes are levied at the same rate in all tax-paying brackets. The second anomaly is that the redistribution of income that occurs through the tax system is not only from the upper-income groups to the lower-income groups but perforce also from earned income, which workers can

---

2   *The Tax/Benefit Position of Selected Income Groups in OECD Member Countries* (Paris: OECD, 1978), pp. 94, 96.

spend or save as they desire, to welfare income, whose availability, form and size are determined by the government.

In consequence, there has been a perceived reduction in the difference between the aftertax disposable income obtained for work performed, on the one hand, and the income in cash and kind of the nonworking recipients of welfare benefits, on the other. Moreover, the differential is preserved or further narrowed by the practice of indexing welfare benefits both to inflation and to the average annual increase in real wages. The result is to strengthen the incentive to live on welfare income and to weaken the incentive to live on earned income, to work overtime and to qualify for more-demanding higher-paid jobs.

In addition, high basic and marginal tax rates have fostered the growth of "black labor," the "hidden economy," barter, and other forms of tax evasion and income supplementation by the lower-income groups. Workers may use their paid sick leave or refuse to work overtime in their regular jobs in order to work part-time at various manufacturing, construction, repair, maintenance, and other service jobs for households and small firms that agree not to report their earnings to the tax authorities. Or, services may be bartered with no money changing hands—an auto mechanic will repair a building contractor's car in return for work on the mechanic's house. The tax revenues lost in these ways are significant—the estimate given by a Swedish government official was 7 percent of total tax revenues, and the percentages are comparable in the other North European countries. While the increase in the "hidden economy" improves the living standards of those who provide and receive the services or products involved, it also has the effect of inducing the government to make up the lost revenue by raising the taxes that can be collected. And, by fostering absenteeism, it increases labor costs and adversely affects productivity.

The differences between earned income and welfare income have also been reduced and the work incentive generally weakened by other developments directly or indirectly related to the growth of the welfare system and the rising pressure for equalization of incomes. One of the most important is a national incomes policy in which the government limits average annual wage increases while expanding the scope or size of welfare benefits. Another is the narrowing of the wage differentials between skilled and unskilled workers—a major manifestation of the equal-income philosophy in European countries with industrial-type unions in which the unskilled members substantially outnumber those with craft or technical skills.

Since the 1974–75 recession, unemployment has been high and the narrowing differences between welfare income and aftertax earned income have had a less important impact on labor availability than they would have in a boom period. Nevertheless, although the supply of unskilled labor has not been seriously affected, there have been and continue to be shortages of skilled labor even in countries, like the United Kingdom, with high unemployment rates.[3] These are attributed in varying degree to the disincentive effects of the reduction in wage differentials, of ceilings on wage increases under incomes policies, and of the loss

3   Gerry Eastwood, *Skilled Labour Shortages in the United Kingdom: With Particular Reference to the Engineering Industry* (London: British-North American Committee, 1976). See also *The Economist*, June 24, 1978, pp. 115–118.

in some countries (e.g., Sweden, Denmark) of income-related welfare benefits—such as housing subsidies and free child-care facilities—when gross earnings rise above a certain level. In other words, the increase in aftertax earnings that could be obtained by promotion to skilled jobs has not seemed great enough to compensate for the effort, expense and time of the training required or to make up for the reduction in welfare income resulting from the loss of income-related benefits. And, when unemployment declines, the potentially adverse effects on labor availability at unskilled and semiskilled levels could become increasingly manifest.

ADVERSE EFFECTS ON CAPITAL AVAILABILITY
AND TECHNOLOGICAL DEVELOPMENT

In addition to labor, the other essential factors of production that could be adversely affected by welfare increases are capital availability and the development of technology. Here, again, the impact can be either direct or indirect via the effect on the incentives for productive investment. Both results occur chiefly through the reduction of the current or projected return on capital. For, in market economies, the rate of profit determines the amount of income devoted to investment and influences the decisions of the owners or managers of capital as to whether it should be invested at home or abroad and, if in the former, in which sectors of the economy. As shown in Chapter 4, profit rates since the early 1970s have declined substantially in most North European countries, although not solely because of direct or indirect welfare effects. Nonetheless, they have been among the main contributory causes.

One important way in which capital availability can be limited or reduced is through government-mandated welfare improvements that increase unit labor costs. If profits are already declining or are regarded as inadequate or if productivity does not increase sufficiently to offset rising labor costs, then legislated reductions in working hours, improved fringe benefits, higher social security taxes paid by employers, increased minimum-wage rates, better on-the-job safety measures, and other legally enforced welfare improvements will reduce the returns on capital and lessen the incentives to save and to invest in the domestic economy rather than abroad. The same effects may result from official incomes policies that involve controls on prices and/or profits, as well as on wages. The question is not whether many of these mandated welfare benefits are desirable per se—undoubtedly they are. The problem is that their costs may substantially exceed their positive contributions to productivity through improved worker attitudes and physical well-being. So long as profits are satisfactory, such increases in labor costs may be absorbed. However, if not, and if price controls or—more commonly—the need to preserve international competitiveness prevent price increases, then the rise in unit labor costs cuts into the already inadequate profits, with a correspondingly adverse effect on investment.

In the 1970s, newer types of mandated welfare improvements that could significantly increase unit labor costs have been adopted or are currently being urged in various OECD countries. Among the most important are job-security laws, or proposals for such legislation, which are designed to prevent or deter companies from laying off workers in consequence of recessions, the closing of uneconomic plants, or the introduction of new machinery and production techniques. These existing and proposed measures generally require that prior government and/or trade-union approval of reductions in force be obtained, and they usually involve heavy compensation to workers who cannot be shifted to jobs elsewhere in the enterprise. In addition to inhibiting productive investment under the conditions specified above, job-security laws in West European countries have tended to limit the expansion of employment when their economies turn upward and to discourage the hiring of school-leavers and young people generally. Since output can often be increased without hiring additional workers, productivity would thereby be raised. But, there are offsetting adverse effects—the failure to reduce unemployment by as much as might otherwise be possible and the resulting higher costs of unemployment compensation.

Also included among the new welfare improvements legally required of market-sector firms are the existing and prospective measures for preventing or eradicating the harmful effects of market-sector activities on the physical environment and on the health and safety of the consumers of their products or services. Such environmental-improvement and consumer-protection measures usually require additional, and often expensive, investment. Again, there is no question that such measures are desirable in themselves. The problem arises when their capital and operating costs are not offset by increases in productivity and hence must be recouped through higher prices, which adversely affect living standards and international competitiveness. Alternatively, profits decline, which adversely affects investment and eventually living standards and competitiveness as well. However, not all environmental and safety measures have such effects. There is evidence that some newly introduced antipollution equipment and techniques can turn out to be more efficient than those they replace either by raising output, lowering production costs, or converting waste materials into salable products.[4]

Positive and negative effects similar to those of mandated environmental and safety measures are also produced by the changes in the organization of the work process that in Western Europe are usually called "humanization of work" and in the United States "the quality of working life." Since in most countries they are not a part either of the government-administered welfare benefits or of those legally required of private enterprises, measures designed to humanize the work process are not, strictly speaking, included in the scope of national welfare systems as defined in this study. But, because they are becoming increasingly important ways of trying to improve the welfare of blue- and white-collar workers, especially in Northern Europe, and hence have significant implications for welfare/efficiency interactions, they cannot be omitted completely. In brief, work-humanization measures are intended to eliminate or reduce significantly the division of the work into psychologically depressing and sometimes physically exhausting simple, repetitive tasks, as in assembly-line production techniques and routine clerical operations. The aim is to introduce greater variety, more interpersonal cooperation, and self and group regulation of tasks into the work process, and thereby

---

4 For examples of technological and product improvements resulting from mandated environmental-protection regulations, see *Government Influence on the Process of Innovation in Europe and Japan* (Cambridge: Center for Policy Alternatives, Massachusetts Institute of Technology, May 1977).

make it more satisfying and less tiring. Mixed welfare/efficiency effects have resulted from the rather extensive efforts of this kind undertaken, in most cases voluntarily, by market-sector enterprises in the Scandinavian countries and Germany over the past 10 years. On the one hand, improvement in workers' morale is reported in many cases, with some reduction in absenteeism and easing of labor-management problems. On the other hand, unit labor costs have usually risen due to smaller output, the necessity of increasing the wages of all members of a production group to that of the previously highest-paid worker, and sometimes the need to purchase new machinery and equipment. And, by no means all workers respond positively to the allocation of tasks and the fixing of production norms jointly by the members of semiautonomous work groups. Nevertheless, as in Sweden, companies have pushed ahead with work-humanization measures as a means of reducing the very high rates of absenteeism and of trying to make factory work less unattractive to young workers better educated and more demanding of psychological satisfactions than their parents. Insofar as it accomplishes these objectives, the humanization of work may produce benefits to both workers and companies that are worth the costs involved.

Another form of mandated welfare benefits consists of employers' social security taxes and required contributions to insurance, retirement and other official or quasi-governmental funds. Such payroll taxes are considerably higher in West European countries than in the United States. In Northern Europe particularly, they have been substantially increased since the mid-1960s to help finance the mounting costs of expanding welfare systems. In contrast, corporate income taxes tend to be lower and/or permitted deductions therefrom more generous in Western Europe than in the United States. Thus, insofar as taxation has been responsible for the decline in retained corporate earnings available for investment in the West European countries, it has done so mainly through rising social security contributions and other payroll taxes rather than because of the corporate income tax per se.

Leaving business taxes aside, the high basic and marginal rates of personal income tax, especially in Northern Europe, have had not only the adverse effect on labor described in the preceding section but also a similar impact on managerial personnel and the owners and managers of capital. Table 2-1 gives an indication of the rapidly shrinking increments of aftertax income as salaries rise. When combined with the tightening restrictions on expense accounts and other perquisites, steep marginal tax rates have weakened work incentives, reduced the willingness to take the risks of aggressive entrepreneurship, inhibited the improvement of skills, and increased the preference for leisure among managerial personnel, especially in countries, such as the United Kingdom, where marginal rates are highest. Moreover, in the United Kingdom at least, these disincentives have fostered a "brain drain" to countries with lower taxes.

Otherwise desirable welfare increases can adversely affect not only the availability of and willingness to invest capital in the domestic economy but also the development of more advanced technology and its application. The latter result can occur through the same process as the former. That is, as profits decline, the funds available for technological research and development may be reduced along with the capital needed to apply new technological innovations and the willingness to invest it for this purpose. However, the rising labor costs and the increasing

Table 2-1. Intercountry Executive Remuneration Comparisons: June 1978

	Gross pay £	Net after tax £	What that buys £	Gross pay £	Net after tax £	What that buys £	Gross pay £	Net after tax £	What that buys £
United Kingdom	8,700	6,450	6,450	12,100	8,145	8,145	16,300	9,680	9,680
Australia	15,087	10,435	9,317	20,668	12,981	11,591	29,192	16,150	14,419
Belgium	27,272	17,432	11,621	40,085	22,619	15,079	55,357	28,146	18,764
Canada	18,300	12,899	13,029	26,570	17,005	17,177	37,585	22,077	22,300
France	21,172	17,836	12,301	29,641	23,781	16,400	41,260	31,629	21,813
Netherlands	23,876	14,392	9,407	34,000	17,866	11,677	48,417	21,985	14,369
Singapore	14,231	10,892	10,373	21,297	15,141	14,420	30,868	20,563	19,584
South Africa	12,731	9,000	10,714	17,666	10,938	13,020	24,513	12,875	15,327
Spain	15,878	11,390	10,079	22,793	14,610	12,929	32,705	18,441	16,319
Sweden	19,097	8,078	5,689	25,602	9,015	6,349	34,204	10,285	7,243
Switzerland	31,237	22,613	12,157	43,775	29,520	15,871	61,346	38,560	20,731
United States	22,143	14,670	13,840	30,385	17,967	16,950	41,692	21,868	20,630
West Germany	27,910	18,865	11,718	38,232	24,010	14,913	52,854	30,660	19,043

Note: The table shows, given U.K. gross pay of (for example) £8,700, what remuneration an executive with a similar level of responsibility might expect to earn in another country. The column headed "What that buys" indicates the comparative purchasing power, that is, a Dutch manager doing the same job in the Netherlands would enjoy a standard of living about 46 percent higher than his U.K. counterpart; an American doing the same job in the United States would have a standard of living more than twice that of his U.K. counterpart.

Source: Inter-Country Executive Remuneration Report for 1978, Employment Conditions Abroad, Ltd. (13 Devonshire Street, London W 1); reprinted with permission.

social security taxes and contributions that have helped to push down profit rates and expectations over the past decade in many OECD countries can also have the opposite effect: they can lead to greater technological innovation in an effort to make up for the loss of efficiency and in this way reverse the downward trend of profits. In fact, as Lindbeck found in the case of Sweden, both types of effect can occur sequentially.[5] In that country, the profit squeeze led in the shorter term to capital deepening—that is, increased investment in the newest machinery and productive techniques—thereby raising productivity but in the longer term to a substantial drop in investment in both machinery and new plant. In the United Kingdom, too, Bacon and Eltis have documented a similar development.[6]

---

5   Assar Lindbeck, *Swedish Economic Policy* (Berkeley and Los Angeles: University of California Press, 1974), pp. 224–225.

6   Robert Bacon and Walter Eltis, *Britain's Economic Problem: Too Few Producers*, 2nd edition (London: The Macmillan Press, Ltd., 1978).

WORKERS' INTEREST IN PRODUCTIVITY

It is clear from the foregoing account of the adverse effects of otherwise desirable welfare improvements that the crux of the problem is the willingness and ability of blue- and white-collar workers and of the owners and managers of capital to maintain adequate rates of growth of both capital-deepening and capital-broadening investment in the market sector so as to keep the rise in labor costs consonant with the increase in productivity and to provide jobs for new additions to the labor force. Whether they want to and can do so are to a very considerable extent affected by government policies. But, their own perceptions and conceptions also importantly influence their behavior, especially with respect to productivity.

In the case of the owners and managers of capital, their attitudes tend naturally to be conducive to a positive approach to productivity growth; if they are not, the competitive pressures of the market economy will sooner or later weed them out. In contrast, the perceptions and conceptions of workers tend to be ambivalent with respect to productivity increases. On the one hand, they have a natural fear that a change in equipment or in the organization of the work process will require them to work harder or faster during any given time period or may eliminate their jobs. On the other hand, they often understand that lasting increases in real wages and salaries depend on improvements in productivity. Constructively resolving this ambivalence is a responsibility not only of the workers themselves but also of management and of labor leaders and others to whom workers may look for advice and help.

Productivity improvements need not require people to work harder or faster. Indeed, their effect is usually just the opposite. Over the past 100 years, technological advances and changes in the work process have made it possible for managements voluntarily or under pressure from workers and unions to reduce very substantially the physical effort required in a great many blue- and white-collar jobs. And, similarly, the income gains resulting from increased productivity have been shared, voluntarily or perforce, between the owners of capital and the workers. Finally, the failure of market-sector firms to keep up with technological innovation in their industries can sooner or later result in bigger job losses than might be incurred if they did. Thus, wherever both managements and workers (and their union representatives) have been alert and forward-looking, productivity improvements have been a positive-sum game, benefiting efficiency and welfare alike, as in Germany.

For such positive-sum outcomes to occur, however, it must also be recognized that productivity advances in most cases require investment in research and development as well as in new machinery and productive facilities. As explained in the preceding section, such investment is not likely to continue over the longer term if profits are declining or are stagnant at a low—or zero—real rate of return and if the attitudes and policies of the government, the major political parties and other influential groups are perceived as hostile to private enterprise and the market sector of the national economy. Among the most significant influences in the latter respect are the labor unions which, in most West European countries, are affiliated with—in some cases are the most important elements in—the Social Democratic and Labor Parties. Although the attitude of trade-union leaders and members toward market-sector investment is by no means the sole determinant of whether productivity grows at an adequate rate, it plays a major role in the process and in certain circumstances can be of decisive importance.

The contrast here between Germany and the United Kingdom has been striking. In Germany since the early 1950s, the unions and their members have recognized that productivity growth is a prerequisite for rising living standards and that economic expansion generally is a prerequisite for full employment. Hence, their attitude toward capital-deepening and capital-broadening investment has been positive. Until recently, they have generally been willing to share with private enterprises the real income gains resulting from rising productivity and economic growth. This attitude has been manifested both in direct wage negotiations and indirectly through their acquiescence in government policies for assuring that adequate resources and incentives for investment remained in the market sector. In the United Kingdom, a contrary situation has prevailed. The attitudes of many trade-union leaders and socialist activists, especially of the powerful shop stewards in certain key industries, have been indifferent—among the left-wing militants openly hostile—to market-sector investment. Instead, they have stimulated and mobilized the pressures for wage increases and government welfare policies that, in many years, have helped to weaken the incentives and reduce the profits available for the investment necessary to increase productivity and expand employment in manufacturing. As explained in Chapter 4, management deficiencies and other factors have reinforced the effects of these pressures in generating Britain's vicious circle of slow or no economic growth, declining or stagnant real income, increased taxes and government borrowing to finance larger nonmarket-sector employment and greater welfare benefits, mounting inflation, demands for higher money wages in the market sector, smaller market-sector profits, inadequate market-sector investment, slow economic growth, and so on. In contrast, Germany has until recently enjoyed a favorable cycle of high growth, rising real incomes and living standards, and adequate market-sector profits and investment, along with substantial increases in government expenditures for welfare and other purposes.

MACROECONOMIC CONSEQUENCES

The contrasts between the German and the British experiences dramatically illustrate the different effects of positive-sum and negative-sum interactions between national welfare systems and the efficiency of national economies as a whole. The effects at the macro level of such interactions vary considerably among countries and some of these differences are explained in the individual country sections in Chapter 4. Here, the general type of negative-sum outcome—or vicious-circle effect—is briefly sketched.

As pointed out in Chapter 1, changes in the relative sizes of the shares of employment and income of the nonmarket and the market sectors can have important consequences, especially for the international competitiveness and balance-of-payments equilibrium of economies heavily dependent on foreign trade. The expansion of nonmarket-sector income involves increasing total wages and salaries as its employment grows, extending and increasing the transfers provided by the national welfare system, and increasing other government transfers and subsidies. The disposable incomes of government employees, welfare recipients and subsidy recipients rise without a corresponding increase in the productivity of the nonmarket sector but with a resulting increase in its demand for the consumer goods and services produced by the market sector and imported from abroad. In addition, the growing demand for market-sector output raises its own imports of materials, equipment and fuel. At the same time, the shift of income from the market sector to the nonmarket sector may reduce the resources available to the market sector and thereby lessen its ability to meet the demands of its own workers and employees for consumer goods and services, its own needs for continuing research and development and capital investment, and the requirements for exports. This restriction tends to result in excessive claims on the national income, rising domestic inflation and a growing current-account deficit, as may be seen in the cases of Sweden and Norway analyzed in Chapter 4. These effects may be experienced even when the market-sector's productive facilities are not fully employed if its unit labor costs increase faster than those of its major international competitors—witness the case of Denmark explained in Chapter 4. Such disproportionate increases may arise from the heavier taxation required to finance the expanding scope of the welfare system and the growing size of the benefits it provides due to their linkage to the consumer price index and/or to the average annual rise in wages. In addition, unit labor costs in the market sector may rise owing to the effort of its workers and employees to match, if not surpass, the wage and salary increases granted in the nonmarket sector, as has happened in the United Kingdom. There and in other OECD countries, increases in government employees' salaries—on which there are no domestic or international competitive restraints—have tended to set the pace for market-sector wage rises.

Once such an interacting process is under way, it can become self-reinforcing. Not only are moral and political considerations conducive to continued expansion of the national welfare system but they might now be buttressed by economic policy constraints as well. The need to contain domestic inflation and cope with the balance-of-payments deficit may lead to restrictions on credit and imports, which would further limit the resources available to the market sector and inhibit its growth. Or, a mandatory or voluntary incomes policy can be made politically less unpalatable, as in Sweden, by improving welfare benefits in kind (e.g., health services and day-care centers), which would have a smaller impact on the demand for consumer goods and services and on imports than would growth of earned disposable income and of the cash benefits of welfare recipients. Similarly, the adverse effects on living standards of a currency devaluation to inhibit imports and make exports more price competitive might be partially offset by expanding welfare benefits in kind and, if political pressures are strong enough, in cash as well. Both types of policy measures would have the effect of increasing the size of the national welfare system and hence would augment the drain on market-sector resources and strengthen the disincentives to work and invest. At a certain point in these adverse interactions between the market and nonmarket sectors, government controls would have to be imposed to assure that the market sector, both internally and in its external relationships, would operate in conformity with the intended distribution and use of the national income while protecting the balance of payments.

The vicious circle sketched above is by no means a hypothetical possibility. In one or another variant and to greater or lesser degree, it has already appeared in the West European countries under study here. Its fullest expressions to date have been in the United Kingdom during the first half of the 1970s and in Sweden in the mid-1970s. Norway and the Netherlands would also be manifesting their own versions of the vicious cycle were it not that the adverse effects on their balances of payments have been obscured by their anticipated or actual earnings from North Sea oil and gas. Without this advantage, Denmark has been openly confronted with severe payments problems that reflect in part the operation of a vicious cycle. Only Germany seems so far to have avoided serious manifestations of adverse interactions between the market and nonmarket sectors.

In sum, national welfare systems may be of such nature and size as to interact positively with the efficiency of enterprises and the productivity of the market sector. But, for all their desirable benefits, welfare systems may also have negative effects on the incentives to work and invest, on employment and price stability, and on international competitiveness and the balance of payments. Thus, the specific kinds of benefits included in the national welfare system, the particular ways in which it is financed and administered, and the increasing relative size of the nonmarket sector can so adversely affect the market sector as to bring about not only a decline in efficiency but eventually a lowering of welfare as well. In that case, the consequence is likely sooner or later to be a growing resort to neomercantilist production, trade and monetary policies.

The Movement for Industrial Democracy

3

The term "industrial democracy" (ID)[1] is used increasingly in Western Europe to refer to a variety of legally required changes in the organizational structure, methods of decision making and ownership of enterprises in the market sector that have major implications for both welfare and efficiency. These changes are justified, their proponents believe, because workers—or their trade-union representatives—have the right to participate in enterprise decisions affecting their employment, incomes and psychic and physical well-being. In contrast, the opponents of these changes fear that they will severely impair the efficiency of the affected enterprises and hence the ability of the economy over the longer term to maintain, let alone raise, the levels of welfare already attained. Because these developments are regarded as welfare improvements and are legally mandatory, they must be included in a study of welfare/efficiency relationships although they are quite different from those ordinarily comprised in the concept of a national welfare system—even when it is defined as broadly as in the preceding chapters.

The changes subsumed under the ID movement result from legislation and occur at three levels in the enterprise: on the shop floor, in the boardroom and at the stockholders' meeting. *At the shop-floor level*, ID refers to the works councils, or analogous bodies representing blue- and white-collar workers, that management must consult or, in some countries, whose consent management has to obtain before instituting changes regarding working hours and work assignments, product lines and production methods, and other management decisions, including in some cases individual hiring and firing, layoffs and the closing of unneeded production facilities. *At the boardroom level*, ID means the election or appointment of a varying number of directors representing blue- and white-collar workers to companies' boards of directors or to the supervisory boards in those countries where two-tier boards are required. *At the stockholder level*, ID relates to the issuance of shares in the enterprise, representing the capitalization of a percentage of the annual profits, to an industry-wide or nationwide fund, whose trustees are elected by the workers and/or appointed by the trade unions, who vote the stock at the annual meeting and thereby obtain an increasing degree of control over the company, and who dispense the dividend income of the common fund for various specified purposes (e.g., augmenting the wages of workers in the lowest-paid industries or categories and supplementing pension benefits). Thus, at all three levels, ID has the effect of reducing the freedom of decision making of the managements and existing owners of private enterprises and, conversely, of in-

---

1   The movement has also been designated by other names, such as codetermination (in Germany) and worker participation in management, but many of its proponents now seem to prefer the term industrial democracy as more expressive of the essential purpose.

creasing the power of the trade unions as representatives of the workers and in certain ways of the workers themselves.

As explained in the next section, the movement for industrial democracy has its historical roots in the institutional and ideological characteristics of West European trade unions, which differ significantly in these respects from those of the United States. The movement's current development has been stimulated by the changing ideas about social justice explained in Chapter 1. And, its rapid spread in Western Europe in recent years has been particularly fostered by the secretariats of three intergovernmental agencies—the Organization for Economic Cooperation and Development, the European Community and the International Labor Organization (ILO)—and by several international trade-union organizations, most notably the European Trade Union Confederation (ETUC). Since the early 1960s, these international organizations have sponsored numerous conferences and seminars and published many reports and policy proposals that have helped to disseminate information and ideas about ID and to stimulate European trade unions, political parties and governments to take actions designed to realize the movement's goals.

BACKGROUND OF THE ID MOVEMENT

Except in the United Kingdom, where there is a multiplicity of trade unions divided along craft and skill lines, the great majority of West European union members belong to industrial-type organizations—that is, they cover all kinds of workers in entire industries, including public-sector employment. Jurisdictional disputes are rare—again, except in the United Kingdom—and the more significant differences and conflicts among unions arise from their affiliations with rival political parties.

In France, Italy and Belgium—and until recently in the Netherlands—the unions are grouped into three confederations affiliated respectively with the Communists, the Socialists and the Christian Democrats or other religious parties. In Scandinavia, Germany and the United Kingdom, the Communists have been and continue to be much too weak to form separate unions and confederations, constituting instead one of the left-wing groups within the dominant national trade-union organizations. In these countries, as also now in the Netherlands, the sole or major national trade-union confederation is affiliated with the Socialist, Social Democratic, Labor, or other Parties committed to a democratic (i.e., noncommunist) form of socialism.

In the North European countries (except the United Kingdom), the large central labor confederations exercise considerable power over their constituent unions. In part, this relationship expresses the historical origin of these organizations in the more hierarchical and authoritarian societies of the 19th century. But, their powers have been perpetuated and strengthened by legislation or administrative action in countries where the negotiations over wages and employee benefits have been made quasi-official proceedings involving national and/or industry-wide employer and union organizations and, in some cases, the government itself. In turn, this quasi-official status both reflects and helps to maintain the numerical strength of the trade unions which, in most of Northern Europe, cover varying majorities of the workers in manufacturing industries, public utilities, the civil service, and parts of the financial and commercial sectors. Thus, even when their affiliated political parties are in opposition, European trade unions, and particularly the central confederations, have a great deal of formal political influence not only in wage determination but also in policies affecting the national welfare systems. A final significant institutional characteristic of the North European trade unions and confederations is the important role in determining their policies played by appointed staffs, as well as by elected officials. Indeed, except in the United Kingdom, many of the latter come from the former rather than up from the "rank and file" of blue- and white-collar members.

These institutional characteristics have been noted not only because they are important for understanding the background of the ID movement but also because they differ substantially from those of U.S. labor unions. Both craft-type and industrial-type unions exist in the United States, grouped into one major national confederation, the AFL-CIO. However, there are important unions not affiliated with it (such as the United Auto Workers and the Teamsters), and the AFL-CIO does not exercise the power over its constituent unions that is customary everywhere in Western Europe except in the United Kingdom. Moreover, the AFL-CIO has no official or quasi-official status nor is it a direct participant in wage and other collective-bargaining negotiations, which are conducted by its constituent unions generally with individual companies and only in a few cases with industry-wide employers' organizations. The appointed staffs of American unions do not have the policy-making power of their European counterparts nor are they elected to the top official posts as frequently as the latter.

Perhaps the most significant differences between the U.S. and the European labor movements are that, in the 20th century, American unions have not had formal affiliations with political parties, although they generally support the Democrats, and they either never have had or have long since abandoned any commitment to socialism. American unions accept the continued existence of a predominantly private-enterprise market economy while generally favoring larger public-sector expenditures and more government regulation of business than do most other groups in the population. But, they do not advocate nationalization of industry and other sectors of the market economy.

In contrast, since their origins in the 19th century, the great majority of European trade unions have been committed to a socialist society regardless of their often bitter disagreements over its form and the means and timing for achieving it. Those affiliated with Socialist, Social Democratic and Labor Parties have in the past generally pressed for gradual nationalization of key industries—"the commanding heights of the economy"—leaving consumer-goods manufacturing, small-scale industry and most services under private ownership and control until the more or less distant future. There have been, however, some significant variations from this generalization. In Sweden and the other Scandinavian countries, socialism has meant until recently the "socialization" of income distribution and of consumption rather than of production. The nationalized portion of industry and services has been until now relatively small but a large part of the GDP is distributed in cash and in services by the government in the form of extensive welfare benefits and subsidies. In Germany, the Social Democrats have hitherto accepted the "social-market economy" developed after World War II by the Christian Democrats; in consequence, when they were elected to office in 1969, they stressed distributional socialism, as in Scandinavia. In the United Kingdom, many unions have remained doctrinairely committed to nationalization while also pressing for increasing measures of distributional socialism. Owing to the dominant positions of the Communist-led trade-union confederations in France and Italy, the ID movement in those countries has been rejected as "a futile effort to bolster an unworkable capitalist system," although the unions participate—however contemptuously—in its institutional manifestations.

Since the late 1960s, however, the conception of socialism to which the European trade unions are committed has been changing. The nature and possible implications of these changes will be discussed in the last section of this chapter. Suffice it to note here that a new generation of trade unionists and political activists educated during the late 1950s and the 1960s has been rising to positions of influence in the labor movements and socialist parties. Among them are a growing number who no longer are willing to preserve the mixed market/nonmarket economy within which the older generation has been content to work since World War II. Instead, they have been putting pressure on the top leadership of the unions and their affiliated political parties to move faster and by novel means toward a fully socialist society. Their conception of such a society has been heavily influenced by the ideas about distributional justice surveyed in Chapter 1, especially the notion that all persons have a natural right to an equitable share of the national income regardless of their contribution to producing it. Concerned about possible natural-resource shortages and environmental deterioration, some of the younger socialists are opposed to continued economic growth and increasing material consumption, which they condemn as immoral. They advocate an authoritarian form of national investment planning to limit growth and consumption. Other socialists are pressing for such planning for the opposite reason—to increase economic growth so as to eliminate unemployment and improve consumption despite prospective supply shortages. These contradictory economic prescriptions reflect not only the new ideological commitments but also the fact that, unlike in the 1950s and '60s, professionally trained economists are no longer accorded the preeminent intellectual role by the new generation. Instead, many of the younger trade unionists and political activists now look for guidance to political scientists, whose economic ideas tend to be neomarxist and who are occupationally, as well as personally, concerned with questions of social justice and natural rights rather than of productivity and investment.

This is not to imply that the older generation of leaders still holding top positions in the trade unions and socialist parties has been completely opposed to the ideas and objectives of the younger generation. The differences between them are in degree, not in kind, reflecting the different educational and life experiences of the former—i.e., the great depression of the 1930s, fascism and nazism, World War II, postwar reconstruction, and the cold war of the 1950s. These have inclined the older generation toward more cooperative relations with other social groups, to compromise for the sake of common national reconstruction and security concerns, and to concentrate on proximate objectives for welfare improvements and rising living standards in contrast to ultimate socialist goals. To the younger generation, however, national recovery was completed before they became adults, the Soviet Union is perceived as a bad example rather than as a menace, and a fully socialist society is regarded as a practicable goal to be achieved as quickly as possible and not in the indefinite future.

Certain of the changes at the shop floor, the boardroom and the stockholders' meeting urged by the proponents of industrial democracy would be among the most important of the accelerated steps toward socialism that have been defined in recent years. Their significance in this respect will be assessed in the last section of this chapter. But, first, the implications of the ID movement as a whole for the welfare/efficiency relationship need to be analyzed.

INDUSTRIAL DEMOCRACY ON THE SHOP FLOOR

There is a wide variety of arrangements for ID at the shop-floor level.[2] Their common element is a works council—or cooperation committee, enterprise committee, shop-stewards' committee, or representative body called by some other name—part or all of whose members are either elected by the blue- and white-collar workers in a corporation or by those in each factory of a large multi-plant company. In other respects they may vary. The works councils may be established directly by law or by a legally required agreement between an individual employer and the union, or between the national employers' organization and the national trade-union confederation. Their membership may be limited only to workers' representatives or they may include members appointed by management as well. Their powers may range, on the one hand, from the right only to obtain information about the company's financial condition and employment policies and to express their views on these subjects, and, on the other hand, to the right to compel the management to negotiate with them on any aspect of the enterprise's operations they wish and to obtain their consent to virtually all existing or proposed policies and activities.

The oldest and most widely known of these shop-floor arrangements are the works councils in Germany. Originally established by law after World War I, they were suppressed by the Nazi regime, revived after World War II, and substantially strengthened in recent years by new legislation. At present, the members are elected every three years by the workers in each enterprise or in each separate plant or branch in large companies. In the latter, the individual works councils may elect a general works council for the enterprise as a whole. The works councils are separate from and complementary to the system of collective bargaining over wages and employee benefits that takes place between the employers' association in each industry and the trade union involved at either national or regional levels. The councils have no direct functions with respect to these negotiations, although they may subsequently handle the specific applications at the plant level of certain aspects of the general collective-bargaining agreements.

Nonetheless, the works councils have very extensive powers of "co-determination"—that is, their concurrence is legally required before management can take various specified actions. They must be given all pertinent information about the company's affairs and, more important, management must obtain their

---

2   The efforts to humanize the work process discussed in Chapter 2 are sometimes regarded as part of the movement for industrial democracy because they often involve self-governing or semiautonomous work groups.

prior consent before making any changes in working hours (including short time and overtime); shop rules; methods of pay and other remuneration; safety measures; services and amenities provided by the company; hiring, classifying and transferring employees; vacation schedules; and in what the Europeans call "social issues"—plant closings, layoffs, individual firings, redundancy payments, and other aspects of job security. Failure of management and the works councils to agree can be resolved either by appeal to the official Labor Court or by binding arbitration of a committee with equal representation from both sides and a neutral chairman appointed by mutual agreement. In addition, management must inform and consult the works councils in advance on changes in work processes and procedures, production and investment plans, mergers, manpower planning, training, educational programs, and "other matters or projects of essential importance to the employees." Although the works councils are forbidden by law to strike, their right to be informed and consulted on these kinds of management decisions often amounts in practice to the right of codetermination because, to win concessions on them, they can withhold their consent on those matters important to management on which the councils legally have to concur.

In Germany, the works councils are separate from and in theory independent of the trade-union structure. By law, the trade-union leadership at the plant level consists of shop stewards, who are elected by the union members to represent them vis-à-vis the regional and national union headquarters and not vis-à-vis the individual company, which is the function of the works councils. In practice, however, the shop stewards exert a powerful influence because they usually nominate the union-supported slates of candidates which normally win about 80 percent of the seats in the triennial works-council elections. Nevertheless, despite the fact that the unions control in this way the great majority of the works councils, there is a certain tension between the latter and the regional and national trade-union leadership. Not formally part of the hierarchical and rather authoritarian trade-union structure, the works councils tend not only to be concerned predominantly with local plant problems rather than with regional or national union strategies but also to be protective of their local autonomy and tactical freedom to act in accordance with their own conceptions of their best interests. At the same time, they look informally to the higher echelons of the unions for information and guidance. And, for their part, the top trade-union leaders are equally ambivalent about the works councils—unhappy that they are legally independent entities but supporting the continuing increase in their powers.

In Scandinavia, the works councils—or equivalent bodies—are even more powerful than in Germany but are organized quite differently. In Sweden, for example, they were originally established by agreement between the employers' associations and the trade unions, with the local union organization becoming in effect the works council. Under a new Act on Codetermination at Work that went into effect at the beginning of 1977, management has the "primary duty to negotiate" with the local union before putting into effect "major changes" in the operation of the enterprise, including but not limited to the conditions of work and employment. The union's concurrence is necessary before the company can proceed with changes directly affecting employment and working conditions. However, the union may request management to enter into a collective-bargaining agreement under which the union's concurrence would also be required before the company could implement changes affecting any or all other specified aspects of its activities. The scope of such collective-bargaining agreements is not limited in the Act and, therefore, depends upon the relative strength of the company and the union. In addition, the Act specifies that management has a "primary duty to inform" the union continuously about all significant developments in the enterprise, including but not limited to personnel and employment policies. The union's representatives must be given access to the books, accounts and other documents of the company, and the extent of their obligation to preserve the confidentiality of this information is also subject to negotiation, with the Labor Court deciding if agreement cannot be reached. Management must refrain from putting into effect any change on which negotiations are being conducted unless "extraordinary reasons" compel immediate action, but questions relating to wages, working conditions and employment policies are excluded from this exception. On the latter, the union's view prevails if agreement cannot be reached in the course of negotiation, but management has the right to appeal to the Labor Court. For its part, the union can appeal to the Labor Court on other matters and, if the subject in dispute is included in a collective-bargaining agreement with the company, the union has the right to strike in order to put pressure on management.

Still another situation has existed in the Netherlands. There, the works councils have included management's representatives as well as those elected by the workers. The councils have had more limited powers than in Germany, let alone in Sweden. They have had the right of codetermination only on matters relating to working hours, vacations and holidays, pensions, and bonus schemes, and the right of prior consultation on hiring and firing, promotions, job evaluation, and training. However, under a proposed law introduced in May 1978 by the centrist coalition government, the councils will have codetermination rights on hiring and firing and on promotion policies and prior-consultation rights on financial cooperation by the firm with other companies and on the firm's use of outside experts. In addition, the management's representatives will cease to be members of the councils but will be eligible to attend important meetings as observers. The Dutch Labor Party is pledged, when it next returns to office, to extend the councils' codetermination powers to other important company activities—such as investment plans, mergers, plant closures, and other social issues—and to strengthen their right of access to information to include all pertinent data on the enterprise's operations. As in Germany, the works councils are not part of the trade-union structure, and Dutch union leaders tend to be even more ambivalent than their German counterparts with respect to the autonomy and powers of the councils, to which relatively few union members have been elected. Thus, for example, the major Dutch labor confederation favors the removal of the management's representatives from the works councils, but it has not been as enthusiastic about substantially increasing the councils' codetermination powers which, it fears, would limit the unions' local effectiveness even further.

These examples illustrate the variety of organizational forms and powers of the works councils, or equivalent bodies, at the shop-floor level in Western Europe today. The trend in most countries is toward continuing expansion of the scope of the councils' legitimate concerns and strengthening of their codetermination rights vis-a-vis management.

It is, however, impossible to present an objective quantitative evaluation of the effect of the works councils on either the increase in employees' welfare or the efficiency of the enterprises involved. Not only are the expansion and strengthening of the works councils very recent developments but also the possible measures of their welfare/efficiency effects—e.g., working days lost due to strikes, output per worker or manhour, rates of absenteeism, and corporate rates of profit—are not available for individual enterprises and, in any case, are influenced by many other factors. In these circumstances, a qualitative assessment has to be made based on interviews with managers, trade-union leaders, government officials, industrial-relations experts, and other knowledgeable observers.

Leaving aside the ideological commitment to socialism that motivates many ID supporters, the benefits sought by the works councils are both psychological and material. As to the psychological benefits, there is general agreement even among managers that the works councils have often helped to resolve difficult issues in the plant, and they have contributed in various ways to more cooperative attitudes on the part of blue- and white-collar employees toward the enterprise. Through the councils, workers are better informed not only about the financial capabilities of the firm but also about its current and prospective problems. Workers generally feel that the councils are a more effective channel than existed in the past for making management aware of their concerns about company policies and practices. Management, too, has benefited in this regard by having to take workers' attitudes and interests explicitly into account in the course of making decisions rather than after the fact, when revisions or reversals might be even more costly. Moreover, the councils often provide the means whereby workers' suggestions for improvements in the companies' operations can reach the attention of management, since suggestion boxes and other devices used in the United States for directly soliciting individual employees' ideas have not been effective in the generally more authoritarian European environment. Both trade-union leaders and managers believe that the existence of works councils has contributed to limiting the frequency and duration of strikes. Finally, the works councils have enabled blue- and white-collar employees in many cases to obtain substantial improvements in working conditions, plant safety, job security, paid leisure, training, and so forth to complement the increased wages and fringe benefits won through national, regional or industry-wide collective bargaining by their unions or national labor confederations.

While readily conceding that the works councils significantly lessen labor-management tensions and contribute in the other ways noted to improving their companies' operations, many managers, as well as outsiders, interviewed thought that these benefits have involved substantial costs and adverse effects on efficiency. Probably the most important impact on efficiency is through the marked slowing down of decision making in the enterprise due to the need to consult the works council and, on an increasing number of matters, to obtain its consent before action can be taken. The result is to reduce management's flexibility to deploy the company's resources in the most efficient manner. In addition, many enterprises report a decline in the authority and morale of middle- and lower-level managers owing to their virtual exclusion from the negotiating process, which is usually conducted directly between the councils and the top management. Finally, managers and outside experts in countries, such as Germany and Sweden, where the works councils or equivalent bodies have extensive codetermination powers, point out that, when their concurrence is requested in a proposed change in company policy, the councils are increasingly conditioning their agreement not only on the modifications they desire in the particular policy but also on concessions with respect to other company practices not then in question. Thus, the works councils use their right to veto or modify proposed changes in company policies as leverage for obtaining other unrelated benefits as well.

That the works councils have resulted in both beneficial and adverse effects on efficiency is beyond question. So far, the positive effects appear at least to counterbalance, if not to predominate over, the negative consequences but the available information is insufficient to make a definitive judgment. Nor, in view of the likely future increases in the codetermination powers of the works councils, can there be any assurance that their net effect will continue to be positive. Indeed, the only safe generalization is that, in the last analysis, it all depends upon the situation of the individual enterprise: on the effectiveness of its management in all significant respects, including its capacity to deal constructively with the works council, and on the extent to which the latter is both willing and able to take adequate account of the company's needs as well as of the workers' expectations.

INDUSTRIAL DEMOCRACY IN THE BOARDROOM

As at the shop-floor level, the boardroom arrangements for industrial democracy vary considerably among the West European nations. The common element is the presence at directors' meetings of persons representing the blue- and white-collar employees of the firm. In some cases, these representatives are simply observers with the right of access to information and to ask questions regarding it; in others, they are members of the board with the right to vote. Their number may range from a small minority to parity with the directors elected by the shareholders. In countries that require two-tier boards, the workers' representatives invariably sit on the upper-level supervisory board, not on the lower-level management board in charge of the firm's day-to-day activities. In most instances, the presence of workers' representatives at board meetings results from specific legislation rather than from the voluntary action of management or pursuant to an agreement with the trade union. The workers' representatives may be elected by some or all of the company's employees, or appointed by the trade unions, or both.

Again, the oldest and best-known example of boardroom ID is in Germany. After World War II, the newly revived German trade unions persuaded the British occupation authorities—who for their part wanted to prevent a Nazi resurgence encouraged by big German industrialists—to take the lead in the passage of a law in 1951 requiring that workers' directors equal in number to the shareholders' directors be elected to the supervisory boards of all companies over a specified size in the coal, iron and steel industries. In the event of a tie, the chairman of the board, who would always be a shareholders' director, would have a casting (second) vote. Even if in a minority, however, the workers' directors were given the right to approve the appointment of the member of the management board responsible for the company's personnel policies.

The Works Constitution Law of 1952, revised in 1972, provided that one-third of the members of supervisory boards should represent the workers in companies not covered by the coal, iron and steel legislation of the previous year. Usually, most of the workers' directors are employees of the company but trade-union officials may also be elected.

Under a new law passed in 1976, near parity for workers' directors with the shareholders' directors was enacted for all German firms employing 2,000 or more workers. Leaving intact the existing arrangements for the coal, iron and steel industries, this law specified a more complex system for the newly covered companies. Although strongly pressed by the trade unions and many Social Democratic politicians, effective parity of representation for the workers' directors was not achieved. The size of the supervisory board varies directly with the size of the company. While shareholders and workers each have the same number of directors, those representing the latter are elected by separate groups of workers, of which one group consists of the management staff. Thus, at least one director sitting on the labor side—the "labor bench"—represents management. Of the others, the majority are elected by the blue-collar (hourly) workers, the next largest number are appointed by the trade unions, and the smallest number are elected by the white-collar (salaried) employees. The chairman is elected by a two-thirds vote of the entire supervisory board but, if that cannot be achieved, by the "shareholders' bench," with the labor bench electing the vice chairman. The chairman has a casting vote in the event of a tie and may exercise it in writing if unable to attend a meeting in person. Even if the chairman fails to specify his decision in writing, the vice chairman cannot cast the deciding vote. In other words, although there is a nominal parity between the two benches, several safeguards protect the decisive vote of the shareholders' representatives.

In contrast to the power of the labor bench in German supervisory boards, the workers' representatives in French companies have hitherto been only observers with the right solely to obtain information on the firm's activities and to offer advice if asked. French companies have unitary boards, whose meetings can be attended by four observers, two representing the blue- and white-collar workers and one each representing the managerial and technical staffs. Their lack of voting rights has reflected both the traditional power and prestige of the patronat—the top-level officers and/or owners of French companies—and the reluctance of the leaders of the two major trade-union confederations (the Communist-led CGT and the left-socialist CFDT) to press for it owing to their ideological concern that voting membership for workers' representatives would constitute endorsement of the "capitalist system" which, they believe, must be replaced, not "propped up."[3] However, certain influential politicians in the Gaullist-centrist coalition, which has governed France for the past two decades, have viewed ID as a means of wooing French workers away from the ideological goals of the dominant unions. In 1975, a government-sponsored committee issued a report—known as the Sudreau Report after the name of the committee's chairman—recommending that up to one-third of the voting directors on French company boards should be elected by the

3   The left-socialist CFDT favors autogestion, worker self-management of enterprises, under which the workers would elect all levels of management and adopt the policies they would have to follow, along the general lines of worker management in Yugoslavia.

workers. However, this and other related suggestions—e.g., for strengthening the works councils and for greater profit sharing for workers—were not enacted due to the attitude of the unions and the opposition of the *patronat*. In March 1978, another government-appointed commission (chaired by Paul Delouvrier, head of the nationalized electric power company) recommended that up to four additional directors with full voting rights should be added to the boards of French companies to represent the various grades of employees, including middle-level managers.

The situation in Denmark and Sweden is intermediate between those in Germany and France. Under laws passed in 1973, Danish workers in companies with 50 or more employees may elect two voting directors if, in a prior election, they decide that they want board representation. Such workers' directors, who serve for two-year terms, now exist in most large and many middle-size Danish firms, and they are usually trade-union nominees in the more unionized industries. Since 1972, the Swedish trade unions have had the right to appoint two voting directors and two deputies to the boards of companies with 100 or more employees. This law was extended and amended in 1976 to apply to Swedish firms with 25 or more employees, to require that at least one union director be a voting member of the executive committee of the board, and to give the deputies the right to speak at board meetings. The leaders of the Swedish Social Democratic Party and of the trade unions have expressed their intention of pressing for near parity for workers' directors, as in Germany, whenever the former is reelected to office.

An unusual arrangement exists in the Netherlands under a law of 1971. Except at the formation of a new company, boards of directors are not elected by the stockholders but are appointed by cooptation by the existing directors. The latter must choose only from lists nominated by the annual shareholders' meeting, by company managements and by the works councils. Those coopted must be outsiders—that is, they cannot be employees of the company or elected officials or staff of the unions—and both the shareholders' meeting and the works councils have the right to object to any of the directors' choices. If such objections cannot be settled by negotiation or substitution, appeal can be made to the national Social and Economic Council, an official tripartite body representing management, unions and eminent persons, such as university professors, that advises the government on many social and economic problems.

These examples illustrate the variety of arrangements for ID at the boardroom level in Western Europe today. There is, moreover, a wide variation in trade-union attitudes regarding the participation of workers' representatives on company boards. In addition to the ideological objections urged by the French unions, other reasons for labor hesitancy or ambivalence exist.

In the United Kingdom, a committee appointed by the Labour government issued a report—known as the Bullock report from the name of the committee chairman—early in 1977. The committee's majority (consisting of representatives of the Trades Union Congress—TUC—and of independent outsiders) argued strongly for full parity for workers' directors on company boards (unitary) and further recommended that they be elected only by trade-union members from slates nominated by the unions—in effect, that they be union representatives. The minority (representing the Confederation of British Industry—CBI) suggested two-tier boards with the top-level supervisory board consisting one-third of directors representing the shareholders, one-third elected by all workers (i.e., whether union members or not), and the remaining third of independents coopted by agreement of the other directors. Interestingly, however, not all of the TUC unions favor workers' directors regardless of whether they have parity and are elected by union members. Several important unions—although a minority within the TUC—fear that representation on boards would give the unions too much responsibility for the companies' performance and would impair their freedom to bargain collectively in the workers' interest.

In May 1978, the Labour government issued a White Paper on industrial democracy in the United Kingdom. Its proposals, although fairly general and open-ended, fell considerably short of the recommendations of the Bullock report. As a first step, the White Paper envisaged that companies with 500 or more employees would form joint representation committees, comprised of trade-union representatives, with which management would be legally obliged to discuss all major policy changes affecting the workforce. Then, after three or four years, the workers in companies with 2,000 or more employees would have the legal right to hold an election to determine whether they wished to appoint one-third of the directors on the top board of a two-tier arrangement or on a unitary board, whichever the company prefers. In the meantime, companies and unions would be free to agree voluntarily on earlier or more far-reaching ID measures. The possibility of parity for workers' directors, as recommended by the Bullock report, was left open to be decided after the foregoing arrangements went into effect. The Labour government stated its intention of introducing legislation along the lines of the white paper in 1979, if it wins reelection.

In contrast to the divided views of the British trade unions regarding workers' directors, the unions in Germany and the three Scandinavian countries attach a great deal of significance to this form of ID. Full parity of representation is a major goal which they expect to achieve in the foreseeable future. Parity of board representation is regarded by German and Scandinavian trade-union leaders, as well as by many in the Netherlands, as much more important than further strengthening of the works councils, about which they have ambivalent views. Indeed, the Norwegian labor confederation contemplates trade-union representatives not only on the boards of locally owned companies and foreign-owned subsidiaries in Norway but eventually also on the boards of the latter's parent multinational firms in the United States, Germany, the United Kingdom, and elsewhere.

The Commission of the European Community has also been pressing for workers' directors. In its draft Statute for European Companies, which it has long been urging EC member governments to approve, the Commission envisaged that the new European-wide companies it proposed to incorporate would have two-tier boards and that the top supervisory board would consist of one-third shareholders' representatives, one-third workers' representatives, and one-third independent members coopted by agreement of the others. Moreover, in the past, it advocated harmonization of its members' own national systems of board representation along the same lines both to assure equal benefits in this respect to all workers and to eliminate any competitive advantages that might result from the persistence of different kinds and degrees of worker participation in the member countries. Recently, however, the Commission recognized that such rigid uniformity was one of the obstacles to acceptance of its proposals, and it has been revising them to take account of members' diversities.

European businessmen are generally opposed to worker, let alone trade-union, directors as full board members. While acknowledging that such participation has helped to ease labor-management tensions, they believe that—as in the case of the works councils—it slows down decision making and reduces management flexibility. Above all, they fear that full parity would mean deadlock. They also point to the conflict of interest involved in having the workers' representatives participate, on the one hand, as company directors and, on the other, as union members in negotiations with the union and the works council. Finally, they are concerned about the confidentiality problem—the disclosure of business secrets and other confidential material to directors who, in turn, are obliged to keep their worker constituents and their unions informed about the company's condition and prospects.

Again, as in the case of shop-floor ID, the question is whether the psychological and material benefits of boardroom ID outweigh the negative effects on efficiency. And, again, quantitative measures are lacking for objectively determining such effects. Nor does the fact that, for the past quarter century, workers' directors have had near parity on the boards of German coal, iron and steel companies provide the evidence for reaching a definitive conclusion on qualitative grounds.

First, although there is a substantial volume of literature on the German experience, it rests ultimately on the personal opinions of the management and labor participants and on the evaluations of their views by outside analysts. Not only is it uncertain that these data provide a truly representative basis for judgment but, more important, they are inevitably biased by the ideological convictions and institutional interests of the participants and sometimes by those of outside analysts as well. The workers' directors and union leaders invariably maintain that the benefits of boardroom codetermination outweigh the ill effects; indeed, many claim, if there are any adverse consequences, they could readily be eliminated by giving the labor bench full parity. Public statements by managements' representatives are also in most cases favorable to workers' membership on supervisory boards—although not to full parity—on the grounds that it eases labor-management tensions and improves employee understanding of company problems. However, in private interviews, many discount their public statements—which they justify as designed to placate the unions and their political allies—and insist that boardroom codetermination has seriously slowed decision making and entailed greater concessions to the unions than were justified by the financial condition and prospects of their companies. It is difficult for an outside observer to make a valid assessment on the basis of such clearly biased participant opinions.

Second, the experience of near parity in the German coal, iron and steel industries may not be typical of what will happen under the extension of near parity to other German industries. Nor are the policies and actions of the German trade unions typical of those in other West European countries. Coal, iron and steel have experienced a great deal more government involvement than most other German industries—e.g., to reduce and rationalize the coal industry during the 1950s and '60s, to assist troubled steel companies during the 1970s—in addition to the supervisory control exercised by the High Authority of the European Coal and Steel

Community. The extent, if any, to which the problems of these industries have
been favorably or adversely affected by near parity in the boardroom is difficult to
estimate in view of the greater governmental and other constraints to which they
have been subjected compared with other parts of the German economy.

However, there is an important exception to these uncertainties that relates to
the attitude of the German trade-union movement during the postwar decades.
This is its sense of national solidarity and responsibility that reflects both traditional
German sociocultural characteristics and the pressing problems of the period of
defeat, occupation and reconstruction after World War II. In consequence, the
German unions have generally attuned their wage demands to the needs and
capabilities of the economy as a whole and have usually favored a high rate of
investment—in the market sector as well as in the nonmarket sector—as essential
for economic growth and hence for both increasing employment and raising living
standards. These policies were major elements in the German economic "miracle"
of the 1950s and '60s. Not only on the supervisory boards but also in the works
councils, both the union members and those representing the plant workers have
generally supported management's investment plans and have often in the past
been willing to limit increases in wages, employee benefits and other welfare-type
costs so that adequate funds would be available for capital investment. Indeed,
some government officials commented during interviews that codetermination
takes the form in some large corporations of collusion between managements and
trade unions to assure sufficient company funds for investment and to raise wages
at the expense of the dividends paid to the shareholders.

Further relevant evidence is the fact—reported by both shareholders' and
workers' directors—that bloc voting by the two benches is by no means the rule.
The workers' directors frequently take different sides, with a split between those
appointed by the unions and those elected by the plant workers particularly
noticeable. The latter tend to be more solicitous of the company's financial well-
being and prospects because they see the increase of employees' real incomes and
the stability of employment as directly related to productivity and investment
whereas the former are more concerned with the union's broader economic and
political goals at industry-wide and national levels. This difference in perceptions
and interests on the labor bench has also been of concern to the leaders of the
Dutch trade unions and, in the United Kingdom, was one of the reasons that led the
pro-Labour majority in the Bullock report to recommend that workers' directors
should be nominated by the unions and elected only by union members.

Some persons interviewed maintained, however, that the broader perspective
of the unions' directors inclines them to cooperate with the management's and the
shareholders' directors on certain common interests vis-à-vis the government and
the consuming public. For example, this cooperation has involved efforts to obtain
protection against foreign competition—a problem particularly important for the
steel industry in recent years—and subsidies and other special treatment from the
government. Several government officials and outside analysts expressed the fear
that, with the extension of near parity to all large German companies, such
management-union collusion would become much more significant in the future
and would seriously impair competition in the market sector through cartel-like
price-fixing and market-sharing arrangements, one of whose major purposes
would be to maintain the employment and incomes of the workers involved.

However, most business spokesmen in Germany tend to minimize this possibility, pointing instead to the danger of another kind of collusive action. With the union members of the labor benches of the companies in a particular industry representing the same union—sometimes being the same individuals—the possibility exists that confidential information obtained at one board meeting would deliberately or inadvertently be revealed at a competitor's board meeting or used in some way by the union to the detriment of the company or companies involved. The question of the confidentiality of the information that must now legally be provided to workers' representatives is especially troubling to business executives not only in Germany but in other European countries as well, for they have customarily been much more secretive about company affairs—even vis-à-vis the stockholders—than has been the case in the United States. Against this background, their alarm at the new requirements for workers' access to information is understandable. But, no instance in the past was cited by the executives interviewed of the disclosure by union representatives of a company's commercial or technological secrets to its competitors. Nonetheless, the fact that the union's directors on the boards of the various firms in an industry will have access to confidential information from all of them may give the union an advantage it has hitherto not possessed in industry-wide negotiations over wages and other matters. Indeed, this is precisely a major reason why the unions have pressed for the substantially liberalized right of access to information that they have recently been granted in one form or another in West European nations.

Financial data and information on other aspects of a company's policies, plans and activities are of little value to those who lack the education or experience for interpreting them. Hence, both businessmen and trade unionists in Western Europe have been concerned that training facilities of various kinds should be established for enabling workers' directors to equip themselves for their board responsibilities. In some cases, these training programs have been provided solely by the unions; in others, they are jointly sponsored by the unions or national labor confederations and the industry-wide or national employers' organizations. Conversely, the presence of knowledgeable workers' representatives on supervisory boards in Germany appears to have improved the participation of the shareholders' directors as well. Not only is their attendance more regular but they are reported to be much better prepared than formerly to discuss the subjects on the meeting agenda. These improvements in the capabilities of both workers' and shareholders' directors should at least partially counteract the ill effects of the slowing down of decision making entailed by boardroom codetermination.

In sum, for the reasons indicated, it is difficult to draw definitive conclusions from the German experience. In the other West European countries, workers' directors are still too new, or too few in number, or too limited in their rights for there as yet to be an adequate body of data to support any reasonable conclusions. That union and/or worker participation—especially as it approaches or achieves parity with shareholders' representation in the future—will slow down decision making in the boardroom and reduce management flexibility appears to be likely. At the same time, there is also a reasonable possibility that collusion between the two benches could lead to restrictionist responses to problems of competition and employment with or without the collaboration of the government. Thus, if the workers' directors achieve full parity, it is likely that boardroom codetermination would impair both the efficiency of individual firms and the productiveness of the national economy as a whole.

Whether full boardroom parity would bring equal or greater welfare benefits, material and psychological, to the workers involved also cannot be definitively determined at this time. Suffice it to say in this regard that the workers themselves appear to attach more importance to shop-floor ID in the forms described in the preceding section than they do to boardroom ID. The reasons are obvious: they are much more closely involved in the former and the benefits they derive from it are obtained much more directly and immediately. Conversely, trade-union leaders and activists—with the exceptions noted above—view boardroom ID as a more important means for enhancing their power and influence while they tend to be ambivalent about the works councils and other manifestations of shop-floor ID. In the years ahead, the trade unions and their political allies in most West European countries will very likely continue to push for full parity for workers' directors on company boards whenever political conditions are propitious for such moves.

INDUSTRIAL DEMOCRACY
AT THE STOCKHOLDERS' MEETING

Industrial democracy at the stockholders' meeting is the newest manifestation of this movement in Western Europe and has not as yet been realized in any country, although it may soon be in the Netherlands. Variously called worker asset-formation, workers' share of capital formation, excess-profit sharing, or simply financial participation, these ideas differ importantly from conventional profit-sharing plans involving stock ownership by individual workers and from pension funds, part or all of whose assets consist of shares of the sponsoring company or of other enterprises.

In the conventional profit-sharing plans established by European and American corporations, the ownership of stock in the company is vested in the individual employee, who acquires his or her shares in accordance with a defined schedule usually related to the company's profits, directly receives the dividends on them, may vote the stock at the annual meeting, and may sell it under specified conditions or after a specified period. In contrast, worker asset-formation refers to proposals under which company stock is not owned by individual employees but is issued in specified amounts to an industry-wide or nationwide fund, whose directors vote the shares, receive the dividends, and dispense this income for certain defined purposes. Again, in partly or wholly funded pension plans holding stock in the sponsoring company or in other enterprises, the trustees who can vote the stock may be officers of the company, or independent outsiders, or employees of a bank or investment firm, or—as in some European countries—managers of quasi-official funds appointed by the government or elected by the various groups contributing to and benefiting from the fund. In many cases, especially in the United States, they do not vote the stock held in the pension plan as a matter of policy. In contrast, the primary purpose of worker asset-formation plans is to enable the trade unions to obtain voting control of the participating companies.

There are two main proposals for worker asset-formation in Western Europe today: the so-called Meidner Plan in Sweden and the draft law now under consideration in the Netherlands. In addition, the national labor confederations in Denmark and Germany have been interested in similar schemes in recent years but no specific legislative proposals are at present pending in these countries. However, the Social Democratic government in Denmark recently expressed its intention of introducing a bill in the near future.

The Meidner Plan—named for the labor economist who was its principal author—was formulated in 1975 and adopted in broad outline as a major policy objective at the 1976 congress of the Labor Organization (LO), the largest Swedish national trade-union confederation, which represents the blue-collar workers and is affiliated with the Social Democratic Party. It was omitted from the Social Democratic platform in the 1976 election for reasons of political expediency.

As originally adopted by the LO in 1976, the Meidner Plan provided that 20 percent of the annual pretax profits of Swedish companies with 50 or more employees would be capitalized.[4] That is, additional shares equal in value to this sum would be issued by each company, with the funds involved being added to its capital to be used for investment. The new shares issued each year in this way would be held in trust by a fund established for each industry, whose directors would be appointed by the trade union in that industry and would vote the stock so acquired. Thus, over a period determined by the amount of company stock already outstanding, the firm's rate of profit, and the specified percentage it had to capitalize each year, the fund in its industry would obtain first a controlling and then a majority interest. Conversely, although the absolute value of the existing stockholders' equity would not be diluted owing to the increase in capitalization, they would sooner or later lose voting control of the company. The dividend income accruing to each industry fund would be transferred by it to a national fund, whose directors would be appointed by the national trade-union confederations. The national fund would use its resources partly to supplement the incomes of workers in the lowest-paid industries and jobs and partly to purchase new issues of stock in Swedish companies and other equities that might become available (such as old shares sold by private investors unwilling to hold stock in companies now controlled by the unions).

In February 1978, a joint committee of the LO and the Social Democratic Party issued a report proposing several revisions and additions to the original Meidner Plan. Only firms with 500 or more employees would be required to capitalize 20 percent of their annual pretax profits and issue voting stock to the union-controlled funds. Smaller companies would instead be subject to an additional payroll tax of 1 percent, which would be transferred to a "codetermination fund" administered by the trade unions and used to finance "union activities for the democratization of the economy." The report also recommended that two national development funds and several regional development funds be established, financed by a further increase of 3 percent in the payroll tax, to supply capital for improving the technological competitiveness of Swedish companies. One of the national funds would be controlled by the trade unions, the others by the government.

---

4   Foreign-owned companies would also be included and special provisions in the law would regulate profit remittances, transfer pricing and other relations with the parent corporation affecting the subsidiary's pretax profits.

Because of their controversial nature, however, these proposals will not be formally adopted by the Social Democratic Party until after the 1979 election. If the Social Democrats return to office then, they intend to introduce legislation along these lines which would be passed after the subsequent election in 1982. Meantime, to mollify the trade unions for this delay, the Social Democratic leadership has promised to institute near parity for workers' directors on company boards if the Party wins the 1979 election.

An "excess" profit-sharing bill was pending in the Dutch Parliament when the coalition government led by the Labor Party fell in the spring of 1977, and the Party is pledged to proceed with such legislation when it next returns to office. Its original scheme would require companies (including foreign-owned firms) to capitalize a portion of their pretax profits—beginning at 20 percent in the first year and rising 1 percent a year for the next four years—with the new shares going into a nationwide central fund, 15 of whose 20 directors would be appointed by the trade unions and the remaining 5 by the government. The central fund's shares would be voting stock, and the dividend income from them would be used to supplement the wages of the workers in the companies involved and the pension benefits of retired workers generally.

In an effort to forestall this far-reaching Labor Party scheme, the centrist coalition government that took office in late 1977 has introduced its own milder, though more complicated, bill. Aftertax profits equal to the yield on government bonds plus 3 percent would be excluded from the plan, but 12 percent of the profits above this amount would have to be divided among the employees in cash or as stock, and a similar percent would be paid into a central fund administered by the trade unions. The unions naturally prefer the Labor Party proposals and, when the latter returns to office, the excess-profit legislation will very likely be revised to conform to its own ideas.

As the Swedish LO stated specifically at its 1976 congress, the primary purpose of its worker asset-formation scheme is the eventual transfer of ownership of the means of production to the workers as represented by the trade unions. This aspect of worker asset-formation is potentially the most significant, involving a fundamental transformation of the nature of the economic system, and it will be discussed in the concluding section of this chapter.

The secondary purpose of the LO scheme is to provide funds for further implementation of the wage-solidarity policy—more fully discussed in Chapter 4—that has long been a major objective of the Swedish trade-union movement, and it has a direct bearing on the welfare/efficiency relationship. An early stage in the development of the idea of the natural right of all to an equal share of the national income, the wage-solidarity policy holds that workers' wages should not be related to the profitability of the companies or industries in which they happen to work. Instead, all jobs should be classified according to skill, with workers in each job category paid at the same rate and, eventually, all job categories paid at the same rate regardless of the skills involved or where and by whom the workers are employed. In accordance with this policy, dividend income under the Meidner Plan would be used in part to raise the incomes of workers in the least profitable companies and the lowest-paid job categories, thereby reducing the differentials between them and those in profitable firms and higher-skilled jobs. Thus, the only welfare improvements under the original Meidner Plan would be those obtained by the lowest-paid workers. In contrast, even though the workers in the more profitable companies and higher-skill categories would make the biggest contributions to the industry and national funds, they would not receive any increase in income and, in addition, they would suffer a narrowing of the differentials between their wages and those of the lowest-paid workers. Both of these effects would significantly reduce their incentives to work conscientiously and productively.

This problem was recognized in the Dutch Labor Party proposal, which would apply at least part of the dividend income of the central fund to supplementing directly the wages of all employees in the companies involved while using the remainder to increase the pension benefits of retired workers. Although many trade-union leaders in the Netherlands are no less committed to the philosophy of ultimately equal incomes for all than in Sweden, the Dutch unions include a much smaller percentage of the working population than is the case in Sweden and, hence, cannot as readily disregard the skilled and semiskilled workers within their own organizations and among the unorganized.

The disincentives for management and investors generally of worker asset-formation and excess-profit schemes are even greater and more pervasive than those for the more productive workers in the Meidner Plan. For, the more efficient the management of a company and the higher its rate of profit, the quicker will the investing shareholders lose control of it. In these circumstances, little, if any, incentive would exist for private organizations and individuals to invest in equities, and there is likely to be a corresponding decline in innovation, the establishment of new enterprises, and other forms of risk-taking that usually depend in substantial degree on the availability of venture capital.[5] Moreover, foreign companies would also be deterred from making new or expanding old investments, with resulting loss of their technological and managerial contributions to increasing the economy's productivity and international competitiveness, and existing foreign investors would seek to transfer some or all of their assets abroad, thereby generating a continuing capital flight.

Proponents of worker asset-formation and excess-profit schemes claim that, once the companies are under the control of the trade unions, no conflicts between efficiency considerations and welfare considerations could possibly arise by definition. That is, the workers, as owners of the enterprise, would be concerned about its efficiency and the directors, as trade unionists, would be concerned about the workers' welfare. But, this a priori assumption of socialist theory is not likely to be empirically valid. The experience of all existing socialist or semisocialist economies indicates that the trade-union directors in control of companies would be no more exempt from the difficult choice between the welfare of the workers whom they represent and the profitability—and hence the efficiency—of the enterprises for which they are responsible than were the previ-

---

5   The national and regional development funds in the revised Swedish LO-Social Democratic Party proposals are designed to meet these objections but would be unlikely to do so because the private stockholders would still lose control of the larger companies. Moreover, increasing by 3 percent the already high payroll tax—currently 35 to 40 percent of wages—would adversely affect the competitiveness of Swedish companies, which would be a further deterrent to investment in them.

ous directors. On the one hand, they would be under pressure and obligation to meet the workers' expectations for increased disposable income and greater paid leisure. On the other hand, they would soon come to realize that their company could continue to provide such welfare improvements and to pay dividends into the industry or national fund only if it is efficient enough to earn the profit necessary for these purposes and, in addition, for financing the research and development and the investment required for its growth and the maintenance of its competitiveness in domestic and foreign markets. Moreover, as explained in the first section of this chapter, many younger trade-union leaders and politicians are opposed to rising material consumption and hence have an ideological reason for holding down increases in workers' disposable incomes.

This choice is difficult enough under the existing system of collective bargaining, in which each side represents only one of these competing interests. How much more difficult will it be when each director is torn between two conflicting obligations, or loyalties. If the directors are believed to be favoring the longer-term interest of the shareowning fund that appointed them, they will sooner or later be regarded by the workers as no different from the old management and hence as adversaries, not allies. If they are liberal in raising wages and fringe benefits or in relaxing work discipline and quality standards, they will find costs mounting and little, if any, profit available for paying dividends to the stockholding fund and for investment. A compromise emerging from an adversary relationship like collective bargaining is much more likely to be acceptable to both sides, because it is believed to be the most that each has the power to get, than is a decision arrived at on rational grounds by trade-union directors who are known to have the power to give more had they so wished. In the former case, the negotiators are perceived to have done their best; in the latter, they will be regarded as having done their worst either for the workers or for the shareholding fund.

In such circumstances, the always latent differences of interests and viewpoints between the local unions and the national trade-union leadership would become manifest even in a country, such as Sweden, where disagreements between the two levels have been minimal—except for the resentment of the skilled workers at the narrowing of their differentials under the wage-solidarity policy. In Germany and the Netherlands, mutual suspicion already exists between the works councils at the plant level and the industry and national trade-union organizations, and their differences would be greatly aggravated by the conflicting interests explained above and the absence of their old common adversary—the directors and managers representing the former stockholders. Given the political power of the trade-union leadership in most European countries, such conflicts between the two levels of workers' organizations would sooner or later impel the central bodies to seek government support, including the necessary legislation, for restricting the freedom of action of local unions and works councils, particularly their right to strike in pursuit of wage increases, improved fringe benefits and greater paid leisure.

THE TRANSFORMATION OF THE WEST EUROPEAN ECONOMIES

The three manifestations of industrial democracy—on the shop floor, in the boardroom, at the stockholders' meeting—can be viewed as progressive stages in a fundamental transformation of the economies of the affected countries from predominantly market to predominantly nonmarket systems.

The shop-floor stage leaves the market system essentially intact. Indeed, although its efficiency costs to the companies involved may be substantial, it may actually help to preserve the market system by reducing labor-management tensions and workers' disaffection. Boardroom ID may also contribute to the latter. But, if the trade-union and/or workers' directors achieve full parity with those of the shareholders, the beneficial effects on individual enterprises and the market system as a whole may be more than offset by the adverse impact. For the companies, such negative consequences would be impairment of management flexibility, slowness of decision making, expensive concessions to obtain agreement on necessary or potentially profitable changes in operating policies and investment plans, decline of middle-level managers' morale, and other effects that raise costs, reduce productivity or cause business opportunities to be missed. Alternatively— or even simultaneously—the companies and unions in an industry might collaborate to maintain or increase profits, wages and employment through open or clandestine price-fixing arrangements, market-sharing agreements and understandings to slow down technological innovations and to obtain government subsidies, protective tariffs or quotas, and other discriminatory and restrictive aids. Thus, whether the two benches disagree or collaborate, there is a strong possibility that full boardroom parity would sooner or later lead to restrictive private and/or governmental actions that would lessen or eliminate competition and undermine the effectiveness of market incentives and pressures.

The third stage of industrial democracy—at the stockholders' meeting—is explicitly intended to transform the nature of European economies through trade-union control of an increasing proportion of the voting stock of the large and medium-size companies. In Scandinavia, the Netherlands and Germany, worker asset-formation schemes are being seriously considered or discussed precisely because a growing number of trade-union leaders and left-wing activists in the Social Democratic and Labor Parties, especially among the younger generation, have come to believe that such measures provide a more certain and desirable means for achieving a socialist society than does the traditional device of nationalization. Government ownership of productive enterprises has not been entirely abandoned—it is still advocated in these countries as a way of preserving employment in declining industries, such as shipbuilding, and insolvent companies unable to cover their costs in competitive domestic or foreign markets. But, increasingly in Northern Europe, nationalization is regarded as a less satisfactory road to and form of socialism than worker asset-formation schemes.

Experience has shown the unions that, despite their political power, they are in many instances no more able to impose their will on the managers of public enterprises than they are on those of private enterprises. With the examples of the Soviet Union, the East European countries and China before them, the trade unions fear that, once most or all of the economy has been nationalized, their freedom of action would be drastically curtailed by the government, and they would become only another control mechanism of the bureaucratic state, with their positive functions limited to dispensing fringe benefits to their members. In their view, worker ownership of the means of production is more democratically and efficiently realized through the agency of the trade unions than through that of the government. For, they hold, the unions are the workers' own organizations and hence are much better aware of and responsive to the workers' needs and aspirations than government ministries could ever be.

These ideas constitute—in essence, if not necessarily in intent—a revival of an early 19th-century form of *syndicalism*.[6] The latter was denigrated as "petty bourgeois" socialism by Marx and condemned by his socialist and communist followers, who believed that the control of state power and the nationalization of the means of production are inseparable measures for imposing a socialist system and preventing a capitalist reaction. Be that as it may, a more relevant criticism of today's neosyndicalists is their refusal to admit that disputes between the trade-union directors in control of companies and the workers and their shop-floor and other local organizations would be likely to arise. The neosyndicalists believe that any significant conflicts are impossible by definition, since all involved would be members of the same union and *ipso facto* would have the same interests. Thus, they insist, there would never be any need to restrict the freedom of action of the works councils or to enlist the power of the state in preventing strikes or enforcing work discipline. Rather, the neosyndicalists envision a harmonious society in which the trade unions, as the organization of the blue- and white-collar workers, by far the largest social group, would play a leading role in settling issues of national policy with the other social groups—such as the small businessmen, farmers, professional managers, and technocrats—through rational agreements that would give adequate weight to all of the legitimate interests involved.

Influenced by such beliefs, neosyndicalist trade-union leaders and socialist activists are among the most ardent advocates today of a more clearly defined and authoritative system of national economic planning than has hitherto been practiced in Western Europe. In the course of the 1970s, there has been gradually growing dissatisfaction with the existing methods of national policy making with respect to two major interrelated problems: investment planning to expand productive capacity so as to reduce unemployment and meet existing or feared supply shortages, and incomes policy (i.e., efforts to limit inflation by controlling wages, profits and prices). A description of the variety of approaches to national investment planning and incomes policy that are currently utilized in Europe is beyond the scope of this study. What is relevant to it, however, is the nature of the supposedly more effective method now being urged by the unions and their political allies, as well as by many government officials, social scientists, journalists, and other opinion leaders.

The various proposals have in common the notion of "tripartite planning by the social partners" at the national level and at the level of the European Community as a whole. By the three "social partners" is meant the trade unions, the managements of large and medium-size companies, and the government, with the

6   The reference is to the ideas of Louis Blanc and to some extent of Fourier and Proudhon in the 1830s and '40s and not to the syndicalist movement of the late 19th and early 20th centuries, which advocated forcible action by the workers to seize and keep control of the enterprises in which they worked. Among the contemporary neosyndicalists, the CFDT's idea of *autogestion* is closer to the early syndicalist notion of direct worker control than are the current views of the Dutch, Scandinavian and German unions, which would vest management control in the trade unions.

latter representing not only the responsibilities of the state for defense, health, education, and so forth but also the interests of the farmers, small businessmen, consumers, and other social groups. First, each partner would concert its own position among its constituent unions, companies and ministries, and then the three partners would negotiate as equals to determine the national investment plan and incomes policy. The resulting agreement would be enforced both by the power of the government and by the strengthened authority of the national trade-union confederations and management associations over their respective members.

In essence, this authoritarian conception is remarkably similar to that of the "corporate state" propounded by the Italian, German and other European theorists of fascism during the 1920s and '30s. Although followed in name only by the fascist regimes of the interwar period, the corporate-state concept envisaged that the main socioeconomic groups—business, labor, farmers, and so on—would be organized into quasi-official associations, or corporate bodies, whose leaders would participate under the controlling direction of the government in the determination of national economic policies and would be given the power to enforce these decisions on their members. Because of this similarity, some European observers refer to the current approach to directive planning as "fascism with a human face."

There are, of course, other forms of national economic planning in Europe that do not involve as tightly organized, centralized and controlling a system as that explained above. Nonetheless, the latter appears to be the method increasingly advocated among younger trade-union leaders, the left wings of the Social Democratic and Labor Parties, and the numerous Marxists in the universities and the communications media throughout Western Europe. It is also supported—though not for the same reasons—by many younger technocrats in the national governments and the EC secretariat, who accept it as the most "rational"—and hence presumably effective—means for coping with the complex socioeconomic problems of the last quarter of the 20th century. Thus, the pressure for a more centralized and directive system of national economic planning is likely to persist in Western Europe and efforts to institute arrangements along these lines will probably be made whenever socialist-led coalition governments feel themselves strong enough to do so.

In sum, the movement for industrial democracy, should it reach the stage of boardroom parity and go beyond it to worker asset-formation, and the related pressure for more authoritarian national economic planning would reinforce each other in sustaining a process of transforming fundamentally the character of European economic systems. By its nature, this gradual transformation would involve increasing centralized control over the economy and the growing restrictions on the internal and external operations of market forces that would be required to implement planning decisions. Controls would be needed, too, to enforce the difficult choices that would have to be made between the demands for greater welfare and earned income and the necessity to maintain some minimum degree of efficiency at macro and micro levels. And, if the views of those opposed to economic growth were to prevail, then even more stringent controls would be needed to hold in check workers' demands for increased disposable income and to shift consumption patterns away from goods and into services, governmental and private, and more *unpaid* leisure. The political, economic and other sociocultural factors likely to affect the probability that such developments would occur in Western Europe over the next decade or so are assessed in Chapter 5.

Welfare/Efficiency Interactions in Selected West European Countries

4

This chapter presents brief analyses of the differing relationships between welfare and efficiency in six West European nations. The purposes are (a) to explain the main factors involved in the changes in this relationship in each country and (b) to ascertain whether negative-sum effects have already arisen or are likely to emerge in the coming years that contribute to neomercantilist trends. For these purposes, it is not necessary to give a comprehensive account of the progress, problems and policies of each national economy. Only those aspects will be covered that help to illuminate the nature and consequences of the welfare/efficiency relationship. However, as explained in Chapter 1, even this limited aim cannot be fully achieved due to the incompleteness of the available data.

SWEDEN

Until recently, no OECD country was more successful than Sweden in reconciling continuing welfare improvements with the maintenance both of an adequate rate of productivity growth and of international competitiveness. Indeed, Sweden was a model in these respects: it developed one of the most comprehensive and generous welfare systems in the OECD region and, until the early 1970s, it had relatively high investment in its export industries and satisfactory growth of their sales to foreign markets. At the same time, it was an innovator in countercyclical policies—particularly in what the Swedes call labor-market policy—which enabled Sweden to maintain very low levels of unemployment throughout recessionary periods without strain on the balance of payments.

In the last few years, however, Sweden has suffered an alarming loss of international competitiveness as its unit labor costs have soared above those of many of its major trading partners and competitors. The question is whether this development is a temporary, largely cyclical phenomenon or whether it reflects the emergence of more basic negative-sum interactions between welfare and efficiency. Some Swedish economists hold that, even by the late 1960s, certain trends had become evident that were beginning to undermine the basis of Sweden's hitherto positive-sum welfare/efficiency relationship. Temporarily reversed by the 1972–73 world export boom, these trends were resumed and reinforced, they believe, during the mid-1970s by the new directions of trade-union and socialist policy internally and by the unfavorable changes in Sweden's external economic environment (e.g., the OPEC price increases and the slow recovery from the 1974–75 recession). Hence, it may legitimately be asked: is Sweden at or even beyond the critical turning point in its welfare/efficiency relationship and, if so, what are the prospects for reversing this process?

Real gross domestic product grew at an annual average rate of nearly 5 percent during the 1960s but fell to half that average annual rate during the first half of the

1970s.[1] Despite this deceleration, the rate of growth was sufficient until 1974 to permit continuing substantial increases in private and public consumption and satisfactory rates of private investment, especially in mining and manufacturing. Public investment, too, grew rapidly during the 1960s largely due to local-government construction programs for hospitals and health centers, roads, schools, and so forth, but its rate declined to a more normal level during the first half of the 1970s.

However, government expenditures as a whole rose rapidly during those years, particularly for transfer payments and other costs of the welfare system and for public employment at national and local levels. Total government expenditures were 35 percent of GDP (at market prices) in 1965, 43 percent in 1970, 52 percent in 1975, and 62 percent in 1977.

This trend both reflected and stimulated important changes in the composition of the labor force. While the total employed increased by over 418,000 from 1960 to 1975, employment in agriculture, fishing and forestry dropped by over 318,000, from 16.5 percent of the labor force to 6.7 percent. Employment in mining and manufacturing hardly changed in size over the period and, in consequence, its share of the total fell from 29.1 percent in 1960 to 26.1 percent in 1975. Private-service employment (including merchandise trade) grew sufficiently to maintain its percentage of the total at about 26.5 during the period. In contrast, the sectors that increased absolutely and together more than doubled in percentage share were central and especially local government, whose combined gains were equal to the total growth in employment plus about half the losses in agriculture, fishing and forestry. Another significant change in the labor force was a small decline of 4 percentage points in the male participation rate from 1965 to 1975 while female participation jumped by 11 percentage points. By 1977, more than 70 percent of the women between the ages of 16 and 64 were in the labor force. Assisted by the increasing provision of day-care facilities for children of working mothers, this growth reflects both the new conception of women's social role and the pressure to maintain real family income in the face of rising taxes and inflation.

Sweden's economic performance during the 1960s and early 1970s expressed not only the developmental potentialities of its economy but also the policies followed by the Social Democrats, who held office continuously until September 1976. Their conception of socialism involved the "nationalization" of income, not of the means of production. Thus, less than 10 percent of goods production has hitherto been carried on by companies taken over or established by the government, mainly in steel, shipbuilding, electronics, and pharmaceuticals. In contrast, the size and scope of the national welfare system have grown continuously, with the percentage rise in transfer income consistently outpacing the large percentage increases in disposable income as a whole and in private consumption. In addition to the national welfare system, the conception of distributional socialism includes

---

1   Unless otherwise specified, all historical series are from *The Swedish Economy 1975–1980: The 1975 Medium Term Survey* (Stockholm: Economic Department of the Ministry of Finance, 1976) and current statistics and forecasts are from *The Swedish Economy 1977: Prospects and Policies* (Stockholm: Ministry of Economic Affairs, May 1977); *The Swedish Budget 1977/78* and *1978/79* (Stockholm: Ministry of the Budget, 1977, 1978); and *Sweden, OECD Economic Surveys* (Paris: OECD, April 1977 and April 1978).

the maintenance of full employment and the increasing equalization of income. Sweden was able until 1977 to hold unemployment to between 1.5 and 3 percent even during recessionary periods, and it ranks second among the OECD countries in having the most equitable distribution of income.[2]

The big increase in central- and local-government employment—which has continued since 1975—reflects the growth in the size and scope of the health-care and educational services provided mainly by county and municipal agencies and in the personnel administering the other national and local welfare programs outlined in Chapter 2. These personnel costs and the benefits provided in cash and in kind by the welfare system constitute the great bulk of public-sector expenditures which totaled SKr 216.9 billion ($48.4 billion) or, as noted, 62 percent of GDP in 1977. Thus, over three-fifths of GDP was expended by the nonmarket sector in 1977. Of total government expenditures, over 46 percent was dispersed as cash transfer payments to households, as subsidies to keep food prices down, and as subsidies to nationalized and private-sector firms to cover their deficits and/or enable them to maintain employment; over 46 percent was used to finance the benefits in kind provided by the educational, health and other social-welfare systems, as well as the other costs of civil government and national defense; and almost 7.5 percent went for public-sector investments.

Of total government revenues of SKr 219.3 billion in 1977, direct taxes yielded 38 percent, indirect taxes 25 percent, employers' social security contributions and other payroll taxes 22 percent, and other revenues 15 percent. Personal income taxes levied by both the central and local governments are high and the local income tax is at a flat rate, varying among localities but averaging almost 27 percent for the country as a whole in 1977 and 29 percent in 1978. The OECD estimated that, in 1976, the average production worker (married and with two children) in Sweden paid 35 percent of his gross earnings in income tax, and the marginal rate on the next 10 percent of additional income was 63 percent.[3] Income taxes in the highest bracket reach a maximum of 85 percent. In addition, the value-added tax (VAT)— currently at a rate of 20.6 percent and affecting two-thirds of consumption—and the excise taxes on beverages, tobacco, gasoline, electricity, and so forth reduce the real consumption of workers' households despite the fact that the prices of various foods are subsidized. It should be noted, however, that employees pay no social security taxes except for a small monthly contribution to the unemployment insurance societies managed by the trade unions.

In contrast to personal income taxes, the corporate income tax is not a major source of government revenue. Although the combined nominal rate of corporate income tax levied by the central and local governments is around 57 percent, the effective rate is in most cases substantially lower due to the generous depreciation and inventory-valuation allowances, the liberal rules governing the shifting of profits among the companies comprising a group, and the countercyclical investment-reserve schemes described below. As employees pay no social security

---

2   See Malcolm Sawyer, "Income Distribution in OECD Countries," *OECD Economic Outlook: Occasional Studies* (Paris: OECD, July 1976), pp. 16–17.

3   *The Tax/Benefit Position of Selected Income Groups in OECD Member Countries* (Paris: OECD, 1978), pp. 94, 96.

taxes, a large proportion of the cost of pensions, health care, and injury and disability payments, as well as of unemployment insurance, is covered by the employers' payroll taxes, which have risen sharply since 1965 and currently add 35 percent to the basic wage cost of blue-collar workers and 40 percent to that of white-collar workers. The remaining cost of these social security programs is met by the government from general revenues.

In addition to using conventional Keynesian fiscal and monetary measures, Sweden has introduced several countercyclical devices that have enabled it to maintain virtually full employment and, until the mid-1970s, relatively high rates of investment during recessionary periods. The oldest is the investment-reserve scheme, under which a company may set aside each year up to 40 percent of its pretax profits, depositing 46 percent of the amount reserved with the central bank and adding the remainder to its own working capital. The corporation is free at any time to use part or all of the reserve but, if it does so without the government's permission, the amount spent plus a 10 percent penalty becomes part of its taxable income. However, when these reserves are utilized for purposes and at times authorized by the government, no tax is levied on them and the company receives in addition a special tax deduction equal to 10 percent of the amount expended. The permitted purposes are limited to investment in facilities and machinery, the promotion of exports, and industrial research and development, and authorizations are granted when increases in such expenditures are desirable for countercyclical reasons. After funds have been in the reserve for five years, the corporation may use up to 30 percent of that amount for permitted purposes without the government's specific authorization and without loss of tax exemption.

In 1974, a supplementary scheme was introduced, permitting 20 percent of pretax profits in excess of SKr 100,000 and 15 percent of pretax profits in excess of SKr 1,000,000 to be deposited at the central bank. With government authorization, the 20 percent portion can be spent on facilities and amenities that improve working conditions in factories and offices and the 15 percent portion for capital investment and to finance the production of goods for inventory. For the latter purpose, too, the government adopted in mid-1975 a plan under which tax-free grants were made to companies to permit them to continue producing for inventory provided they undertook not to reduce employment. The Swedish government estimated that, over the 18 months to the end of 1976, inventory accumulation amounting to over 2 percent of GDP was financed under this tax-free grant scheme, which was continued at a reduced level in 1977 to prevent too rapid liquidation of excess inventories and a resulting adverse effect on output and employment.

In addition, subsidies are given to companies increasing their employment of young people entering the labor force. These measures, combined with extensive labor training and retraining programs, involved some 4 percent of the labor force in 1977. Along with additional job creation in the public sector—which increased by some 50,000 a year in 1976 and 1977 and is estimated to add the same number in 1978—these steps held unemployment to 1.6 percent of the labor force in both 1975 and 1976 and to 1.8 percent in 1977. Thus, the real rate of unemployment in Sweden would have been close to 6 percent in 1977 in the absence of the special labor-market measures. On the one hand, these measures have certainly maintained the morale and improved the skills of the workers involved, thereby contributing to both welfare and efficiency. On the other, they have led to overmanning and pushed up production costs, which the subsidies do not cover fully. Whether the benefits to welfare and efficiency exceed the adverse effects on the latter cannot be determined.

The Swedish government's expectation was that, after the 1974–75 recession, the recovery of world demand for Sweden's exports of semiprocessed and manufactured goods would absorb the accumulated stock of these products along with the continuing current production, thus preventing any drop in domestic output and employment. However, world demand for imports failed to grow at the anticipated rate and, more important, Swedish products suffered a substantial loss in competitiveness in both foreign and domestic markets. In recent years, the volume of Sweden's manufactured exports to the other OECD countries, its principal markets, increased at a much lower rate than the latter's total imports of such products. The OECD estimated the loss of market shares for Swedish manufactured exports at 8 percent in 1975, 7 percent in 1976 and 4 to 5 percent in 1977.

In the domestic market, the government's countercyclical policies and big increases in wages and welfare benefits pushed up real private and public consumption by a total of 12 percent during the three years 1974 through 1976. Although private consumption dropped by an estimated 1.5 percent in 1977, public consumption continued to rise by an estimated 3 percent, due mainly to rising local-government employment and welfare expenditures. The growth in domestic demand for manufactured goods combined with the loss of competitiveness of domestic producers resulted in a 5 percent greater increase in imports in 1976 than Sweden's normal import propensity for such goods would have indicated.

Beginning in 1975, the loss of both foreign and domestic market shares by Swedish industry led to a continuing decline in industrial production despite the large inventory accumulations. Industrial production dropped by an estimated 4 percent in real terms during 1977 and a further—although smaller—decline is expected in 1978.

Before analyzing the reasons for Swedish industry's loss of competitiveness in both foreign and domestic markets, the effect of exchange-rate changes needs to be noted. Until 1977, Sweden's inadequate export performance and greater than normal import demand may have resulted in part from the excessive appreciation of its currency due to its link to the rising deutschemark in the European "snake." However, successive devaluations of the krona occurred in October 1976, April 1977 and August 1977, when the krona was removed from the "snake" and its rate was permitted to float downward even further. By the end of 1977, the krona had declined by about 17 percent below its level at the end of 1976. These devaluations and the phasing out of the tax-free inventory-accumulation grants during 1977 have been helping to reduce the stock of unsold semiprocessed and manufactured goods accumulated since the 1974–75 recession and to improve Sweden's export performance. But, because imports normally average about 30 percent of GDP, a devaluation of this magnitude will aggravate the effects of the other factors that have been pushing up Sweden's costs and prices relative to those of its trading partners. In the latter connection, it may be noted that the consumer price index rose by 9.8 percent in 1975, 10.3 percent in 1976, 11.4 percent in 1977, and is expected to go up by 9 to 10 percent in 1978.

The first factor affecting costs and prices was the big increase in wages in the mid-1970s, reflecting the pressure for rising real aftertax income and the commitment to equalization of income as expressed in the wage-solidarity policy that the trade unions have pursued since World War II.

This policy envisages "equal pay for equal work" regardless of the profitability of the industry or enterprise within which the work is performed. It is supposed to be implemented through a comprehensive evaluation of all jobs in the market and nonmarket sectors so that differences in wages can be used to offset inequalities in the work effort required, in the cost of the necessary education and training, in the physical conditions of work, and in the psychological satisfactions involved. Such a classification has never been made nor, even if it could be, is it likely that there would be general agreement on the evaluation of most jobs. In practice, the wage-solidarity policy has meant substantial reduction of the differentials among skilled, semiskilled and unskilled workers achieved primarily by raising the wages and salaries of the lowest paid at accelerated rates. But, the actual narrowing of differentials has been less than the nominal equalization specified in the national agreements negotiated with the Swedish Employers Federation due to the effects of wage drift. At the industry and enterprise levels, skilled workers and white-collar employees have insisted upon bigger increases for themselves to restore at least part of their former differentials, and they have sometimes resorted to wildcat strikes to obtain them. And, until recently, many employers acquiesced in these demands owing to the greater losses they might suffer if production were to be halted by strikes. Wage drift increased costs not only directly in this way but also because the higher rates won by skilled workers in one year tended to become the standard that, in accordance with the wage-solidarity policy, the trade unions sought to achieve for the lower-paid workers in the next year's negotiation.

The second factor pushing up costs in the market sector in recent years has been the increase in the social security contributions and other payroll taxes paid by the employers. These totaled about 11 percent of wages and salaries in 1965 and rose only to 18 percent by 1972.[4] But, since 1973, they have increased rapidly and, as already noted, currently add 35 percent to blue-collar wages and 40 percent to white-collar salaries. Total payroll taxes would have risen even higher in 1978 had the government not offset the mandatory increases in specific employer contributions by eliminating the 4 percent general payroll tax. If all mandatory, contractual and voluntary fringe benefits, including pay for time not worked, e.g., holiday, vacation and sick pay, are combined, the U.S. Bureau of Labor Statistics estimated that the percentage rose to around 50 percent of the wage cost for time actually worked in manufacturing in Sweden in 1976.

The third set of factors increasing costs in the market sector comprises the negative-sum effects of the national welfare system in addition to those already covered. Among the most important is the high rate of absenteeism that is encouraged by the very liberal sick-leave policy. In 1976, for example, the average number of days of paid sick leave used per insured person was 26 in Stockholm, 28 in Malmo and 29 in Göteberg (the three largest industrial centers), with short periods

---

4   Skandinaviska Enskilda Banken, *Some Data About Sweden, 1977–1978*, p. 12.

of sick leave accounting for two-thirds of the total. In some of the biggest industrial firms, rates of absenteeism of over 20 percent of the labor force have been reported. To schedule and maintain uninterrupted production despite high absenteeism requires a considerable degree of overmanning, which raises wage costs and reduces output per manhour.

These factors have combined to make total labor costs in Sweden's manufacturing industry among the highest in the OECD area. In 1975, hourly compensation rose 21 percent in kronor (30 percent in dollar terms); in 1976, 19 percent (13 percent in dollar terms); and, in 1977, an estimated 12.5 percent (10 percent in dollar terms). Unit labor costs increased 23 percent, 17 percent and an estimated 10 percent in kronor (31 percent, 11 percent and 7 percent in dollar terms) in those years.[5] However, the negotiated hourly wage rates that became effective in mid-May 1978 are substantially less than in previous years.

One result of rising costs and the loss of export and domestic market shares was the emergence of a profits squeeze. The returns on investment in the market sector were high throughout the 1960s and early 1970s. The Swedish government estimates that, during the early 1970s, the operating surplus in the manufacturing and mining sector averaged nearly 25 percent of value added. But, from 1973, the wage share rose rapidly, while that of capital dropped correspondingly, amounting to only 5 to 10 percent of value added in 1977. By another calculation, the gross profit margins of industrial enterprises with over 500 employees fell from 13 percent in 1974 to 9 percent in 1975 and 6.5 percent in 1976, and dropped further in 1977. Despite the fall in profits and the decline in industrial output, the rate of investment in machinery and equipment—although not in new plant—in manufacturing remained high in 1975 and most of 1976 largely because the government authorized the use for these purposes of the tax-free company funds in the countercyclical investment-reserve scheme described above. By late 1976, however, manufacturing investment was slackening, and the Swedish government estimated that investment in plant and machinery dropped by 15 percent in 1977 even though the authorization to withdraw tax-free funds from the investment reserve continued during the year. The government and the Federation of Swedish Industries both project a further large decline in industrial investment in 1978 of 15 percent.[6]

Another result of Sweden's declining international competitiveness was the deterioration in its balance of payments. After current-account surpluses in the early 1970s, Sweden experienced current-account deficits of $936 million in 1974, $1.6 billion in 1975, $2.4 billion in 1976, and $3.2 billion in 1977, or about 4.25 percent of GDP. A somewhat smaller deficit is forecast for 1978.

---

5   U.S. Department of Labor, Bureau of Labor Statistics, Office of Productivity and Technology, May 4, 1978. Compensation is defined as all payments made by employers directly to their employees, before deductions of any kind, plus employer contributions to legally required insurance programs and contractual and other private welfare plans for the benefit of employees. For Sweden and the United Kingdom, the figures also include taxes (other than social security contributions) levied on payrolls or employment rolls that are paid by the employer. For intercountry comparisons of hourly compensation and unit labor costs, see the Tabular Note at the end of this chapter.

6   *Nordic Economic Outlook, May 1978* (Stockholm: Federation of Swedish Industries), p. 38.

Before it was defeated in the September 1976 elections after 44 years in office, the Social Democratic government began to be concerned about Sweden's worsening balance of payments and it started to tighten up on bank credit. However, it was not until the centrist coalition took office after the election that policy changes were instituted to lessen the rate of increase of private and public consumption and of imports. The present centrist government is well aware of the nature of the problems facing the Swedish economy and of the policies necessary to cope effectively with them. But, it is equally cognizant of the sociopolitical limitations on the measures that could be adopted to remedy Sweden's decline in international competitiveness as well as of the uncertain prospects for faster growth of world trade. This understanding confronts it with a double dilemma: the more realistically it assesses the medium-term international economic outlook, the greater the internal adjustments need to be; but, the more drastic the internal remedial measures it applies, the greater will be the frustration of popular expectations and the less likely will be its reelection in 1979. Already, the needed adjustments it has had the courage to institute have caused it to fall behind the Social Democrats in recent opinion polls.

Since World War II, Swedish blue- and white-collar workers have been accustomed to annual real increases in wages and salaries as well as in employee benefits (for example, four weeks of paid vacation a year, to which a mandatory fifth week was added in January 1978). For their part, the managers and owners of Swedish enterprises have generally acquiesced in these real-income gains because they believed them to be desirable and the increased costs could usually be recovered in the buoyant international and domestic markets of the period from 1950 to 1974. Even in the depressed conditions of 1975 and 1976, large increases in real wages were conceded by the Swedish Employers Federation. However, in 1977 their resistance stiffened. The annual wage negotiation was exceptionally bitter and took an unprecedented seven months; before agreement was reached, a general strike was threatened and sporadic strikes had already occurred. But, the agreed-upon increase in wages and the ensuing wage drift, while smaller than in the preceding years, nevertheless had an adverse effect on costs and profits. Nor did the increase prevent a small decline in workers' real disposable income due to the continuation of inflation at over 11 percent, a 3 percent rise in VAT in mid-1977, and the fact that the cut in the central government's personal-income tax rate was partially offset by increases in local taxes. A further reduction in real income will probably result from the 1978 wage negotiation, which provided for increases of only 4.25 percent for white-collar workers and 5 percent for blue-collar workers over the 17-month period through October 1979, as well as from the increased cost of imports due to the krona devaluations.

A critical question of national policy is whether subsequent wage negotiations will continue to result in sufficiently moderate settlements to help check the recent explosive rise in unit labor costs. Judging from their behavior in the 1977 and 1978 negotiations, the managers and owners of Swedish enterprises seem determined to break with their previous pattern of acquiescence in high wage increases. And, although they fought hard for their wage demands, especially in 1977, many Swedish trade-union leaders, too, have become aware of the international and domestic limitations on future rises in unit labor costs and private consumption. Some have even stated publicly that, in these circumstances, their objective must be to minimize declines in real income, not to increase it. This realistic viewpoint would be strengthened if, as expected, unemployment rises above the 1977 rate of 1.8 percent due to the projected decline in 1978 GDP of 0.5 percent, the continuing fall in industrial production, and the termination of the inventory-accumulation grants in 1977. All other things being equal, these attitudes on both sides of the negotiating table could hold down future increases in wage rates to amounts consistent with productivity gains. Thereby, they would continue to contribute to the gradual improvement in the international and domestic competitiveness of Swedish industry.

The major uncertainty relates to the attitudes of the blue- and white-collar workers. Accustomed to three decades of rising real disposable incomes and increasing government-financed social-welfare benefits, they may not tolerate for long enough a reversal of this process. Since all political parties are convinced that any significant reduction in the national welfare system would be politically impossible, much depends, therefore, on how direct and indirect taxes affect the level of real disposable income and household consumption in the next few years. The question of tax policy is crucial also to the problem of unit labor costs since rising social security contributions and other payroll taxes have contributed to making these costs among the highest in the OECD region.

With central-government budgetary deficits equal to about 4 percent of GDP in 1975, 2 percent in 1976, 5 percent in 1977, and estimated to rise to 8 to 9 percent in 1978, there are powerful constraints on fiscal policy in the next few years. Nonetheless, the cost of the national welfare system mounts annually due to the indexing of benefits to inflation, the absolute and relative expansion in the size of the non-working portion of the population, and the already mandated improvements over the next few years, such as the extension of supplementary pensions (ATP) to all retired persons, the big construction program for day-care centers, and the improvements in other welfare standards. This annual growth in the welfare system is largely responsible for the actual and projected increases in government employment of about 50,000 a year during the second half of the 1970s. To avoid bigger inflationary budget deficits, the Swedish government has ended the grants for inventory accumulation and reduced some other expenditures. But, it has had to continue the worker retraining and other programs, which have been preventing a rise in unemployment, and the subsidies to the nationalized industries and market-sector firms adversely affected by imports and the loss of exports. Therefore, unless a substantial increase in the level of economic activity occurs to generate much larger tax receipts, a further rise in tax rates may be unavoidable. Given the limitations on the stimulation of domestic demand, the main hope for achieving a higher level of economic activity is a substantial increase in the exports of semiprocessed and manufactured goods, which normally account for 40 to 50 percent of Sweden's total output of these products. In turn, such an improved export performance depends either on an unlikely boom in world import demand, or, more realistically, on a rapid recovery of Sweden's international competitiveness.

Thus, Sweden is confronted with a series of interdependent policy dilemmas which reflect the fact that, in the mid-1970s, it entered the early stages of a vicious circle of negative-sum welfare/efficiency interactions. The nonmarket sector has grown both absolutely and relative to the market sector and, as noted, already preempts three-fifths of GDP. This trend has been having adverse effects on the incentives for research and development and investment in the market sector and on its international competitiveness. Unless the rise in public expenditures can be limited, tax rates will probably have to be increased, which would not only strengthen the disincentives to work but also adversely affect Sweden's international competitiveness by further raising costs. The resolution of these dilemmas can only be accomplished by slowing down, if not halting for a time, the improvement of the national welfare system and the increase of unit labor costs until productivity gains in the market sector, especially in traded-goods production, can offset their adverse effects on international competitiveness. It will also be necessary to correct some of the other ways in which the national welfare system has been adversely affecting the productivity of the economy and the efficiency of market-sector enterprises. Data is lacking for evaluating quantitatively the precise effects on unit labor costs of high absenteeism, skilled labor shortages, longer vacations, earlier retirements, and other components or consequences of the welfare system. Nonetheless, it cannot be doubted that they have tended to increase unit labor costs directly, as well as indirectly by weakening the incentives to work, to innovate and to invest. The need is not to reduce, let alone abolish, the welfare benefits involved but rather to change their forms or the conditions under which they are provided so as to lessen their negative impact on productivity.

With respect to restoring and maintaining Sweden's international competitiveness, a possible future development that would have a major adverse effect on the incentives of the managers and owners of market-sector enterprises to undertake the requisite investment and technological research is the intention of many trade-union leaders and Social Democratic politicians to resume the movement toward the more extreme forms of industrial democracy when the socialists return to office. The prospect that legislation along the lines of the Meidner Plan (explained in Chapter 3) would be enacted during the early 1980s is especially worrisome to Swedish industrialists, as is also the promise of the leader of the Social Democratic Party to raise the number of trade-union representatives on company boards to near parity. If by either or both of these changes trade-union control over market-sector enterprises appears likely to be achieved over a period of time, there would be a corresponding weakening of the incentive for their present managers and stockholders to undertake the research and development and to make the new capital investments required to help restore and maintain Sweden's international competitiveness. The adverse impact would be especially serious in those branches of industry responsible for the high-quality and high-technology products that have earned excellent reputations in foreign markets and have enabled Swedish firms to win large international contracts. The uncertainty regarding future developments in industrial democracy may be the most difficult negative influence for the existing coalition government to counteract.

Negative-sum welfare/efficiency interactions have already helped to make Swedish policy much more neomercantilist than it was a decade ago. The counter-cyclical subsidies to finance inventories and the wages of workers who would otherwise be laid off or not hired constitute in effect, if not in intent, subventions to its exporting and import-competing industries. In addition to the investment-reserve scheme explained above, the Swedish government provides generous depreciation allowances for investment in machinery and equipment and cash grants for this purpose to loss-making companies unable to benefit from such tax reductions. More directly related to foreign trade, subsidies in the forms of loan guarantees, soft loans and grants are made to industries facing stiff competition in foreign and domestic markets, with shipbuilding, iron and steel, and textiles and clothing obtaining 85 percent of this aid. The government intends to reduce the size of these and other distressed industries and to make the remaining portions of them more competitive. It estimates that subsidies and other assistance to them would be over $1 billion a year in 1977 and 1978 and that shipbuilding and iron and steel—most of which are nationalized—would receive an additional $2.25 billion of loan guarantees from 1977 through 1979.

In sum, Sweden's centrist government has succeeded in checking the vicious circle in which the economy was caught during the mid-1970s. It is currently trying to reverse this process by relating increases in welfare benefits and earned incomes to productivity growth and by restructuring industry to restore Sweden's international competitiveness. If these efforts can overcome the policy dilemmas noted, the trend toward neomercantilist aids to production can be halted; if not, this trend will in all probability continue.

UNITED KINGDOM

That the United Kingdom has been experiencing earlier and more severe negative-sum welfare/efficiency interactions than the other OECD countries surveyed here may seem strange in the light of some of the indicators noted in Chapter 1. Public expenditures have been a smaller percentage of GDP than in some of the others, and social security contributions, payroll taxes and other fringe benefits add less to basic wage costs than in any of them. This indicates, however, that institutional and cultural factors have made the United Kingdom susceptible to vicious-circle effects at a lower point in the relative increase of nonmarket-sector income and employment than are the other countries.

By the first half of the 1970s, the United Kingdom was well into a vicious circle of inadequate market-sector investment, slow economic growth, rising inflation and unemployment, recurrent balance-of-payments strain, increasing nonmarket-sector expenditures, mounting taxation and deficit financing, falling industrial profits, declining market-sector investment, and so on, with resulting loss of both real income and efficiency. Beginning in mid-1975, however, efforts were made to check this vicious circle and considerable success was achieved over the next two years in slowing the rise of nonmarket-sector expenditures and government employment, reducing the rate of inflation, and allowing industrial profits to increase so as to stimulate market-sector investment and employment. Thanks largely to the growing flow of North Sea oil after mid-1977, the balance of payments showed a small surplus by the end of the year. Hence, the overriding question facing Britain's policy makers and opinion leaders in the years ahead is whether the mounting resources from the North Sea will be used to provide a breathing spell for the basic reconstruction work of transforming the hitherto negative-sum welfare/efficiency interactions into positive-sum effects (i.e., continuing improvements in both productivity and living standards) or merely to suspend temporarily the operations of the vicious circle without eradicating its underlying causes.

The statistical demonstration of the vicious circle in which the United Kingdom was enmeshed from the mid-1960s to the mid-1970s has been presented in detail by Bacon and Eltis and only the main outlines of their findings can be summarized here.[7] In brief, they explain that the root of Britain's problem lay in the relatively more rapid growth of nonmarket-sector income and employment since the early 1960s and its consequent preemption of an increasing share of the goods and services produced by the market sector, thereby reducing both the available resources and the incentives for job-creating investment in the latter. Whereas in 1961 the nonmarket sector's gross claims (i.e., before tax) on marketed output were 41.5 percent, they rose to 62 percent by 1975. Over the period, central-government employment increased by 27 percent and local-government employment by 70 percent, while employment in the services part of the market sector rose by only 11 percent and industrial employment fell by 15 percent. In other words, nonindustrial employment, mainly public-sector employment, increased by 40 percent relative to industrial employment—a very large shift in so brief a period.

The big expansion of nonmarket-sector employment was mainly justified as needed to provide greatly increased welfare benefits in kind and in cash. To acquire the resources for these mounting expenditures for the salaries of government employees and for welfare benefits, direct and indirect taxes were increased substantially and large budgetary deficits were incurred. In turn, higher taxes and inflation impelled those trade unions with effective bargaining power to press for wage increases to preserve, and where possible to increase, the real disposable income of their members. Thus, not only was the relative share of resources available to the market sector declining but also a disproportionate part of those that remained was obtained by the more powerful unions. Conversely, the relative shares available for market-sector profits and investment and for exports were declining. Net profits of market-sector companies as a whole were 17 percent of value added in 1964 and only about 3 percent in 1974 and 1975; for manufacturing companies, the decline was even more severe—from 17.9 percent in 1964 to an estimated net loss of 6 percent in 1974 (allowing for the effects of inflation). Net investment in industry dropped from 8.2 percent of sales of industrial production in 1961 to 3.5 percent in 1973 and rose only to 6.8 percent in 1975 (with half this increase for North Sea oil) and, over the period, the nonpetroleum investment was largely for capital-deepening rather than for capital-broadening purposes. The proportion of industrial production exported, net of industrial imports, fell from 15.5 percent of total industrial production in 1961 to only 11 percent in 1975.

Among the important consequences of these trends pointed out by Bacon and Eltis are:

---

7   Robert Bacon and Walter Eltis, *Britain's Economic Problem: Too Few Producers*, 2nd edition (London: The Macmillan Press, Ltd., 1978), Chapter 1. For a dissenting view, see A.P. Thirlwall, "The U.K.'s Economic Problem: A Balance-of-Payments Constraint?", *National Westminister Bank Quarterly Review*, February 1978, and the further exchange between him and Bacon and Eltis in the May 1978 issue of that *Review*.

. . . [that] while Britain was investing enough to raise industrial production 3 per cent per annum or 35 per cent in a decade until the mid-1960s, the rate of growth of industrial capacity is only about two-thirds of this today. This means that when demand is expanded . . . the plant is just not there to meet the country's requirement for goods. Hence articles which are normally produced in Britain have to be imported and the goods are just not available to exploit export opportunities. . . . This has become true over an increasing range of industrial products. In consequence, attempts by government to move toward full employment produce vast balance of payments deficits. . . . In addition, the deep problem that declining industrial investment is producing is unemployment which is becoming increasingly structural. . . .[8]

The effects of these trends on the international competitive position of the United Kingdom have been particularly marked. A large part of Britain's manufactured output is exported, comprising over four-fifths of U.K. merchandise exports. Thus, manufactured exports provide a substantial share of the employment and incomes in the market sector and help importantly to finance Britain's merchandise imports, which are currently 27 percent of its GDP. Yet, even with capital-deepening investment, output per worker in manufacturing grew from 1955 to 1973 at an average annual rate of only 3.2 percent while increasing at rates of around 5 percent in the other major European industrial nations. From 1964 to 1974, Britain's unit labor costs in manufacturing rose at an average annual rate of 7.1 percent while those of its five major international competitors were significantly lower, averaging only two-thirds the British rate. Despite recurrent sterling devaluations, Britain's share of world exports of manufactures dropped from nearly 16 percent in 1960 to 10.5 percent in 1970 and 8.5 percent in 1976 but recovered by about 1.5 percent in 1977. The OECD estimates that, over the past 10 to 15 years, the U.K.'s imports of manufactures have risen on a trend basis at rates 4 to 5 times higher than the growth of its industrial production.[9]

The effects of the OPEC price rise and of the world recession of 1974–75 superimposed on the adverse trends within the British economy sketched above resulted in a stagnant GDP, which fell by 0.6 percent (at factor cost on an output basis) in 1974 and a further 1.7 percent in 1975 but increased by 1.1 percent in 1976 and 1.6 percent in 1977. The impact on manufacturing output, however, was much more adverse: it declined by 1.5 percent in 1974 and a further 6 percent in 1975, while rising by only 0.7 percent in 1976 and 0.6 percent in 1977. Excluding school-leavers, unemployment increased gradually from a little under 5 percent at the end of 1975 to 6 percent during the latter part of 1977, and it would have been 1 percent higher had it not been for the large-scale wage subsidies given for job creation and for the training programs instituted in mid-1975 to slow the rise in unemployment. After the explosive increase of money wages in the early 1970s, the index of real

---

8   Bacon and Eltis, *Britain's Economic Problem*, p. 19.

9   Unless otherwise specified, the statistics on the United Kingdom are derived from *United Kingdom, OECD Economic Surveys* (Paris: OECD, March 1977 and March 1978); *National Income and Expenditure, 1965–75* and *1966–76* (HMSO); and recent issues of the U.K. Treasury's *Economic Progress Reports, Economic Trends* (HMSO) and the *Department of Employment Gazette* (HMSO).

average earnings (with the second half of 1973 as 100) fell from the high of 106 at the end of 1974 to 95 in 1977.

The U.K.'s poor economic performance since the early 1960s has continued under both Labour and Conservative governments and, insofar as it results from policy decisions, both must share in the responsibility. On the one hand, neither party has been able to formulate and implement an effective program of incentives and aids for revitalizing British industry—for raising its unsatisfactory rate of investment and improving its ability to export and to compete with imports in the domestic market. On the other hand, each party has tried to outbid the other in expanding the size and coverage of the national welfare system, with consequent increases in government employment, expenditures and taxation. In addition, the left-wing politicians and activists in the Labour Party and the trade unions have remained dogmatically committed to nationalization of the means of production as the road to socialism.

About 10 percent of GDP is produced in the 20-odd public corporations and nationalized companies in electricity, gas, coal, steel, railroad, automobile, aerospace, shipbuilding, machine-tool, and other industries. Many of these enterprises were nationalized as part of the Labour Party's move toward socialism, but others—such as in automobiles, shipbuilding and machine tools—were taken over by the government to avert unemployment in uneconomic or inefficient enterprises. Many of them have required government loans and grants to cover their deficits, whose combined total amounted to an estimated 2 percent of GDP in the recession year 1975. The revenues of public corporations were depressed during the first half of the 1970s by the government's policy of refusing to allow them to raise their prices to consumers so as to hold down the increase in the rate of inflation. Since then, this policy has been reversed and the deficits have declined or disappeared. But, the continuing subsidies are still substantial. Programs for rationalizing the deficit-ridden enterprises and improving their productivity and competitiveness, particularly shipbuilding, automobiles and steel, have too frequently been either unrealistic or largely frustrated by political and trade-union opposition to the required reduction in their labor forces.

To illuminate the role played in Britain's unsatisfactory economic performance by adverse welfare/efficiency interactions, as distinct from cyclical and other economic influences, the analysis will focus on two sets of factors that particularly reflect the rising pressures for both improved welfare and greater aftertax earned incomes. The first set, relating to improved welfare income, involves the ways in which the rapid growth of the nonmarket sector and the methods of financing it have drained resources from the market sector and adversely affected its productivity, investment and international competitiveness. The second set, relating to greater aftertax earned income, includes the factors that have shifted an increasing proportion of the resources remaining in the market sector into rising consumption by market-sector workers in the more powerful unions through higher wages and employee benefits.

As to the first set of factors relating to the growth of and methods of financing the nonmarket sector, the total expenditures of the central government and of local governments increased as a percent of GDP (at market prices) from 37 percent in 1965 to 41 percent in 1970 and to 50 percent in 1975. After the change in policy discussed later, they dropped to 48 percent in 1976 and the proportion was further reduced in 1977 to 44 percent.[10] Direct and indirect taxes and social security contributions financed four-fifths of total expenditures in 1965, three-quarters in 1975 and four-fifths in 1977. The public-sector borrowing requirement rose from 3.4 percent of GDP in 1965 to 10 percent in 1975; it is estimated to have dropped to a little over 4 percent in 1977, due in part to the sale of a portion of the government's holdings of British Petroleum stock, and is projected to increase to 5.25 percent in 1978.

Over the period, most of the increase in government expenditures was necessitated, as already noted, by the growing volume of benefits in cash and kind provided by the welfare system,[11] the rising salaries and benefits of the growing number of nonmarket-sector employees, and the public-sector investment and indirect costs (e.g., for the mounting debt service) thereby entailed. Most welfare benefits are indexed either to the rate of inflation or to the rate of wage increases, whichever has been greatest over the preceding 12 months. Thus, over time, welfare benefits increase more than wage earnings, which in some years rise less than inflation.

The rising costs of the welfare system have necessitated general increases in taxation. Personal-income tax rates in the United Kingdom have been among the highest and most steeply progressive in the OECD region. The basic tax rate in the lowest-income bracket was 35 percent of income above the tax threshold until the rate was reduced to 34 percent, effective in April 1977. (As explained below, further reductions were proposed in the 1978 Budget.) According to the OECD, the portion of gross earnings paid by the average production worker in the United Kingdom (married and with two children) in income tax and social security contributions rose from 19 percent in 1972 to 26 percent in 1976 while the marginal rate on the next 10 percent of additional income went from 34 percent to 41 percent over the period.[12] For people in the higher-income brackets, the top marginal rate reaches 83 percent for earned income and all unearned (investment) income from £2,000 is taxed a further 15 percent, bringing the combined top rate to 98 percent. In addition, the indirect taxes on consumption are high; although the rate—8 percent—and coverage of the VAT are less than in most continental countries, the excise taxes (on tobacco, alcoholic beverages, gasoline, and other consumer products) are substantial and cut significantly into the actual consumption of blue- and white-collar workers. Combined with the very high rates of personal income tax in the middle-income brackets, the indirect taxes even adversely affect the consumption of many junior- and intermediate-grade managers, technicians, teachers, and professionals. The corporate-income tax rate in the United Kingdom

---

10   These percentages reflect the change in the presentation of government income and expenditure in the national income accounts made by the British government in 1977. Under the change, public corporations are no longer consolidated with general government, except in the financial accounts. On the previously consolidated basis, the percentages given above would have been higher.

11   Nevertheless, the British welfare system is not as comprehensive nor are its benefits as large as Sweden's. But, the U.K.'s 1977 per capita GDP (at market prices and average 1977 exchange rates) was less than half that of Sweden—$4,360 versus $9,490—and hence the latter can afford a higher absolute level of welfare expenditures.

12   See footnote 3, p. 64.

is currently 52 percent, except that some small companies are taxed at 42 percent.[13] Recently, however, the depreciation allowances, investment tax credits and other deductions and exemptions have been made more generous.

Employers' social security contributions, payroll taxes and other fringe benefits were estimated to total around 31 percent of the wage cost for time actually worked in industry in 1975.[14]

The growing size of and the methods of financing the welfare system produced a variety of adverse and sometimes contradictory effects. On the one hand, the heavy burden of taxation has impelled blue- and white-collar workers to press for continually rising money wages so as to increase their aftertax incomes. On the other hand, the steeply mounting marginal tax rates have deterred many workers from qualifying for higher-paid skilled jobs, leading to shortages in these categories despite a comparatively high rate of general unemployment.[15] Combined with the loss of certain income-related welfare benefits (e.g., child benefits and rent subsidies), high personal-income tax rates may make it more advantageous for the head of a family to live on tax-free unemployment payments (for as long as they last) than to accept a nominally higher-paying job.[16]

There have been analogous effects on management in the market sector. Among the most important has been the "brain drain," for which Table 4–1 presents the available statistics. It is generally maintained in the United Kingdom

Table 4–1. Net Migration of United Kingdom Managers and Administrators, 1964–76
(Thousands)

1964	1965	1966	1967	1968	1969	1970	1971	1972	1973	1974	1975	1976
+0.4	−1.3	−1.1	−1.1	−0.6	−1.0	−1.4	+0.2	−0.8	−0.2	−2.2	−4.5	−3.0

Notes: Negative sign indicates a net outflow from the United Kingdom. Excludes migration to and from the Republic of Ireland and Ugandan Asians entering the United Kingdom in 1973.

Source: International Passenger Survey (IPS), conducted by U.K. Office of Population, Censuses and Surveys. From *Department of Employment Gazette* (London: HMSO, September 1977), p. 903; reprinted with permission.

13   Other small companies, however, come under the Inland Revenue's "close-company" rules, under which a certain proportion of their profits are assumed to be distributed and hence are taxed at the higher rates of unearned income.

14   *Labour Costs in Industry in 1975, Statistical Telegram*, 1–1978 (Luxemburg: European Community), Table 5. Fringe benefits include all legally mandatory, contractual and voluntary benefits, including pay for time not worked, e.g., holiday, vacation and sick pay.

15   Gerry Eastwood, *Skilled Labour Shortages in the United Kingdom: With Particular Reference to the Engineering Industry* (London: British-North American Committee, 1976); and *The Economist*, June 24, 1978, pp. 115–118.

16   In his Budget Speech in April 1978, the Chancellor of the Exchequer stated that the income tax rate levied on people in the lowest income bracket is the highest in the world, in consequence of which "many of the low paid are little better off in work than on the dole" and their rate should be cut.

that the high tax rates in the medium- and upper-income brackets, reinforced by the recent taxing of certain hitherto tax-free perquisites, are among the most important reasons for the steady emigration of business managers, scientists and technicians, doctors, university professors, journalists, entertainers, and so forth to other OECD countries, in which both their gross and aftertax incomes would be substantially greater. Another important effect has been to strengthen the preference for leisure of many owners and managers of small and medium-size enterprises, which leads to inadequate management control and competitive capability. Better management performance is also discouraged by the fact that managers would gain too little in increased aftertax income for taking the risks involved in more innovative and dynamic behavior or for the expense and disruption of moving to nominally higher-paying positions in other parts of the country.

The size of and methods of financing the welfare system and certain of the economic policies adopted to cope with related budgetary and balance-of-payments deficits have also had adverse consequences, directly and indirectly, on market-sector enterprises. Although the resulting low rate of investment in plant and equipment has limited the borrowing requirements of manufacturing firms, they were also until recently deterred from borrowing by the prevailing high nominal interest rates. High nominal interest rates reflected not only the high rates of inflation but also a monetary policy designed to attract short- and long-term portfolio-investment funds from abroad so as to reduce the balance-of-payments deficits and ease the downward pressure on the floating pound sterling. Thus, the high nominal interest rates of past years both raised costs further in the market sector and helped to deter new investment in plant and equipment.

The adverse effects of the first set of factors relating to the size of and methods of financing the welfare system have been compounded by those of the second set of factors relating to the pressures to raise money wages and salaries so as to increase—or at least maintain—the real purchasing power of aftertax earned incomes. Here, the institutional characteristics of the British trade-union movement and the attitudes and motivations of many workers, especially those active in union affairs, have been of crucial importance, as also have been the deficiencies of many owners and managers of manufacturing enterprises.

About half of the total workforce belongs to trade unions, but the proportion is over three-quarters in manufacturing companies with over 100 workers and around 90 percent in those with over 200 workers.[17] The unions are more fragmented and power within them is more decentralized in Britain than in any of the continental countries surveyed here or even in the United States. There are over 460 separate unions in the United Kingdom—compared with 19 in Germany—divided along both industrial and craft lines. Individual plants may contain a dozen or more unions representing different skills and/or stages of the production process. Demarcation disputes among them have been recurrent, often resulting in work stoppages. The struggle to hold on to members or to expand membership at the expense of other unions tends also to reinforce the resistance to reducing restrictive labor practices, feather-bedding and other forms of overmanning that

---

17   *Report of the Committee of Inquiry on Industrial Democracy* [Bullock Committee Report] (London: HMSO, January 1977), p. 14.

arises from the general fear of unemployment. Competition within and among unions has fostered the concentration of power at the plant level, which is in effect the "front line" in the rivalries among unions, on the one hand, and in their struggles with management, on the other. While they may use their leverage on management to help protect or advance their own union's interests vis-à-vis their rivals in a plant, the shop stewards may at the same time combine in a plant-wide committee to exact concessions from management for one or more of their unions.

Thus, on most matters affecting worker productivity and unit labor costs, the most powerful voices on the labor side are those of the shop stewards—the local union leaders—whose influence on wage bargaining, job classification, work and shift assignments, introduction of new technologies, hiring and firing, layoffs, and other determinants of productivity and labor costs is often more important than that of the top officials of their unions. In turn, the latter are much more influential than the leaders of the national labor confederation, the Trades Union Congress, which has far less control over its constituent unions than do its continental counterparts. The TUC's main effective role is as the spokesman for the labor movement as a whole vis-à-vis the government in office, the national organizations on the management side, especially the Confederation of British Industry, and the public generally.

Rivalries among unions at both local and national levels are one major cause of wage drift. In many cases, the effective bargaining agents for the workers in negotiations regarding wages and benefits are the shop stewards. Often, these negotiations are conducted independently in each plant by the local shop stewards and not on a company-wide—let alone an industry-wide—basis. The size and frequency of the increases obtained are influenced by three interrelated forms of mutually stimulated escalation of demands: the rivalry among the different unions within the same factory, that among the same union's local organizations in the different plants of the same company, and that among the same union's local organizations in different companies in the same industry. And, at the national level, rivalry among different unions or top-level union leaders leads to similar efforts to outdo one another in wage and benefit settlements. The other major cause of wage drift is the effort to preserve the traditional differentials in wages among various skills and between skilled and unskilled workers generally that have been eroded by the wage-restraint policy discussed below and the egalitarian convictions of certain trade-union leaders.

The effects on industrial productivity and labor costs of these institutional characteristics of the British trade-union movement are reinforced by the motivations and attitudes of many workers, especially union activists and shop stewards. Some of the latter, who were especially influential during the first half of the 1970s, held left-wing political convictions that impelled them to press militantly for maximum demands without regard to the broader economic consequences. And, most workers, although moderate in their own political views, are naturally interested in obtaining higher wages and other benefits, which inclines them to support the local union leaders most effective in winning such gains. During the 1960s and early 1970s, there was a pronounced leftward drift in the leadership of several of the largest and most powerful unions that, in turn, strengthened the influence of left-wing socialists in the Labour Party. This trend appears to have been reversed in recent years and support for the more moderate trade-union leaders has been growing.

Another factor affecting workers' and trade-union attitudes is the class consciousness that is still evident in the United Kingdom. This is expressed, on the one hand, in the sense of superiority of those owners and managers of enterprises who regard themselves as members of the "Establishment" by birth, education or economic attainment; and, on the other hand, in the sense of resentment of many workers and employees who regard themselves, and are treated by their employers, as members of a "lower class." Moreover, unlike in past centuries, the resentment is no longer tempered by respect for the "Establishment's" successful guidance of the nation's destinies. Since the end of World War II, the loss of empire, the decline of Britain's importance in the international system and, above all, the failure to manage the U.K. economy so as to realize popular expectations for continuing rises in levels of living without excessive inflation, unemployment or balance-of-payments problems have helped to diminish the "Establishment" in the eyes of many workers and intellectuals. And, their resentment has been aggravated by the attitude still prevalent in the managements of a substantial—although declining—number of British companies that their workers should accept deferentially whatever decisions their "superiors" choose to make. Finally, unskilled workers' expectations are stimulated by the support for further equalization of income and wealth that is widespread not only in the Labour Party and the trade-union hierarchy but also in the civil service, the universities and the communications media.

On the management side, class consciousness is often accompanied by a lingering quasi-aristocratic preference for leisure and prejudice against aggressive entrepreneurship and technical proficiency. The negative effects of these attitudes on efficiency and profitability have been reinforced by the disincentives to work, investment and technological innovation discussed above. The resulting entrepreneurial shortcomings can be found in a substantial number of companies, especially among the small and medium-size enterprises. However, there are many outstandingly successful corporations not only among the large multinational companies but also among the smaller firms, particularly those started or acquired by the dynamic group of new postwar entrepreneurs. Nevertheless, the owners and managers of too many companies share some or all of the deficiencies noted in business attitudes and capabilities. The results have been inadequate knowledge of and control over developments within their companies, lags in the adoption of new technologies and management methods, inability to cope with the changing attitudes of workers and trade-union leaders, lack of information on the conditions and prospects in foreign and even in domestic markets, and unwillingness to compete abroad and at home with the more aggressive and efficient managers of other countries.

The fragmented and decentralized character of the British trade-union movement and workers' attitudes, on the one hand, and the inadequacies of many British managers, on the other, have contributed to official and, especially, unofficial strikes and work stoppages. Neither the total number of working days lost to strikes nor their frequency has been large in the United Kingdom compared with other OECD countries. But, a work stoppage of only a few days by a small number of key workers can halt an entire production line or can do so indirectly by preventing an outside supplier from producing or delivering necessary materials and parts. Work stoppages having such effects have unfortunately been endemic in certain industries and companies important for Britain's export capabilities and for competing with imports in the home market (e.g., automobiles, steel). Not only have they helped to raise costs but they have also contributed to Britain's poor competitive performance with respect to delivery reliability and product-quality control.

The cumulative effects of the two sets of factors affecting labor costs and market-sector productivity were reflected in the dramatic rise in hourly compensation in manufacturing of close to 300 percent in sterling (153 percent on a dollar basis) from 1967 to 1977. In real terms, hourly compensation in manufacturing rose only 34 percent over the period. In part, of course, the increase in money terms was a natural result of the pressures to maintain both real income in a period of high inflation and aftertax earned income in a period of rising taxes. But, it was accelerated by the rivalries within and among unions, the attitudes of their members, and the ineffectualness of many managements in wage negotiations. From 1967 to 1977, unit labor costs rose by 215 percent in sterling (100 percent in dollars).[18] The adverse effects on the price competitiveness of British exports and the ability to compete with imports in the home market were only partially offset by the successive devaluations of sterling during those years. The sharp upward movement in labor costs also contributed importantly to inflation and, in turn, the high inflation rate helped to generate pressures for additional increases in wages and benefits.

The vicious circle in which negative-sum welfare/efficiency interactions played major roles during the 1960s and early 1970s was greatly accelerated by the adverse impact on the British economy of the OPEC price rise and the 1974–75 recession. By mid-1975, the further substantial deterioration of the U.K.'s economic performance produced a growing sense of crisis as inflation rose at one point to an annual rate of nearly 30 percent and the public-sector borrowing requirement reached an annual rate of 10 percent of GDP while a large current-account deficit in the balance of payments persisted. From mid-1975 to mid-1977, the Labour Party government took various drastic actions designed to check and, it hoped, eventually to reverse the process of economic deterioration. One of the most important was the so-called pay-restraint policy, under which annual wage increases were to be limited in accordance with voluntary pledges by the TUC and the CBI. Both at its own initiative and to meet the conditions for obtaining a large loan from the International Monetary Fund (IMF), the Labour government imposed ceilings on certain increases in public-sector expenditures. In addition, efforts were initiated to eliminate some of the inefficiencies in the welfare system and to lessen its disincentives to work. A new "industrial strategy" was formulated to try to improve the competitiveness of selected industries in both foreign and domestic markets. A variety of tax incentives and subsidies was adopted to stimulate market-sector investment and employment both generally and in economically depressed regions.

These and other measures instituted during the second half of 1975 and in 1976 began to produce beneficial effects in the course of 1977, and the sense of crisis

---

18   U.S. Department of Labor, May 4, 1978. See footnote 5, p. 68, for details of coverage.

accordingly abated. By mid-1977, the inflation rate fell to half the mid-1975 level, helped also by the decline in international commodity prices in 1976. Market-sector profits started to rise in late 1976 from their very low—for many industries, negative—rates in 1975 and most of 1976, while investment in manufacturing plant and equipment increased by 8 percent in volume in 1977 after declines in 1975 and 1976 of 14 percent and 4 percent, respectively. And, due both to the continuing effects of the 20 percent devaluation of sterling during 1976 and the accelerating flow of North Sea oil after mid-1977, the balance-of-payments showed a small surplus on current account for 1977.

Reflecting these and other favorable trends—e.g., the drop in inflation to an annual rate of under 10 percent early in 1978—the April 1978 Budget proposed considerable easing of the restraints imposed on the British economy during the two preceding years. In place of the 34 percent tax rate for the lowest income bracket, a new basic rate of 25 percent on the first £750 of taxable income would be introduced while a rate of 33 percent—voted as an amendment to the government's bill by all of the opposition parties—would be applied to incomes from £750 to £8,000. In the upper-income brackets, the bands would be widened, thereby reducing the numbers of people subject to the highest tax rates, which remain at 83 percent for earned income and 98 percent for investment income. Some tax relief would also be granted to small businesses. To make up for part of the revenue loss resulting from the opposition's amendments, the Labour government proposed to increase the employers' social security contribution (currently 8.75 percent) by an additional 1.5 percent of basic wages and salaries. On the expenditure side, a substantial expansion of the pension system also was initiated—to take effect progressively in the coming years—granting supplementary income-related pensions in addition to the flat-rate weekly benefit hitherto received by all retired persons. It will be financed by increasing the social security contributions by a further 1.25 percent of basic wages and salaries for the employers and by 0.75 percent for the employees.

The Labour government's efforts after mid-1975 to revitalize British industry constituted a significant beginning in the difficult and prolonged task of reversing the vicious circle sketched above. Perhaps the most encouraging development was the willingness of the majority of British workers to observe the pay-restraint agreement despite the 7 percent decline in their real earnings while it was in effect.

Nevertheless, now that the general sense of crisis has passed, the outlook for the future is very uncertain. Productivity in manufacturing has not grown since 1973. Due mainly to sterling devaluation, exports of manufactures increased in volume by 8 percent in 1977, thereby raising Britain's world share by an estimated 1.5 percent. However, imports of manufactures continued to grow even faster—by 10.4 percent in volume—despite their higher prices in sterling and the 1 percent decline in private consumption in 1977 as a whole. This trend indicates that important sections of British industry are still losing their ability to compete with imports in the domestic market.[19] Increases in real disposable income are undoubtedly occurring in 1978 due both to the tax cut and to the fact that, mainly owing to wage drift,

---

19   See *The Economist*, May 27, 1978, pp. 74–75, for details on the industries that are still losing shares of domestic and export markets.

increases in earnings have been averaging more than the official "guideline" adopted in mid-1977 of 10 percent for wage settlements. Private consumption is accordingly increasing, as is also import demand for manufactured goods. Since rising manufactured imports will probably be at least equal to—if not greater than—the increase in manufactured exports resulting from the fall in the sterling exchange rate, Britain's hopes for achieving a sufficient surplus in its balance of payments to repay its massive external borrowing of the past few years depend largely on the growing flow of North Sea oil.

Thus, the United Kingdom appears at best to have only checked the vicious circle on which its economy has been embarked since the early 1960s. Nothing is as yet evident to support a conclusion that the process of deterioration has been effectively reversed. The question is whether the vicious circle will be resumed or whether the fundamental institutional and attitudinal elements that largely generate it will be transformed or eradicated. To the extent that policy decisions play an essential role in determining the outcome, the United Kingdom faces critical choices in the next few years that mainly relate to the uses to be made of the bonanza of North Sea oil.

On the one hand, these resources can be allotted to financing the internal and external costs of a continuing major expansion of the welfare system simultaneously with continuing large rises in real aftertax wages and employee benefits and continuing equalization of incomes. By heavily favoring consumption in these ways, policy makers and opinion leaders would be limiting the resources and reducing the incentives required for the structural redevelopment of British industry and the strengthening of its international competitiveness. Such a course of action would perpetuate both the institutional deficiencies of the U.K. economy and the counterproductive (in the literal sense) attitudes in British society that underlie negative-sum welfare/efficiency interactions. Once the resources available from the North Sea begin to decline in the late 1980s or the 1990s, the still latent vicious circle would again become manifest. In this context, the increase in real public-sector spending projected in the Labour government's 1978 Budget statement and the rise in payroll taxes provide cause for concern.

On the other hand, policy makers and opinion leaders have the opportunity to use a large part of these resources to foster the transformation of the basic institutional and attitudinal factors while allocating smaller amounts to finance some continuing moderate improvements in the welfare system and in real disposable income. The Labour government's White Paper of March 1978 stated in broad outline that a substantial portion of North Sea oil resources would be used to increase subsidies and other aids to encourage industrial investment. But, it will also be necessary to provide greater incentives to the market sector for both job-creating investment and continuing technological modernization and innovation. In addition, progress in reforming the institutional structure and functioning of the trade-union movement and in eradicating the attitudinal and technical deficiencies of British management would be required for the success of these efforts.

On balance, there is a clear risk that Britain will drift into the first alternative of using its North Sea resources to boost public-sector expenditures and private consumption. Given the strength of the pressures that led in the past to negative-sum welfare/efficiency interactions, the temptation to take the easy way will be strong even on the part of those political and opinion leaders who understand the adverse longer-term consequences of such actions. At the same time, however, the fact that a Labour government was able from mid-1975 to mid-1977 to follow policies that halted the vicious circle enhances the possibility that it or a new Conservative government would have the will and the ability after the next election—in October 1978 or in 1979—to apply the policies needed to reverse the decline in the future. The determining factor may well be whether, in the minds of Britain's leaders and people, the realism of 1975–77 inculcated by mounting inflation and declining productivity and real income will be swept away by unrealistic expectations generated by the golden flood of North Sea oil in the years ahead.

Despite the greater severity of Britain's economic difficulties in recent years, it is noteworthy that U.K. trade policies have not hitherto been conspicuously more protectionist than those of other major industrial nations. Like them, it has resorted to voluntary restraint agreements and other arrangements to limit imports of textiles and clothing, footwear, steel, televisions, automobiles, and other products from various developing countries and Japan. Nonetheless, to the extent that the United Kingdom fails to make progress in improving the competitiveness of its industries, the pressures will mount in the coming years for a more overt and extensive system of import restrictions. Indeed, this is the policy that is already being advocated as an essential precondition for economic growth by an influential group of British economists in Cambridge University's Department of Applied Economics.

Again as in the other West European nations surveyed in this study, Britain's system of subsidies to market-sector enterprises and nationalized corporations for employment, investment and regional-development purposes—or simply to cover their operating deficits—constitutes in effect, if not in intent, a more subtle and significant form of neomercantilism than the tariffs, import quotas and restrictive agreements per se. Unless the declining competitiveness of British industries in their home market, as well as abroad, can be reversed, the pressures to increase the scope and size of the subsidies will intensify. Moreover, in these circumstances, the resort to greater subsidies would be likely to occur even if the balance of payments as a whole were not in difficulty. Thus, breaking out of the vicious circle of negative-sum welfare/efficiency interactions is a prerequisite for preventing a steady drift of the United Kingdom into neomercantilist production, as well as trade, policies in the coming years.

GERMANY

Germany's experience of welfare/efficiency interactions has hitherto avoided the adverse effects on its external economic relations that both Sweden and the United Kingdom have suffered. Germany's international competitiveness and export capabilities appear to be as strong as ever, despite the appreciation of the deutschemark, and it has continued to earn substantial balance-of-payments surpluses. After Switzerland, its inflation rate is the lowest in the OECD region. Yet, despite these notable successes, the German economy may not be immune to certain negative-sum welfare/efficiency interactions that could cause increasingly serious problems in the future.

Germany was the pioneer in social-welfare legislation, starting with Bismarck's accident, sickness and retirement programs in the 1880s. Ever since, Germany has continued to have one of the most extensive and liberal national welfare systems in the OECD region. As presently constituted, health services and sick pay, accident and disability payments, unemployment compensation and training, and retirement pensions are financed and administered through quasi-official insurance funds deriving their incomes from mandatory contributions by both workers and employers. Each pays 9 percent of the basic wage or salary for retirement and disability, 6 percent for health services and sick pay (after the first six weeks of illness), and 1.5 percent for unemployment and training, with the employer alone contributing an average of 1.5 percent to the accident and disability fund. The employer pays full wages and normal overtime during the first six weeks of illness; thereafter, the worker receives 80 percent of regular earnings from the health insurance fund for up to 18 months for each illness. The percentages contributed by employers and employees have been periodically raised, and the number of beneficiaries and the size of the benefits they receive have been increasing even faster, resulting in sizable annual deficits in the various funds that have had to be covered by government subventions. In consequence, the government took action in 1977 and early 1978 to reduce the deficits of these funds by postponing the automatic increase in benefits scheduled for mid-1978 by six months and lowering those scheduled for the next three years, while raising the pension-insurance contribution by 0.5 percent beginning in 1981.

The rising costs of the national welfare system reflect both demographic changes and the so-called reform program instituted by the Social Democrats when they took office in 1969. Germany had its post-World War II "baby boom" later than most other OECD countries and it is now experiencing unusually large new additions to the labor force that will continue into the 1980s. The Economics Ministry estimated that 2.5 million new jobs would be needed between 1976 and 1985. However, as explained below, job-creating investment has been low since the early 1970s, resulting in continuing high rates of unemployment—currently around 4.5 percent—especially among young people and the foreign workers. Unemployment remains high despite the increase in the ratio of workers reaching retirement age and of those retiring early due to generous disability benefits. The ratio of the employed portion of the population to the economically inactive portion has been falling and hence the costs of the national welfare system to the active labor force have risen.

The reform program instituted when the Social Democrats took office in 1969 consisted mainly of expanding the scope and improving the benefits of the national welfare system, as well as extending the arrangements for industrial democracy (codetermination) explained in Chapter 3. Under the so-called dynamic formula, pensions and disability payments were indexed not only to inflation but also to increases in real gross (i.e., beforetax) wages, and other welfare benefits have been periodically raised. For example, the Economics Ministry estimates that improvements in health care and increases in the number and salaries of the people employed in the health services have been raising costs by 20 to 25 percent a year since the early 1970s. Total health costs in Germany are currently over 10 percent of GDP.[20]

The rising costs of the national welfare system have been the main factors in the increase in federal, state and local government expenditures, which amounted to 37 percent of GDP in 1965, 38 percent in 1970, 48 percent in 1975, and 47 percent in 1977. Taxes have had to be increased accordingly. The OECD tax/benefit study shows that the average production worker (married and with two children) in Germany paid in central- and local-government income taxes and social security contributions 21 percent of his gross earnings in 1972 but that the percentage increased to 27 by 1976 while the marginal rate on the next 10 percent of additional income rose from 26 percent to 34 percent over the period.[21] The VAT is currently 12 percent—scheduled to rise to 13 percent in 1979—but food items are taxed at half that rate. At the higher-income levels, income taxes rise to a maximum of 56 percent regardless of whether income is earned or comes from investments. As to the corporate income tax, undistributed profits are taxed at 51 percent and distributed profits at 36 percent. However, liberal deductions for reserves, investment credits and other concessions substantially reduce the effective rates for most large companies. Employers' contributions to the various national insurance funds currently represent a payroll tax amounting to 18 percent of basic wages. If other mandatory, contractual and voluntary benefits are added, the EC's 1975 survey indicated that basic wage costs in industry for time actually worked were increased by 58 percent.[22]

German managers are by and large innovative and dynamic and their skills have played major roles in Germany's spectacular postwar economic growth. They are well compensated for their efforts and generally enjoy high prestige in German society.

In recent years, however, business investment has been at low levels, reflecting not only the uncertain sales prospects for German manufactures in foreign and domestic markets but also the fact that the net rate of return in the business sector (excluding finance and housing) fell from 13 percent in 1968 to 8.5 percent in 1975. After rising to 10 percent in 1976, the rate declined again in 1977. In turn, as shown in Chart 4–1, the rate of change of investment in industry was on a downward trend from 1969 to mid-1975 but has since been recovering. Also, as indicated in the chart, capital-broadening investment has gradually fallen from over 50 percent of the total in 1970 to about 15 percent in 1976 while the share of capital-deepening investment and replacement has risen accordingly. This shift, which has still not been reversed, has been an important factor in the growth of unemployment and of the problem of providing jobs for the increasing numbers of new entrants into the labor force in the years ahead.

---

20   Unless otherwise indicated, data on Germany are derived from *Germany, OECD Economic Surveys* (Paris: OECD, July 1977); *Economic Outlook* (Paris: OECD, December 1977 and July 1978); and recent issues of the *Monthly Report of the Deutsche Bundesbank* (Frankfurt: Deutsche Bundesbank).

21   See footnote 3, p. 64.

22   See footnote 14, p. 77.

Chart 4-1. Investment Motives and Business Fixed Investment

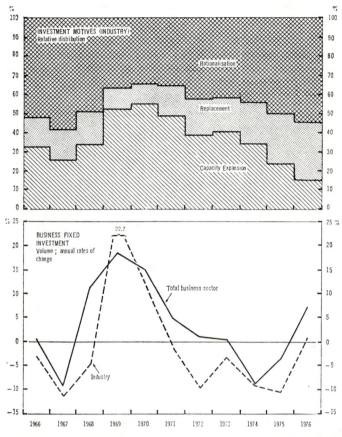

Sources: Ifo; DIW; Statistisches Bundesamt. From *Germany, OECD Economic Surveys* (Paris: OECD, July 1977), p. 25; reprinted with permission.

The heavy emphasis on capital-deepening investment results from the effort to limit the rise in production costs so as to preserve international competitiveness despite the appreciation of the deutschemark. Wage rates rose moderately in 1976 and 1977, and the negotiated increase for 1977 averaged slightly below that of the preceding year. Hourly compensation in industry increased over the past 10 years by 190 percent in deutschemarks (almost 398 percent in U.S. dollars). But, thanks to the beneficial effects of capital-deepening investment on productivity—as well as to the work attitudes of German labor and the constructive policies followed by the trade unions—unit labor costs rose by only 71 percent in deutschemarks (193 percent in dollars).[23] Hence, Germany was able to preserve its market shares, both domestic and foreign, for most manufactured goods. In fact, Germany's share of world exports of manufactures increased from 18.1 percent in the fourth quarter of

23   See footnote 5, p. 68.

1975 to 19.1 percent in the third quarter of 1977.[24] More recent figures on market shares are not yet available but, judging from the continuing merchandise surplus in Germany's balance of payments, it seems reasonable to conclude that it has been maintaining, if no longer increasing, its international competitiveness despite the appreciation of its currency.

Nor do other indicators of welfare/efficiency interactions show adverse effects. Germany's inflation rate has been the second lowest in the OECD region during the 1970s, falling from the high annual rate of increase in the consumer price index of 7 percent in 1974 to 3.5 percent by the end of 1977 and to under 3 percent in mid-1978. The German Employers Association estimated that absenteeism in manufacturing averaged around 7.5 percent until 1975, when it fell to 6 percent.

In short, except for unemployment, the absence so far of any significant negative-sum welfare/efficiency interactions in Germany even though the non-market sector preempts nearly half of GDP would appear to result from three favorable sets of institutional and cultural factors. The first has been the fact that taxes have not hitherto been so high as to reduce too severely the economic incentives of market-sector enterprises and of their owners and managers, whose motivations and skills also continue to be conducive to dynamism and entrepreneurial vigor. The second, as explained below, has been the policy of the German trade unions and the attitudes and behavioral norms of German workers generally that, since World War II, have been essential elements in the growing productiveness of the economy as a whole and the efficiency of its market-sector enterprises. Third, these capabilities and policies, as well as the more basic postwar attitudes of the German people that they reflect, have made possible the realistic macroeconomic-management policies of Christian Democratic and Social Democratic governments alike, particularly their efforts to avoid domestic policies that would trigger inflation and to offset as best they could inflationary impulses coming from abroad.

Given Germany's continuing international competitiveness and the apparent absence of other indicators of negative-sum welfare/efficiency interactions, why should there be such widely expressed concern in business circles and even in government ministries not simply about persisting unemployment but about the nation's economic future as a whole? Three related factors are involved in these worries: the need to cut export prices to offset the appreciation of the deutschemark with a consequent squeeze on the already low rates of profit of market-sector enterprises; the fear that the current and projected rises in government expenditures and cut in taxes next year would eventually result in higher taxes and inflation; and an apparent change in the objectives and attitudes of the trade unions.

As noted, the recent appreciation of the deutschemark against the U.S. dollar and most other currencies—including even the Scandinavian currencies that are normally tied to it in the European "snake"—has not so far adversely affected German manufactured exports. However, exporters maintain that they have been

---

24   *International Economic Indicators* (Washington, D.C.: U.S. Department of Commerce, June 1978), p. 59.

shaving their prices in marks in order to remain competitive in terms of dollars and other currencies, which has been helping to hold down their already low rates of return and hence their investment. The profits squeeze in exported goods is expected to persist due to further appreciation of the mark.

The second reason for concern relates to the likely consequences of the current and projected rises in government expenditures designed to stimulate domestic demand. Since the OPEC price rise and the onset of the recession in 1974, the government has been trying to reduce both inflation and unemployment, with outstanding success in the former. The latter objective, however, has not been realized despite recurrent government efforts from 1975 to early 1978 to stimulate domestic demand for both capital and consumption goods—and hence increase employment—through tax reductions, increases in family allowances, and a series of special expenditure programs aimed at improving labor skills and creating jobs in construction and other fields. As a result, the combined deficits of the federal, *Länder* (state) and local governments in 1978 will amount to over 4 percent of GDP. In view of the likelihood that GDP growth will be under 3 percent in 1978, there have been continued domestic and foreign pressures for further increases in government expenditures and for tax reductions to stimulate demand. In July 1978, the government announced that personal income taxes would be cut in 1979 and government expenditures increased by improving certain welfare benefits and providing subsidies to industry for research and development. The business community has mixed reactions, welcoming the reduction in taxes but also fearing that larger budgetary deficits would contribute to a resumption of inflation and might eventually necessitate higher taxes than Germany has hitherto had to impose.

The third cause of concern is an apparent change in the attitudes and policies of the trade unions. The persistence of high unemployment and the halt in the expansion of the national welfare system resulted in growing trade-union dissatisfaction with the policies of the Social Democratic government in recent years. The national trade-union federation, the DGB, maintains that welfare programs should increase faster than GDP, thus redistributing income not only from higher- to lower-income groups but also from workers' earned income to welfare benefits. It has also been pressing for much bigger government expenditures to reduce unemployment. The unions fought for wage increases in 1978 more strongly than in previous years and accepted a lower average rise than in 1977 only because the fall in the rate of inflation and the tax reduction would result in higher real incomes. The concern in business circles and among many government policy makers is that these trade-union pressures and the exigencies of partisan politics—important elections occur each year in one or more *Länder* governments and/or in the federal government—will sooner or later constrain the Social Democrats to legislate even bigger increases in welfare and other expenditures that would revive inflation and make eventually higher taxes inevitable. Also, the business community is concerned that the unions will seek larger wage increases in the future, as well as stricter employment guarantees to prevent job losses due to capital-deepening investment. Such concessions, businessmen believe, would defeat their efforts to improve productivity and maintain international competitiveness.

The fear is that current trade-union policies may reflect a basic change in the attitudes and objectives of the German unions. As explained in preceding chapters, German trade-union leaders and the workers themselves have recognized since World War II that a high rate of market-sector investment is a prerequisite for adequate new job creation and that rising productivity is a prerequisite for increasing real income. In consequence, they have been willing in most industries to limit their annual demands for wage raises and improved employee benefits to amounts consonant with the maintenance of satisfactory profits and, hence, of an effective investment incentive. This trade-union policy played a major role in the German "economic miracle" of the 1950s and '60s and has been an important factor in the productivity increases that have preserved—in fact, improved—Germany's international competitiveness in the 1970s. In turn, it reflects the more fundamental commitment of German workers generally to diligent work effort and conscientious performance of assigned tasks that has been a psychocultural characteristic of the German people for generations.

In the course of the 1970s, however, a growing number of younger trade-union leaders—supported by younger socialists in politics, the communications media and the universities—have become more militant in pressing for greater trade-union power at both micro and macro levels. The unions were very disappointed at not achieving full parity on company boards, they are bitter over some employers' attempts to resist or evade the existing near-parity arrangement, and they are continuing to pressure the Social Democrats for additional legislation to achieve full parity. Several years ago, some union leaders and socialist activists also advocated the establishment of worker asset-formation funds, like those envisaged in the Netherlands and Sweden, that would eventually give the unions voting control over companies in their industries. However, the Social Democratic leadership refused to adopt this proposal, opting instead for the so-called 624 Law, under which companies can distribute a portion of their pretax profits each year in the form of stock issued directly to their workers and employees. Nevertheless, the pressure for a trade-union-dominated scheme is likely to be revived if and when similar arrangements are established in the Netherlands and Sweden. Finally, union leaders are among the leading advocates of the current movement for directive planning by the "social partners" which, as explained in Chapter 3, would involve control over market-sector investment by a central planning body composed of representatives of the government, the unions and the employers' and industry associations.

To many businessmen and government policy makers, these objectives of the trade-union militants and socialist activists mark their abandonment, in fact if not in name, of the "social-market concept" that was developed in the 1950s and '60s by the Christian Democrats and maintained by the Social Democrats after they took office in 1969. Under this concept, favorable government policies would reconcile profit making and social welfare so that a vigorous market sector would produce the increasing resources required to raise living standards substantially and distribute income more equitably while supplying growing exports and meeting investment needs for future expansion and job creation. In contrast, the policy now advocated by the trade-union militants and socialist activists would involve raising wages and increasing welfare expenditures combined with growing trade-union domination of market-sector enterprises and central control over their investment plans, which would push up their taxes and labor costs, reduce their profits, and erode their entrepreneurial vigor. So far, those pressing for this policy have been a minority in the Social Democratic Party and the trade-union leader-ship. But, there is fear that their views may gradually become predominant and that the long-term result would be increasing negative-sum welfare/efficiency interac-tions and the replacement of the "social-market" economy by a neosyndicalist type of nonmarket economic system.

This concern reinforces the effects of low profit margins and the uncertain prospects in many foreign markets in weakening the incentives for capital-broadening investment in German industry, thereby contributing to the persis-tence of high unemployment. In turn, the latter intensifies the pressures for the kinds of policies that have generated businessmen's fears. One consequence of this mutually exacerbating interaction is the notable increase of German invest-ment in the United States and other countries in recent years. Another is the fact that the freedom of action of the present government has been reduced by the nervousness of the market sector, on the one side, and the rising militancy of many of the administration's younger trade-union and party supporters, on the other side. Thus, despite the fact that Germany has hitherto avoided any significant negative-sum welfare/efficiency interactions, its ability to do so over the next 5 to 10 years is by no means assured.

NETHERLANDS

Paradoxically, the Netherlands' experience of welfare/efficiency interactions in recent years resembles that of Germany, on the one hand, and those of the United Kingdom and Sweden, on the other. It is like Germany's externally: the Netherlands, too, had trade and current-account surpluses until 1977, a strong currency and rising foreign-exchange reserves. But, internally, the Dutch economy has exhibited some of the symptoms that have plagued the British and Swedish economies: rising labor costs due to high payroll taxes and increasing wage rates; declining profits and investment in the market sector, particularly in manufactur-ing; and persisting high unemployment and inflation. Until 1977, the coexistence of these apparently incompatible external and internal trends was made possible in large part by two special assets of the Dutch economy: the natural-gas deposits that supply nearly 60 percent of the Netherlands' own energy requirements at prices considerably below petroleum-based fuels, as well as 5 percent of Dutch exports; and the foreign-exchange earnings of the Rotterdam-Rhine entrepôt complex, the biggest on the planet, which help to push Dutch exports of goods and services to well over half of GDP. Mainly for these reasons, the adverse effects of rising costs and the appreciation of the guilder on the international competitiveness of important sections of Dutch industry only reached serious proportions in 1977, when manufactured exports suffered a 6 percent loss of foreign-market shares.[25]

---

25   Unless otherwise noted, the statistics on the Netherlands are derived from the English translations of *Introduction and Summary, Central Economic Plan, 1976* and *1977* (The Hague: Central Planning Bureau, June 1976 and May 1977); *Note on the Dutch Economy* (The Hague: Central Planning Bureau, October 1977); and *Netherlands, OECD Economic Surveys* (Paris: OECD, February 1977 and March 1978).

The uncertainty confronting Dutch policy makers and opinion leaders in the coming years is whether market-sector profitability and job-creating investment can be increased, rising costs and inflation can be checked, and international competitiveness restored while meeting popular expectations for continuing improvements in welfare benefits, aftertax earnings and income equalization.

Both the problem which such measures have to overcome and the difficulty of instituting them spring fundamentally from the same source. This is the widespread commitment in contemporary Dutch society to increasing welfare and equality with too little regard to the effects on efficiency and international competitiveness. Among policy makers and opinion leaders, this commitment is felt not only by socialists but also by many nonsocialists in government, politics, business, the communications media, and the universities. In consequence, Dutch society has become more and more egalitarian and permissive since the completion of postwar recovery in the late 1950s. Income distribution is already the most nearly equal in the OECD region, with the proximate goal to reduce the highest income to no more than five times the lowest and the eventual goal to even less. The national welfare system ranks with those of the Scandinavian countries in the scope and size of the benefits provided for retirement pensions, health care, sick pay, unemployment compensation, disability payments, family allowances, housing subsidies, education, and so forth. For example, the unemployed receive 80 percent of previous earnings for up to six months and 75 percent for an additional two years. Blue- and white-collar workers can retire early on as much as 80 percent of previous earnings for generously defined physical or mental disabilities. Living allowances are provided to people engaged in artistic and literary pursuits. These and other welfare benefits are indexed to inflation and to increases in average real wages. The ratio of the economically active portion of the population to the inactive portion has fallen to 2 to 1 due not only to demographic shifts but also to the changing attitudes toward work and leisure.

The Dutch government estimated that the cumulative increase in the real disposable income of the "modal worker" (a statistical concept similar to the OECD's "average production worker" but at a somewhat lower level of earnings) was 10.3 percent from 1973 to 1977, while the increases for workers earning lower wages were greater—for example, 17.8 percent in real terms for workers receiving the minimum wage. For retired people, the cumulative increase in the real value of their pension benefits was 27.3 percent from 1973 to 1977. In contrast, a person earning four times as much as the "modal worker" suffered a real income loss of 0.5 percent.[26]

Increasing welfare and equalization of income have necessitated rising central- and local-government expenditures. Total government expenditures were 38 percent of GDP in 1965, 44 percent in 1970, 55 percent in 1975, and 55 percent in 1976, the latest year for which figures are available. To help finance these increases, the income taxes and social security contributions paid by the average Dutch production worker (married and with two children) were 30 percent of gross earnings in 1972 and 31 percent in 1976, while the marginal tax rate on the next 10 percent of additional earnings rose more sharply from 35 percent in 1972 to 42

---

26   Ministry of Finance, *The Netherlands Budget Memorandum 1978* (abridged), p. 10.

percent in 1976.[27] For the higher incomes, the top marginal rate is 72 percent. The VAT amounts to 18 percent, except for certain basic foods on which the tax is 4 percent. On automobiles, an additional sales tax has to be paid, ranging from 16 to 17.5 percent, depending on the price of the car. Excise taxes are also levied on both alcoholic and nonalcoholic beverages, tobacco, petroleum products, and sugar. However, the income-tax schedule is partly indexed to inflation.

The corporate income tax is 48 percent but the effective rate is significantly reduced by accelerated depreciation allowances, investment allowances, liberal inventory evaluation provisions, and allowances for special reserves. However, the employers' share of social security contributions and other payroll taxes totals 27 percent of basic wages and salaries. According to the EC's 1975 survey, the percentage in industry would rise to 74 percent of basic wages for time actually worked if other mandatory, contractual and voluntary benefits were included.[28]

Hourly compensation has been rising rapidly in the Netherlands. In manufacturing, it increased 250 percent in guilders from 1967 to 1976 (around 84 percent in real terms.). However, due to the strength of the guilder, the rise was 378 percent on a dollar basis. Unit labor costs rose 76 percent in guilders over the period (140 percent in dollars).[29] Rising labor costs have contributed to the decline in the rates of return on manufacturing investment and their adverse effects have been reinforced by an extensive system of price controls. Due in part to the 1974–75 recession, the Central Planning Bureau concluded that, in 1975, the aftertax returns to capital invested in "trade and industry as a whole (excluding natural gas, public utilities and housing) was almost zero, and the return on equity capital was negative."[30] Although the overall figure of aftertax return did improve in 1976, the Central Planning Bureau explained "it is somewhat misleading to speak of increased profit margins, since in many cases it must have been a matter of smaller losses rather than of greater profits."[31] The OECD estimates that a small increase in industrial profits may have occurred in 1977.

Unsatisfactory profit expectations combined with excess productive capacity in many industries held down investment in plant and equipment in 1975 and 1976. In 1977, however, industrial investment rose substantially due in part to the subsidies provided for this purpose as explained below. In recent years, much of the net investment in manufacturing has been labor-saving (capital deepening), which has contributed to the current unemployment rate of 6 percent and the likelihood that the rate would remain around that level into the early 1980s.

These unfavorable trends have been accompanied by other negative-sum welfare/efficiency interactions. Sick leave used as a percentage of total hours worked increased by 50 percent from 1967 to 1976. Unofficial estimates are that the "hidden economy"—i.e., moonlighting by employed workers and remunerated work done by the unemployed not reported to the tax authorities—may amount to

---

27   See footnote 3, p. 64.

28   See footnote 14, p. 77.

29   See footnote 5, p. 68.

30   *Introduction and Summary, Central Economic Plan*, June 1976, p. 3.

31   Ibid., May 1977, p. 8.

as much as 10 percent of GNP and cost the government 5 percent of tax revenues. Some large companies report growing reluctance on the part of their Dutch managers serving abroad to return to the Netherlands owing to the high marginal tax rates to which they would be subjected.

The fact that Dutch investment in the United States has grown so rapidly in recent years can be regarded as at least partly a negative-sum reaction. The OECD reported that, in 1977, the Netherlands overtook Canada and the United Kingdom as the largest single foreign direct investor in the United States. However, it must also be noted that the Dutch government has been encouraging investment abroad both to offset the current-account surplus and to provide foreign-exchange earnings in the future when the income from natural gas declines.

In 1977, the volume of merchandise exports fell by over 2 percent, reflecting the loss of export market shares, while that of merchandise imports rose by 1.5 percent in consequence of the increase in disposable incomes. Although no figures are given, the OECD noted growing penetration of manufactured imports into the domestic market. For 1977 as a whole, the size of the trade surplus fell substantially from the levels normally recorded since 1971, when natural-gas exports began to rise. The current-account surplus dropped from Gld. 6.65 billion in 1976 to only Gld. 1 billion in 1977.

In 1976, the left-center coalition government led by the socialist Labor Party became aware of the adverse trends within the Dutch economy and their likely unfavorable effects on its international competitiveness. In consequence, policy changes were instituted that were designed to check the hitherto rapid expansion of the national welfare system, thus limiting the rise in government expenditures. Known as the "1 percent policy," it aimed to hold the annual increase in the tax and social security burden to no more than 1 percent of net national income while slowing the growth of the welfare system and providing subsidies and other measures to stimulate job-creating investment and greater employment in the market sector. A medium-term program of direct wage and investment subsidies was adopted to continue through 1980. The wage subsidies are to total Gld. 4.3 billion ($1.9 billion) through 1980. The investment subsidies are much larger. From 1978 through 1980, they are expected to total Gld. 12.1 billion ($5.4 billion). Including other grants to enterprises for structural changes, research and development and regional development, and for improving labor mobility and working conditions, the grand total of the medium-term subsidies will be over Gld. 18.5 billion ($8.3 billion) from 1978 through 1980. Whether this program will achieve its objectives of raising market-sector investment and employment and restoring international competitiveness while permitting desirable, though limited, increases in welfare benefits and real wages depends as much upon political and social factors as on economic developments per se.

After long negotiations following the election in May 1977, the Labor-led coalition that had held office since 1973 was unable to form a new government mainly because the Christian Democrats refused to go along with the Labor Party's proposed legislation establishing the profit-sharing scheme described in Chapter 3. Instead, the Christian Democrats formed a new centrist coalition that took office in December 1977. It is pressing ahead with—indeed, has strengthened—the previous government's program for limiting the rise in taxes and government expenditures and subsidizing wages and investment. In addition, it is attempting to eliminate some of the disincentives to work, innovation and investment inherent in the national welfare system.

To respond to widespread expectations for greater equalization of income and wealth and to forestall the Labor Party's more drastic scheme, the centrist government has introduced a profit-sharing plan of its own—described in Chapter 3—providing for much smaller percentages of aftertax corporate profits to be issued as stock to trade-union-controlled funds. However, businessmen fear that, when it next returns to office, the Labor Party would substantially increase the percentages and revise other provisions of the legislation to conform with its original proposals. They are also concerned that the Labor Party and the trade unions would press ahead with their ideas for centralized directive planning of market-sector investment. These fears counteract much of the positive effects on business confidence of the present government's measures. Moreover, they underlie the apparent reluctance of foreign companies to make new investments in the Netherlands and the willingness of some to dispose of their existing subsidiaries if they can do so on reasonable terms.

Thus, the uncertain longer-term political and social prospects are exerting an adverse effect on economic trends. Since both socialists and centrists now recognize the need to restrain the growth of government expenditures, it seems probable that future increases in the benefits provided by the national welfare system would be moderate under either type of regime. However, the support for the natural-right egalitarian conception of income distribution and for profit-sharing schemes that would involve eventual trade-union control of market-sector enterprises comes not only from militant socialists and labor activists eager to establish a nonmarket socialist economy but also from many nonsocialists in Dutch society motivated by moral considerations. They believe that equality of income for all, including the sharing of ownership of market-sector enterprises by the workers and pensioners, is justified in itself and they either do not recognize or are resigned to accepting the fact that the eventual outcome of such measures would be a neosyndicalist form of socialist society. Unless these attitudes and expectations become less prevalent, they will continue to erode confidence in the longer-run prospects of the market sector and to generate negative-sum welfare/efficiency interactions. Thus, the sociopolitical trends toward egalitarianism and socialism are likely to affect more profoundly the development of the Dutch economy over the longer term than any failure of economic policy per se to prepare for the depletion of the North Sea natural-gas reserves in the 1990s.

In either event, however, there would be growing pressures for increasingly neomercantilist production and trade policies. Already, the Netherlands has one of the biggest subsidy programs among the OECD countries not only relatively but in absolute size. The program is designed in part to improve the efficiency of market-sector enterprises and hence their competitiveness in domestic and foreign markets. But, it is also intended to serve other desirable social purposes: not only maintenance of employment opportunities for those wishing to work but also development of lagging regions, environmental improvement, encouragement of psychologically satisfying labor-intensive activities, and other noneconomic goals. The costs of achieving these objectives may lessen or even exceed the positive effects of the investment subsidies on productivity. In such cases, the assisted enterprises would not be able to exist without continuing subsidies and tax concessions. And, if the kind of directive investment planning sought by the socialists and trade-union activists should be instituted in the next few years, both internal and external controls would be required to assure implementation of planning decisions, to reduce the disruptive effects of imports, and to offset the loss of competitiveness in export markets.

DENMARK

About a third of Denmark's total output is normally exported; hence, the country's rate of economic growth depends importantly on its international competitiveness. Denmark needs a rate of economic growth sufficiently high to provide job opportunities for those willing and able to work and to meet the widespread expectations for continuing increases in both welfare benefits and earned disposable incomes. But, the resulting high levels of demand stimulate growing imports, especially when Danish producers become less competitive in the domestic market as well as internationally. Thus, the competitiveness of Danish industrial and agricultural producers has been the key to maintaining satisfactory levels of domestic economic activity and reasonable equilibrium in the balance of payments.

The problem confronting Danish policy makers after the 1974–75 recession was that Danish exports were not growing sufficiently to prevent increasing unemployment, rising balance-of-payments deficits, and popular dissatisfaction over high taxation, on the one hand, and the limitation of improvements in living standards, on the other. In part, the failure of Danish exports to increase at the necessary rate resulted from sluggish import demand in its major trading partners in the European Community and Scandinavia. In part, however, it reflected the fact that costs and prices in Denmark have risen faster in recent years than in some of its competitor countries.[32] Denmark has been fortunate in that a solid core of its exports has consisted of specialized industrial products, of which it has been the sole or the most technologically advanced supplier. But, even this advantage is beginning to be threatened by the rising costs of research and development and new productive investment and by the efforts of other industrial producers in Europe, Japan and the more advanced Asian and Latin American nations to develop new exports under the increasingly severe competition prevailing in international markets.

Although Denmark's exports of goods (excluding ships) grew in volume by 4.2 percent in 1976 and by 4 percent in 1977, the volume of imported goods rose by 18.2 percent in 1976 and fell by no more than 1.5 percent in 1977.[33] The import boom

---

32   Appreciation of the Danish krone along with the other "snake" currencies has not been a major factor in Denmark's loss of competitiveness because a large part of its trade is with the other members of the "snake." Moreover, it devalued, along with Sweden and Norway, against the remaining strong "snake" currencies in 1976 and again in 1977 and this adjustment should help its exports in 1978.

33   The statistics on Denmark presented here come from *Nordic Economic Outlook, May 1978* (Stockholm: Federation of Swedish Industries), and *Denmark, OECD Economic Surveys* (Paris: OECD, April 1977 and April 1978).

reflected the high levels of domestic demand resulting from the government's countercyclical policies in 1975–76 and the increase in disposable income due to rising wages and welfare benefits. In consequence, the current-account deficit reached an all-time high of 5 percent of GDP in 1976 but then fell to 3.5 percent of GDP in 1977. During the 1960s, Denmark's current-account deficits were of moderate size and were financed by private-capital inflows. But, since 1973, the much larger deficits have had to be financed by a growing volume of government borrowing abroad. Denmark's net foreign liabilities were 18 percent of GDP at the end of 1977 and are expected to rise to over 20 percent in 1978.

Total central- and local-government expenditures were 31 percent of GDP in 1965, 40 percent in 1970, 46 percent in 1975, and were at the same level in 1977. Although tax revenues have increased to finance these mounting expenditures, the central government's borrowing requirement also rose, reaching 4.5 percent of GDP in 1976 and 6.5 percent in 1977 and it is projected to be as high as 10 percent in 1978.

The main reason for the growth of government expenditures has been the expansion of the national welfare system and the increasing number of govern-ment employees needed to administer it, as well as the other activities of the central and local governments. Welfare benefits have been the fastest-growing component of consumption expenditures, with transfer payments increasing at rates 4 to 5 percentage points higher than total consumption expenditures in recent years. Welfare benefits are comparable in scope and size to those of Sweden—indeed, are more ample in some cases. For example, unemployment compensation amounts to 90 percent of previous earnings (up to a maximum of 90 percent of the average industrial wage) and may continue for as long as three and one-half years. Housewives who have never had paid employment nonetheless receive full pension benefits after 40 years of household work. The health services generally and the child-care facilities for working parents are said to be more extensive than those in Sweden. Since 1975, the personal-income tax schedules have been indexed to past increases in the average wages of industrial workers, and pensions and other welfare payments are indexed to consumer prices.

The average Danish production worker (married and with two children) paid 34 percent of his gross earnings in central- and local-government income taxes and social security contributions in 1972 and the marginal rate on the next 10 percent of additional earnings was 54 percent in that year. These rates rose in 1974 to 38 percent and 60 percent, respectively. However, to stimulate domestic demand after the 1974–75 recession and to mollify the rising antitax discontent, the rates were reduced to 33 percent and 55 percent, respectively, where they have re-mained despite the more recent effort to limit the rise in consumption and imports.[34] Instead, the VAT was raised in mid-1977 from 15 percent to 18 percent and the excise taxes on particular products and services were also increased. Upper-income earners pay income taxes that may be as high as 57.5 to 65 percent, depending on the local-income tax rate.

Business profits are taxed at 37 percent after liberal depreciation allowances and investment tax credits. Employers' social security contributions and other

---

34   See footnote 3, p. 64.

mandatory, contractual and voluntary fringe benefits were estimated to add 23 percent to the wage cost for time actually worked in industry, according to the EC's 1975 survey.[35]

Employers are required to pay directly the sick benefits received by employees: 90 percent of earnings (up to a maximum of 90 percent of the average industrial wage) for the first five weeks of each absence from work due to illness, injury or childbirth. However, after five weeks, sick benefits are paid by the government, as are all medical and hospital costs. In January 1978, the government undertook to reimburse employers on request for the fourth and fifth weeks of sick pay so as to offset some of the increase in labor costs.

High tax rates, even though indexed to wage increases, and sick pay and unemployment benefits equal to 90 percent of previous earnings have encouraged absenteeism and the growth of unreported "black labor," on which no taxes are paid. Adverse welfare/efficiency interactions also result from the fact that, when incomes rise above a certain level, housing and education subsidies decline and a charge is made for the use of child-care facilities, which tend to discourage workers from qualifying for higher-paying jobs. The same effect results from the narrowing of the wage differentials among skilled and unskilled workers that has occurred over the past decade in response to egalitarian pressures in the trade unions and the leftist political parties.

From 1974 through 1977, the increase in real wages has exceeded the growth of real national income by 17.5 percentage points. As the OECD comments, "real wages have not been adjusted to the decelerating productivity trend, nor to the deterioration in the terms of trade."[36] Not only was total business fixed investment (excluding ships and aircraft) in 1977 less than 2 percent above the 1970–73 average, representing a fall in its share of GDP from 10.5 percent to 9 percent, but also much of it was in capital-deepening investment as the elasticity of demand for labor fell relative to output and the substitution ratio between capital and labor in manufacturing became close to unity. The impact has been particularly marked in manufacturing, where the number of persons employed fell by 10 percent from 1973 to 1977. At the same time, the labor force has grown, reflecting the increase in new entrants from the earlier postwar baby boom and the rising female participation rate. In consequence of these trends, unemployment averaged 6 percent in 1977 and rose to 7.5 percent early in 1978.

The Danish government has been endeavoring to cope with the large payments deficit and mounting external debt by abandoning its earlier countercyclical demand-stimulation efforts, pushing both short- and long-term interest rates up to 16 to 17 percent, limiting the growth of government expenditures, raising indirect taxes to reduce consumption, and instituting an "incomes policy" under which a portion of the automatic wage increases that are indexed to the cost of living are paid into the pension fund and not directly to the workers. In consequence, real GDP rose by only 2 percent in 1977 after increasing by 4.9 percent in 1976. Investment subsidies in addition to generous depreciation allowances and investment tax credits have also been provided to assist market-sector enterprises to

---

35   See footnote 14, p. 77.

36   *Denmark, OECD Economic Surveys* (April 1978), p. 27, fn 41.

become more competitive in foreign and domestic markets. Wage subsidies have been instituted to slow the rise in unemployment by enabling employers to retain workers who might otherwise have to be laid off and to hire young people and the so-called long-term unemployed whose benefits are expiring. The employment subsidies are budgeted to cost over 10 billion kroner ($1.8 billion) during 1978–80.

However, these policy changes have been having mixed effects. While real disposable income rose by more than 6 percent a year in both 1975 and 1976, the restraints resulted in an estimated drop in real disposable income of 0.5 percent in 1977 and it is projected to fall slightly again in 1978. The increase in consumer prices, which was over 15 percent in 1974 but fell to 9.6 percent in 1975 and to 9 percent in 1976, rose again to 11.1 percent in 1977 (partly due to the increase in the VAT), and it is estimated to be only slightly below this rate in 1978. While hourly compensation in manufacturing increased by 250 percent in kroner (307 percent in dollar terms) from 1967 to 1977, unit labor costs rose 89 percent (120 percent in dollars) over the period.[37] A deceleration in the increase in unit labor costs is projected for 1978, which should improve the competitive position of Danish industry. But, the continuing sluggish import demand in Denmark's major trading partners, the policy changes limiting the growth of disposable income, and the other noncyclical factors noted above are projected to keep unemployment at high levels during the next few years.

The mixed results of these policy changes reflect the narrow social and political constraints within which any Danish government—whether socialist or centrist—must operate. As elsewhere in Scandinavia and in the Netherlands, the commitment to rising real wages, continuing welfare improvements, and increasing equality of incomes is felt by a large majority of the population. But, in Denmark, dissatisfaction with both the benefits and the costs and the consequent political fractionalization and polarization have become more pronounced than elsewhere in Northern Europe. On the one side, left-wing groups that are more radical than the Social Democratic Party are supported by about 10 percent of the voters, mainly young people, academics and other intellectuals. Their articulate criticisms exert a restraining influence on the capacity of the existing minority government of the Social Democrats to restrict the increase of real wages and other labor costs and of welfare benefits. On the other side, the antitax movement headed by Mogens Glistrup captured around 15 percent of the vote in recent elections, reflecting the opposition to the high income taxes not only of the upper-income earners but also of many industrial workers and farmers. The likelihood that this disaffection would spread if taxes were raised still higher to finance increased government expenditures on welfare limits the ability of the government to satisfy left-wing demands. Thus, the government is constrained to follow a narrowly defined middle course which, while avoiding unfavorable domestic political consequences, may be insufficient to restore and preserve international competitiveness under the prevailing world economic conditions.

Danish trade-union leaders do not have as large a degree of support from the rank and file as do their Swedish or German counterparts. In opposition to the official position of the LO (the national labor confederation), the skilled workers

---

37   See footnote 5, p. 68.

have resisted the effort to narrow wage differentials; their often unofficial work stoppages have been responsible both for preventing greater reductions in differentials and for the wage drift that has been a major element in the rise of hourly wage rates. The workers attach a great deal of importance to their plant-level works councils—called cooperation committees in Denmark—which are not always controlled by the local unions and hence are viewed with some reservation by the union leaders. The workers also tend to be less enthusiastic about labor representation on company boards but the LO has been pressing for new legislation that would give workers' directors full parity. Although both the LO and the Social Democratic Party are committed to an asset-formation scheme like those contemplated in Sweden and the Netherlands, they have been constrained by the preference of the workers themselves to concede that only one-third of the shares would be owned and voted by a central union-controlled fund while two-thirds would be issued directly to the individual employees of each company involved. Until recently, the opposition of the other parties in the Parliament, as well as Denmark's economic difficulties, deterred the minority government and the trade unions from pressing ahead with the necessary legislation. However, the Social Democrats and the LO are currently seeking ways to activate their asset-formation scheme as a substitute for the large increases in welfare benefits and aftertax earnings that workers expect but which the economy cannot now afford.

These divergences between trade-union leaders and members contribute to the other inconsistencies and constraints of the political situation noted above. Workers generally want greater welfare benefits and rising wages and most of them vote for the Social Democratic Party in expectation that it will continue to make these gains possible. But, at the same time, they complain about the high income taxes that limit their disposable incomes and, in consequence, some support the Glistrup antitax movement. In turn, the widespread objection to increased taxation imposes restraints on the ability of the Social Democrats—or of a centrist government—to expand the welfare system. And, the large balance-of-payments deficit and mounting external indebtedness limit the extent to which any government can permit import demand and the production costs of traded goods to rise in consequence of further large increases in disposable incomes. Thus, Denmark is experiencing a halt in its efforts to improve welfare and equality that is likely to persist until changes in the world economy or in its own productivity and international competitiveness make possible a substantial increase in its exports and hence in its rate of economic growth. Until then, it will continue to rely on subsidies and other neomercantilist production and trade policies to hold down unemployment, assist noncompetitive industries, and counteract the impact of any adverse developments in the world economy.

NORWAY

Norway's situation contains elements that resemble those of both Denmark and the Netherlands. As in Denmark, rising domestic demand has stimulated consumer imports while increasing costs and prices have impaired the competitive position of industry not only in export markets but also in the domestic market. In addition, Norway's large imports of oil-extracting and -processing equipment—

although by now past their peak—contributed to the growing balance-of-payments deficits and mounting external debt. Like the Netherlands, Norway has a natural resource—North Sea oil and gas—that, in the next few years, is expected to eliminate its payments deficit, begin to reduce its external debt, and make possible continuing improvements in living standards and the quality of life. Thus, the danger facing Norway is the same as that confronting the Netherlands and the United Kingdom: that too much of the wealth derived from its natural resource "windfall" will be used for the latter purposes and not enough for the incentives, investment and research and development needed to restore and maintain the international competitiveness of its traditional (nonpetroleum) market-sector producers, on which it will have to rely once its oil and gas reserves begin to decline.

In 1977, Norway's current-account balance-of-payments deficit amounted to well over 14 percent of its GDP, the highest ever recorded by an OECD member country.[38] Norway had been incurring increasingly large deficits since 1972 as its imports of equipment to develop the North Sea reserves grew and its earnings from ship sales and shipping declined during and after the 1974–75 recession. However, in 1976 and 1977, the deficits were pushed to unprecedented magnitudes by the loss of international competitiveness of its nonpetroleum exporting and import-competing industries combined with high levels of private consumption, which further stimulated import demand. In 1977, Norway's manufactured exports—which in total dropped by over 4 percent in real terms—to its major trading partners are estimated to have fallen 7 to 8 percentage points below the weighted average of their total imports while its own imports rose by 7 percent in real terms. Underlying both the declining international competitiveness and the rising consumption were big increases in hourly wage rates and unit labor costs. Consumption was also stimulated by the rapid expansion of welfare benefits, as well as by the extensive inventory, wage, investment, and other subsidies designed to keep the unemployment rate under 1 percent.

From 1974 through 1977, domestic demand rose four times faster in Norway than the combined average of the other OECD countries. Over the four years, the wage earnings of industrial workers advanced at an average annual rate of 16.5 percent, compared with 10 percent during the preceding four years. From 1974 to 1977, the OECD estimates that Norway's industrial unit labor costs rose by 25 percent relative to the weighted average of unit labor costs in its major trading partners due both to wage increases and to appreciation of the krone in 1974 and 1975. During these years, Norwegian wage earners enjoyed average annual gains in real disposable income of 4.5 percent along with a 4.5 percent reduction in working hours in 1976. Pensioners and others dependent on welfare benefits obtained real-income increases of around 7 percent a year. In addition, a special program of income supplements and subsidies raised financial support to the agricultural sector to more than 100 percent of the factor income of that sector, with farmers' real disposable income increasing by as much as 20 percent in 1977 alone. In contrast, real national income grew at an average annual rate of only 1.5 percent from 1974 to

---

38   Unless otherwise stated, the statistics for Norway are from *Norway, OECD Economic Surveys* (Paris: OECD, January 1978), and the *Nordic Economic Outlook, May 1978.*

1977. Consumer prices rose by over 9 percent a year in 1976 and 1977 and are expected to increase by about 11 percent in 1978 due partly to the devaluations of the krone in 1977 and 1978.

Between 1974 and 1976, the OECD estimates that profits fell by 40 percent in the export industries. In contrast, profits rose by 47 percent in the import-competing industries and by 54 percent in the so-called sheltered industries—shipbuilding, textiles and clothing, iron and steel, and so forth—due largely to the high levels of domestic demand and the extensive subsidies discussed below. Excluding the oil and gas sector, in which investment has been very high but is now declining, industrial investment fell by 3.4 percent in 1976, increased by over 15 percent in 1977—with construction of a large petrochemical complex at Rafnes accounting for much of the increase while investment in machinery and equipment advanced only modestly—and is expected to drop again by 10 percent in 1978. Total production in traditional manufacturing and mining (i.e., excluding the oil and gas sector) is not expected to increase in 1978, but the rising output of oil and gas should result in real GDP growth of something over 5 percent.

The channeling of increasing domestic and imported resources into rising consumption by wage earners and welfare recipients reflects the attitudes and expectations not only of the Labor Party and the trade unions but also of the workers and of many people in government service and business and professional circles. The intensity of Norwegians' commitment to improving the quality of life and equalizing the distribution of income is striking compared even with the Netherlands and the other Scandinavian countries.[39] Since the discovery of North Sea oil and gas, Norwegians have been inclined to believe that there are few, if any, desirable social goals that their economy could not afford to achieve. Hence, well before the North Sea resources could be developed to the point where they would yield the necessary income, the national welfare system was substantially improved, real wages were allowed to increase rapidly, and other measures were adopted to enhance the quality of life without regard to their effects on the productivity of the economy and the efficiency of exporting and import-competing enterprises. But, the development of the North Sea resources has turned out to be both slower and more costly than the Norwegians anticipated. Meantime, negative-sum welfare/efficiency interactions have manifested themselves.

Norway's welfare system has been expanded to roughly the scope and size of that of Sweden and is even more generous in some respects. Under a new law effective in mid-1978, sick pay was increased from 90 percent of regular earnings to 100 percent and the limitation on the duration of sick leave was abolished. The income subsidization of farmers and fishermen is also much greater than elsewhere in Northern Europe. In part, it reflects the conviction that the incomes of rural families should be equal to the average incomes of those engaged in industry and commerce regardless of the differences in productivity among these sectors. In part, it is designed to prevent migration to the urban areas, especially the depopulation of the northern part of the country which might open the way for Soviet expansion into the region.

---

39   Norway ranks after the Netherlands and Sweden in the degree of equalization of income distribution. See footnote 2, p. 64.

The expenditures of the central and local governments are largely for the national welfare system broadly defined, for subsidies to private-sector and nationalized industries, and for municipal services. These expenditures amounted to 34 percent of GDP in 1965, 43 percent in 1970, 50 percent in 1975, and 51 percent in 1977. The average production worker (married and with two children) in Norway paid 27 percent of his gross earnings in income taxes and social security contributions in 1972 and the marginal rate on the next 10 percent of additional earnings was 42 percent. These rates were raised to 29 percent and 43 percent in 1973. However, in 1976, they were cut to the 1972 level in an effort to restrain the pressure for wage increases.[40] In addition, a VAT of 20 percent has to be paid on most consumer purchases, and excise taxes on gasoline, tobacco products, alcoholic beverages, and other products are also levied. For upper-income earners, central- and local-government income taxes rise to a maximum of 71 percent in the top bracket.

Corporations pay a total of 54.8 percent in direct taxes on undistributed profits and only 27.1 percent on distributed profits (dividends). Purchases of capital goods have been subject to a 13 percent investment tax (in lieu of the VAT) but it was reduced to 9 percent in 1978 to encourage investment. In addition, accelerated depreciation allowances for investment and other tax concessions ease the burden of taxation on profits. The government also provides directly or through the banks a variety of subsidies to private-sector and nationalized industries. An inventory-accumulation scheme like that of Sweden has helped to keep unemployment to 1 percent of the labor force, as have subsidized training programs. Wage subsidies are provided to the sheltered industries adversely affected by imports or declining export demand; in textiles, for example, the subsidy amounts to nearly 10 percent of average hourly wages. In 1977, wage subsidies in the forms of loans, loan guarantees and grants affected a quarter of the total manpower in manufacturing and mining. Subsidies partly offset the effect on manufacturing costs of the rapidly rising wages and also of the social security contributions and other welfare benefits that market-sector enterprises must provide, which add an estimated 42 percent to the basic wage bill.

Tax concessions and subsidies are also being granted to pay part of the costs that enterprises must incur to meet the recently adopted environmental standards and the requirements that physical working conditions be upgraded and that "efforts be made to avoid undiversified, repetitive or machine-controlled production processes"[41] so as to improve the safety, health and psychological well-being of the workers. Norway has gone further than any of the countries surveyed in this chapter in legally requiring enterprises to make investments to eliminate or reduce air and water pollution and for the "humanization of work." The OECD estimated that, in recent years, 10 to 15 percent of total investment in manufacturing probably related to environmental-quality requirements. Even with the help provided by the government, humanizing changes in the work process are often costly and the beneficial effects on productivity, if any, may take considerable time to manifest themselves. In the short run, therefore, environmental and work-humanization

---

40   See footnote 3, p. 64.

41   The Working Environment Act of 4 February 1977, Chapter I, 12, 2.

requirements have contributed to the rising production costs in exporting and import-competing industries.

Norway's coalition government dominated by the Labor Party has been reluctant to reverse its generally expansionary economic policy. But, the unprecedented size of the balance-of-payments deficit and the loss of international competitiveness have constrained it to try to limit wage and price increases and to slow the expansion of domestic demand. One important step has been the devaluation of the krone by about 5 percent (on a trade-weighted basis) during 1977 and by an additional 8 percent in February 1978. Credit restrictions have been imposed and excise taxes raised to limit consumption. The 1978 wage settlement mandated by the government after the unions and the employers failed to reach an agreement was substantially smaller—an estimated average rise of 8 percent, including wage drift—than in preceding years.

However, the Norwegian government's efforts to check the rise in private consumption and reverse the decline in Norway's international competitiveness have not hitherto been as restrictive as those in Sweden and Denmark for two main reasons. First, the prospect of rapidly increasing earnings from North Sea oil and gas has both prevented the development of a sense of crisis and sustained the willingness of foreign lenders to finance Norway's growing external indebtedness. Second, the Labor Party has been under increasing internal strain from its own left wing and that of the LO (the trade-union confederation), which provides much of its support. In both institutions, many of the younger, upcoming activists want to press ahead more vigorously than the older, top-level leaders in achieving a fully socialist society with a more nearly equal distribution of income along the lines of the neosyndicalist conception explained in Chapter 3. In addition, Trotskyist, Maoist and other extremist New Left groups have infiltrated the LO unions and the Party and keep up a continuing agitation for more militant efforts to raise wages and welfare benefits as a means of winning greater rank-and-file support. This twofold pressure from the left has the effect of restraining the leadership of the LO and the Labor Party from adopting more restrictive economic policies. It also impels these organizations to press for greater industrial democracy—called enterprise democracy in Norway—and more rapid improvements in the quality of life than their counterparts are currently seeking to achieve in Sweden, Denmark or even the Netherlands.

Norway's enterprise democracy takes a unique form. Companies with 200 or more employees must establish a "corporate assembly," two-thirds of whose members are elected by the shareholders and one-third by the workers. The assembly in turn appoints the management board and exercises general powers similar to those of the supervisory boards in countries with a two-tier arrangement. However, a majority of the management board of the banks is appointed by the government. Works councils exist at the plant level and multiplant companies have a central meeting for their representatives. Management representatives attend the meetings of both bodies, and the latter have the legal right to discuss any aspect of the company's activities except wages, which are negotiated annually at the national level by the LO and the Norwegian Employers Federation. The Norwegian LO has not pressed as strongly for parity with the shareholders' representatives in the corporate assemblies as have the trade unions in some of the other countries surveyed here. However, it has been advocating that workers' directors be elected to the boards not only of foreign subsidiaries in Norway but also of their parent companies in other European countries and the United States.

Assuming no substantial decline in the international prices of petroleum and natural gas in the next four or five years, foreign lenders will undoubtedly be willing to continue financing Norway's deficits, which should decline and perhaps disappear over the period as its energy exports rise. At the same time, given the Norwegian attitudes and expectations sketched above, the government will have difficulty in strengthening very much its efforts to restrain the disproportionate increase in Norway's costs and prices relative to those of its major trading partners and competitors. Therefore, living standards will probably go on rising and the quality of life improving as resources continue to be channeled into increasing and equalizing the real income of both the working and the nonworking portions of the population. But, it is by no means as probable that, in the coming years, the resources and the incentives will also be made available to Norway's traditional market-sector enterprises for recovering and preserving their efficiency and international competitiveness so that they can sustain these benefits when the income from North Sea oil and gas begins to decline. Thus, as in the Netherlands, the restoration of balance-of-payments equilibrium would not eliminate the pressure for continuing subsidies and other neomercantilist production and trade policies to assure that industries unable to export or to compete with imports will maintain desired levels of employment and wages and forms of enterprise democracy.

STATISTICAL NOTE

Table 1.   Hourly Compensation in Manufacturing, National Currency Basis
(Index: 1967 = 100)

	Denmark	Germany	Netherlands	Sweden	United Kingdom	United States
1970	145.0	133.5	146.2	131.4	132.1	121.7
1971	157.2	151.2	167.1	147.7	150.1	129.8
1972	176.1	169.1	191.5	168.8	168.6	137.0
1973	203.4	192.2	228.4	184.7	188.2	147.0
1974	244.9	221.9	272.2	215.7	240.4	161.4
1975	291.2	250.2	313.8	261.6	306.8	179.8
1976	323.7	265.2	350.3	311.3	362.4	195.6
1977	350.4	289.7	n.a.	350.2	398.6	213.3

Table 2.   Hourly Compensation in Manufacturing, U.S. Dollar Basis
(Index: 1967 = 100)

	Denmark	Germany	Netherlands	Sweden	United Kingdom	United States
1970	135.0	145.9	145.6	130.8	115.1	121.7
1971	148.2	173.4	172.5	149.4	133.4	129.8
1972	176.8	211.4	215.0	183.1	153.3	137.0
1973	235.8	289.3	296.1	219.0	167.7	147.0
1974	281.1	342.5	365.4	251.2	204.5	161.4
1975	354.5	406.2	448.0	326.0	247.8	179.8
1976	373.9	420.1	477.6	368.8	237.8	195.6
1977	407.5	497.5	n.a.	404.6	252.9	213.3

Table 3.   Real Hourly Compensation in Manufacturing, CPI Basis
(Index: 1967 = 100)

	Denmark	Germany	Netherlands	Sweden	United Kingdom	United States
1970	121.8	125.1	126.6	116.2	111.8	104.7
1971	124.7	134.8	134.7	120.6	115.9	107.0
1972	131.1	143.2	143.1	130.0	121.3	109.3
1973	138.5	152.4	158.1	131.0	123.9	110.5
1974	144.7	164.7	171.8	139.2	136.3	109.3
1975	157.0	175.0	179.7	153.8	140.5	111.5
1976	160.1	177.3	184.4	166.0	142.2	114.7
1977	156.0	186.9	n.a.	167.7	133.7	117.5

Note: Compensation is defined as all payments made by employers directly to their employees, before deductions of any kind, plus employer contributions to legally required insurance programs and contractual and other private welfare plans for the benefit of employees. For Sweden and the United Kingdom, the figures also include taxes (in addition to social security contributions) levied on payrolls or employment rolls that are not compensation to employees but are labor costs to employers.

Table 4.   Unit Labor Costs in Manufacturing, National Currency Basis
(Index: 1967 = 100)

	Denmark	Germany	Netherlands	Sweden	United Kingdom	United States
1970	112.2	115.0	109.1	105.6	121.7	116.5
1971	113.3	124.5	116.9	114.5	132.9	117.6
1972	116.8	131.4	124.1	122.4	139.2	118.1
1973	127.3	140.7	134.2	125.2	149.1	123.2
1974	148.3	153.1	147.7	141.8	188.4	143.1
1975	165.8	166.3	173.3	173.9	246.6	152.4
1976	172.2	162.9	176.1	203.6	281.5	158.4
1977	189.3	170.8	n.a.	223.7	314.8	168.3

Table 5.   Unit Labor Costs in Manufacturing, U.S. Dollar Basis
(Index: 1967 = 100)

	Denmark	Germany	Netherlands	Sweden	United Kingdom	United States
1970	104.4	125.7	108.7	105.1	106.0	116.5
1971	106.8	142.8	120.6	115.8	118.1	117.6
1972	117.3	164.3	139.2	132.8	126.6	118.1
1973	147.6	211.7	174.0	148.5	132.8	123.2
1974	170.2	236.3	198.3	165.2	160.3	143.1
1975	201.8	270.0	247.5	216.7	199.2	152.4
1976	198.9	258.1	240.1	241.3	184.7	158.4
1977	220.2	293.4	n.a.	258.5	199.7	168.3

Source for all five tables: U.S. Department of Labor, Bureau of Labor Statistics, Office of Productivity and Technology, May 4, 1978; U.S. figures as of July 1978.

Prospective Developments and Policy Implications 5

The country analyses in Chapter 4 indicate that all of the nations surveyed here, except Germany, have been experiencing in different ways and varying degrees the adverse effects of negative-sum welfare/efficiency relations in the course of the 1970s. These have been aggravated by and in turn have magnified the impact of other developments in the international economic system in recent years—notably the tripling of the real price of energy, the slow recovery from the 1974–75 world recession, and the increasing competition from the more advanced developing countries in Asia and Latin America. The combined effects of these interacting developments on employment, real incomes and balances of payments of the West European nations have led since 1975 to two kinds of changes in their national policies. The first include remedial measures for halting or drastically slowing the rise in government expenditures, for reducing the rate of inflation in this way and by restraining the increase in labor costs, for trying to restructure noncompetitive industries and stimulate market-sector investment, and for reinforcing the resulting favorable effects on balances of payments by appropriate exchange-rate adjustments. The second consist of palliatives by which national governments have been endeavoring to ease the difficulties arising from the persistence of substantial unemployment and the continued declining competitiveness of important industries despite the foregoing remedial efforts. These palliatives include measures to protect domestic manufacturers against imports and to subsidize production in various direct and indirect ways, as well as orderly marketing agreements and other restrictive arrangements affecting international trade.

The questions to which answers must now be suggested are: (1) how are these two policy trends likely to develop in the future, especially with respect to their relative importance, and (2) what are the implications for U.S. policy? This chapter analyzes the political as well as the economic factors likely to be involved, outlines the more and the less probable ways in which they could interact over the next decade or so, and suggests policy measures by which the United States might cope, positively and negatively, with prospective developments.

ECONOMIC LESSONS AND BUSINESS ATTITUDES

One of the most important developments since the onset of the 1974–75 recession has been the recognition by an increasing number of political leaders—including those in the social democratic and labor parties—and senior civil servants that adverse welfare/efficiency interactions played a major role in the difficult economic problems with which the West European nations were struggling in the second half of the 1970s. The growth of nonmarket sectors, mainly due to the expansion of national welfare systems, to preempt half or more of GDP left insufficient resources and incentives in the market sector for investment and innovation, especially in traded-goods production. At the same time, the size of and liberal conditions for obtaining certain welfare benefits, the narrowing of wage differentials, and the steep marginal tax rates have adversely affected the incentives of many blue- and white-collar workers. These negative effects have been most conspicuously manifested in Sweden and the United Kingdom; they are evident also in Denmark, as well as in Norway and the Netherlands, where their adverse consequences are obscured by the North Sea resources; and some may begin to emerge in Germany in the coming years. The extent both of the recognition of these negative welfare/efficiency interactions and of the willingness to adopt remedial measures roughly parallels the degree to which they have been manifested, with two exceptions. One is Germany where, despite the still latent character of adverse welfare/efficiency interactions, political leaders and senior civil servants have been aware of such possibilities and have been trying to prevent them from becoming manifest. The other exception is Norway, where many political and opinion leaders appear to be noticeably less concerned about the effects of negative welfare/efficiency interactions than in the other countries due both to ideological convictions and to the expectation that North Sea resources would be adequate to pay for the achievement of desired social goals.

However, the need to check or reverse negative-sum welfare/efficiency interactions has generally been regarded as temporary. The assumption has been that, as the recovery from the 1974–75 recession progressed, the resulting higher rates of economic growth would provide the annual increments of resources required to increase government expenditures once again, and hence to resume the expansion of national welfare systems, and to raise wages, and hence aftertax earned incomes, while dampening down inflation, achieving adequate rates of investment, and maintaining balance-of-payments equilibrium. Thereby, the deeply rooted expectation of blue- and white-collar workers for continuing improvements in both welfare benefits and real wages would be realized and their political support would be assured for whichever party or coalition was in power and could take credit for such successful policies. Unfortunately, economic growth has been slower than anticipated, and concern is now rising in Western Europe that a new downturn may ensue even before unemployment and inflation have fallen and real incomes have increased to the expected rates.

One reason for lagging growth has been that market-sector investment— particularly capital-broadening investment in manufacturing—has not increased sufficiently despite the measures hitherto employed for stimulating it. A variety of economic, political and psychological factors has been involved.

Among the most important has been the fall in the rates of return on investment in manufacturing since the late 1960s or early 1970s and the resulting inadequate resources and incentives for further investment, especially in new factories. In turn, this development reflects the rise in production costs resulting from higher energy prices, wages and payroll taxes and the resulting decline in competitiveness in both international and domestic markets, as well as the slower growth of world trade generally since the 1974–75 recession. Among other economic considerations influencing the rate of investment have been the unwillingness of market-sector enterprises to borrow at the high nominal interest rates prevailing in some of these countries and the fact that the costs of building and equipping new factories have risen more than the prices of most other goods and services. The foregoing factors have combined to restrict capital-broadening investment and to channel much of the investment that has occurred in recent years into capital-deepening purposes, i.e., to replace worn-out or obsolete machinery and equipment, to offset increasing energy and labor costs, and to conform to the environmental-protection standards that are now beginning to be imposed in a growing number of West European countries. The dominant view among European industrialists has been that any likely expansion of foreign and domestic demand in the next few years could be met from currently unutilized productive facilities and the increase in their existing capacity resulting from capital-deepening investment.

The inhibiting effects of these economic considerations have been compounded by political uncertainties and related psychological anxieties. A major concern of businessmen in the Scandinavian countries, the Netherlands, the United Kingdom, and even Germany is that the socialist parties—in office now or likely to return to power in future elections—would be constrained by their trade-union members and left-wing activists to press ahead toward the more drastic forms of industrial democracy described in Chapter 3. They are especially worried that future legislation would require full parity for workers' and/or unions' representatives on company boards and the establishment of union-dominated shareholding funds that would sooner or later acquire voting control over their firms. Other important causes of concern are the prospect of even greater restrictions on and mounting costs of discharging redundant workers and closing uneconomic plants, mandatory work-sharing arrangements involving reductions in working hours without corresponding reductions in earnings, overtime bans, higher payroll taxes to help finance future increases in welfare benefits, and centralized directive planning of market-sector investment.

Reinforcing these specifically focused worries are more generalized anxieties about the apparent condition of the international economic and political system. Among the economic concerns are the future course of petroleum prices once demand overtakes supply, the pressure from the developing nations for "a new international economic order," the rising competition from the manufactured exports of Japan and the more advanced Asian and Latin American countries, the uncertainties of floating exchange rates, the movement toward increased trade barriers of various kinds, and the longer-term possibility of raw-material and energy shortages. Chief among the political worries are the prospect of communist participation in and eventual domination of left-coalition governments in Italy, France and other South European nations, the possibility of another Arab-Israeli war, the increasing military capabilities of the Soviet Union, and the weakened confidence in the realism of U.S. foreign policy and the reliability of American commitments to European defense.

The nature and depth of the pessimism that has been pervading European business circles, especially on the continent, during the second half of the 1970s are reminiscent of those prevailing during the immediate post-World War II years, when the European economies were prostrate, a Soviet advance to the Atlantic seemed possible, and the West European communist parties were pressing for power through strikes, mass demonstrations and the undermining of weak coalition governments. One consequence of the current pessimistic mood is the marked increase in European investment in the United States in recent years through the purchase of urban real estate and farms and the takeover of American companies. As well, this flow of European investment funds to the United States reflects the higher rate of U.S. economic growth since the 1974–75 recession and the substantial depreciation of the dollar.

FUTURE UNCERTAINTIES AND PROSPECTIVE DEVELOPMENTS

Undoubtedly, higher economic growth and increasing market-sector rates of return in the next few years would dispel much of the current gloom in Western Europe. It is beyond the scope of this study to assess the likelihood of the factors involved in world and regional growth rates over the next 5 to 10 years and to make projections of their effects. Suffice it to note that a return to the real average annual OECD growth rates of the 1960s—say 4.5 to 5.5 percent—is within the limits of the possible. A return to this range during the next decade would be conducive to realization of the aspirations noted in the preceding section—that is, continuing expansion of national welfare systems and increasing real wages for blue- and white-collar workers along with adequate resources and incentives for market-sector investment and exports. But, despite the efforts to achieve them, higher average annual growth rates have hitherto eluded policy makers in most West European countries and the prospect of attaining them over the next decade must be regarded as quite uncertain. Based on the experience of the second half of the 1970s, it would seem to be more realistic to envisage continuation of lower average annual growth rates—say in the range of 2.5 to 3.5 percent. In such circumstances, the need to observe the lessons of negative-sum welfare/efficiency interactions learned during the 1970s would be even more urgent in the 1980s. The major uncertainties involved are political, rather than economic per se, and vary among the countries surveyed in this study.

Based on their behavior to date, it may be safe to predict that, insofar as macroeconomic policy is concerned, most German political leaders and government policy makers would continue to try to limit increases in welfare benefits and earned disposable incomes to those consistent with the maintenance of adequate rates of investment in the market sector and of international competitiveness. However, the success of their efforts would depend not only on developments in external markets but also on the changes that might take place within Germany at the micro level—specifically, the extent to which they would have to accede to the pressure to institute the more extreme forms of industrial democracy described in Chapter 3. This possibility as it would affect Germany and the other countries covered in this study is assessed in the next section.

In Denmark and Sweden, too, the chances are reasonably good that efforts would continue to be made to observe the welfare/efficiency lessons of recent years. Both countries lack oil and gas resources that might tempt them to disregard adverse welfare/efficiency effects and both recognize that their dependence on foreign trade requires them to maintain competitiveness in international and domestic markets. In Denmark, policies aimed at restoring international competitiveness in recent years have been undertaken by the minority government of the

Social Democratic Party, which enhances the likelihood that administrations of the left—as well as of the center—would be willing to make similar efforts in the future. In Sweden, however, the probability is lower because the lessons of the 1970s have been applied by a centrist coalition government, whose attempts to limit increases in welfare benefits and earned disposable incomes have been generating growing popular dissatisfaction. In these circumstances, the return to office of the Social Democrats in 1979 or a subsequent election could entail changes in macroeconomic policies that could restart the vicious circle of negative-sum welfare/efficiency interactions of the mid-1970s. Finally, in Denmark and especially in Sweden, the likelihood that future left-wing governments would decide to press ahead toward the more drastic forms of industrial democracy is considerably greater than in Germany.

The major uncertainties relate to prospective developments in the United Kingdom, the Netherlands and Norway, the countries in which the flow of North Sea resources reduces the need to prevent adverse welfare/efficiency interactions and dulls the sense of urgency to do so before their oil and gas incomes begin to decline. There appears to be more awareness of the nature and seriousness of this prospect among political leaders of both major parties in the United Kingdom than in the other two countries, but the difficulties of overcoming the U.K.'s problems of lagging productivity and declining competitiveness are also more severe than in the others. In the Netherlands, the centrist coalition government in office since late 1977 has recognized the dangers of negative-sum welfare/efficiency effects but its remedial measures have been limited by the widespread egalitarian convictions of the Dutch people and its consequent fear of losing popular support. And, as in Sweden, the return to office of a socialist-led coalition in a subsequent election could mean the relaxation of these efforts. In Norway, both recognition of the danger and willingness to adopt the requisite policies are markedly less than in the Netherlands and the efforts to improve the productivity and international competitiveness of the nonpetroleum industries have hitherto been superficial. Also, both the Netherlands and Norway are likely to move ahead faster toward the more extreme forms of industrial democracy than is the United Kingdom.

In varying degree, the policies that have so far been adopted in all of these countries to deal with adverse welfare/efficiency interactions and to improve productivity and international competitiveness have been of two general types, as noted at the beginning of this chapter. The first are remedial, the second are essentially palliative. Under the first type, the relative growth of the nonmarket sector has been halted or substantially slowed, except in Norway; the increase in consumption has been reduced, and even temporarily reversed in the United Kingdom and Sweden; and, in the latter countries particularly, currency devaluations have also helped toward restoring competitiveness. Nonetheless, all of these countries have had to limit the severity of such remedial measures—mainly preventive measures in the case of Germany—by palliatives of various kinds. Among the most important of the second type of policies are the subsidies and tax concessions granted to market-sector enterprises to offset in whole or in part the adverse effects on their ability to compete in foreign and domestic markets resulting from the disproportionate rise in their unit labor costs relative to those of other producers in Europe, Japan, the United States, and the more advanced Asian and Latin American nations. Other palliatives that have helped to reduce the severity of domestic remedial measures include limitations on imports and direct assistance to exports, and the restrictive and cartel-like arrangements jointly adopted by the members of the European Community.

Such palliatives do not result from ill will or irrationality, as some Americans are inclined to believe. Rather, as explained in the individual country sections in Chapter 4, they reflect the narrow limits on policy makers' freedom to impose fundamental adjustments in societies in which expectations for greater welfare and equality have been rising, the diversity of other desired social goals and the intensity with which they are pressed have been increasing, and the process of resource allocation has thereby been more highly politicized, especially in the strongly democratic countries of Northen Europe. Thus, efforts to remedy the effects of existing or future negative-sum welfare/efficiency interactions are bound to be limited and they will be supplemented by measures designed to palliate in greater or lesser degree their adverse impact on employment, earned incomes and welfare benefits. This means that the West European nations will in all probability continue to resort to subsidies and to other preferential and restrictive measures that have the effect—even though it may not be their main purpose—of distorting their trade both with the rest of the world and with one another.

In addition, through the European Community, they have already concerted or are seeking ways to devise cartel-like arrangements for controlling output and allocating market shares in steel, shipbuilding, synthetic fibers, petrochemicals, and other industries. Although intended to be temporary, such EC measures could be perpetuated and expanded if growth rates remain within the lower range. In such circumstances, these agreements would represent a significant first step toward the kind of centrally directed trading practices characteristic of nonmarket economies, like those of the COMECON countries.

In sum, over the next 5 to 10 years, the extent of unilateral and joint neomercantilist production and trade policies in Western Europe will vary not only with the strength of the political pressures and ideological convictions of the countries involved but also inversely with their rates of economic growth—the higher the growth rate, the less the need for such palliatives, and vice versa.

SOCIALISM, DEMOCRACY AND NEOMERCANTILISM

The foregoing assessments indicated that, except in Norway and perhaps also in the Netherlands, there is a reasonable probability that serious negative-sum welfare/efficiency interactions at the macro level would be prevented during the next decade or so. The question may now be considered of the likelihood that they would occur as a result of policies directed to the micro level, specifically by the imposition on market-sector enterprises of the more extreme forms of industrial democracy. Such a development could lead to the eventual transformation of the existing mixed market/nonmarket economies into socialist systems organized along neosyndicalist lines.

As explained in Chapter 3, the proponents of industrial democracy include not only trade-union leaders and socialist politicians but also many national-government and international-organization officials, journalists, university professors, students, and other intellectuals. The movement has support among the nonsocialist parties (e.g., the British Liberal Party) and there are even some European business leaders who favor the more extreme forms, notably parity for workers' directors on company boards and worker asset-formation schemes, though not under exclusive trade-union control. These diverse proponents of industrial democracy are generally articulate, capable of sustained political efforts and, therefore, exert substantial influence on popular expectations and national legislation. Moreover, the more ardent supporters regard industrial democracy as the major means for attaining the ultimate socialist goal and, hence, view the achievement of lesser objectives as only temporary way stations in an ongoing process that should be resumed as soon as the most recent gains have been consolidated. Thus, the moderate nonsocialist proponents are continually being pushed ahead by the socialists further and faster than they intend to go.

If the higher range of growth rates were to prevail in the 1980s, the advocates of more drastic ID measures would be likely to argue that far-reaching changes in market-sector enterprises could safely be implemented even though some adverse effects on productivity might ensue. Conversely, as already evident in Denmark and Sweden, such steps would seem particularly attractive means for offsetting the disappointment that would be generated if the expansion of welfare systems and the increase of real wages had to be narrowly limited because growth rates were in or near the lower range. In the latter case, too, the sluggishness of market-sector investment and the continuation of high unemployment would lend plausibility to and provide political support for those urging adoption of directive planning of market-sector investment and employment by the government alone or with the participation of the "social partners." And, in either event, existing or newly elected socialist or socialist-led coalition governments would be more responsive to these pressures than would the coalitions of centrist parties.

Adoption of parity on company boards for workers' directors and of arrangements under which union-directed funds would sooner or later acquire voting control over market-sector enterprises would represent decisive steps toward the neosyndicalist version of socialism that is becoming increasingly influential in the North European countries. Hence, this possible course of development needs to be briefly explored, as do its likely implications for the future of democracy in Western Europe and for the nature of European participation in the international economic system.

In the years immediately following World War II, the socialist, social democratic and labor parties in office or participating in coalition governments pressed for nationalization of market-sector enterprises in basic industry and banking in order to socialize "the commanding heights of the economy." But, by the early 1950s, the reestablishment of effectively functioning national governments, the acceleration of economic recovery under the Marshall Plan, and—above all—the onset of the cold war combined to moderate the drive for public ownership of the means of production and to focus socialist efforts upon the development of the national welfare systems described in previous chapters. After the immediate postwar nationalizations, the generation of socialists then in leadership positions in the political parties, the unions, the universities, and the communications media was in the main prepared to go along with a predominantly private-enterprise market economy provided that its operations were regulated and supplemented in accordance with broadly defined welfare objectives. Indeed, as in Sweden and Germany, even the socialists favored and implemented measures designed to foster investment and productivity growth in the market sector.

This acquiescence in a mixed market/nonmarket economy began to change in the late 1960s and continued to erode in the course of the 1970s. As noted in Chapter 3, the new generation of activists in the socialist parties and trade unions born or educated after World War II has become increasingly dissatisfied with the approach of the older generation of party and union leaders, whom they regard as ineffectual. Although, as explained below, the new socialists differ on specific goals and means, they agree that the time has now come to abandon the tacit commitment to maintain the mixed economy and to move ahead once again to full socialism. Their views are influential because of the increasingly important positions they are beginning to occupy in the parties, the unions, the communications media, the universities, and intellectual circles generally. And, even though the majority of the ordinary party and union members, let alone of the voters as a whole, do not share their ideological commitment to full socialism, enough of them may support the younger socialists and the remaining left-wing militants in the older generation whenever popular expectations for increasing welfare and greater earned disposable income appear to be frustrated by the policies of the moderate socialist or centrist coalition governments.

Thus, in the course of the 1970s, the concept of socialism has been infused with new significance and the drive to achieve the goals involved has won new adherents and has been pursued with increasing vigor. Essentially, the concept embraces three distinguishable meanings, one or more of which may characterize the ideas expressed by individual socialists and the objectives professed by socialist parties.

One meaning, largely derived from the teachings of Marx and Engels, is nationalization, or public ownership, of all or a substantial portion of the means of production. This has been the predominant meaning attached to socialism not only by the communist parties but also by many noncommunist socialists, such as the left wings of the British Labour Party, the French Socialist Party and others. This essentially Marxist concept continues to shape the thinking of most socialists in Southern Europe, France and the United Kingdom.

The second meaning is that of the socialization of distribution—the division of national income in accordance with the principles of equality and natural right. As explained in Chapter 1, it derives from a much older intellectual tradition than Marxism and, therefore, can be and is held by many people who do not regard themselves as Marxists and in some cases not even as socialists. Since World War II, distributional socialism has predominated in the three Scandinavian nations, the Netherlands and Germany. In those countries, government ownership of the means of production has not been a major goal of the social democratic, socialist and labor parties. Nationalizations have largely been limited in recent years to companies unable to adjust to competitive conditions and hence threatened with substantial job losses (e.g., as in shipbuilding) and to industries (such as North Sea oil production in Norway) in which the natural resources involved are widely regarded as belonging to the nation as a whole.

The third meaning is the neosyndicalist idea that the workers themselves should own and control the enterprises in which they are employed. It derives from pre-Marxist conceptions of socialism developed during the first half of the 19th century mainly in France—for example, by Louis Blanc, Fourier, Proudhon, and others. Superseded for a long period by the forcible-action approach of late 19th-century syndicalism, these earlier ideas reemerged after World War II in Yugoslavia, where a significant degree of worker management was introduced, and more recently in Scandinavia, the Netherlands and Germany in the form of the worker asset-formation schemes promoted by the movement for industrial democracy.

The resurgence of socialism in the first and third meanings during the 1970s reflects in considerable measure the maturing of the generation educated or born after World War II and the reactions and aspirations that shape the thinking of its politically active and intellectually influential members. The younger socialists reject private enterprise and the market system which, they believe, depend upon the ignoble motivation of self-interest and, therefore, distribute income unjustly, deny employment to people willing and able to work, waste increasingly scarce natural resources, and pollute the physical environment. These gross deficiencies, they insist, can only be eliminated in a socialist system that, by definition, would be motivated by mutual concern and cooperation, and which, therefore, would distribute income equally to all as a matter of natural right, would provide psychologically satisfying employment to people who work and adequate incomes to those who do not, and would effectively conserve natural resources and protect the environment. In essence, there is nothing new in these convictions, which express in contemporary forms aspirations for human perfectibility, social justice and equality, and economic abundance that have played major roles in Western culture since the 12th century.[1]

There are today two important disagreements within the ranks of the West European socialist militants. One cuts across the Marxist/neosyndicalist difference and relates to the desirable rate of economic growth. On the one side are those Marxists and neosyndicalists who favor low or no economic growth on the grounds that material consumption is already so high as to be morally harmful to human beings and destructive of natural resources and the environment. On the other side are those who want to maintain high growth rates to provide the increased resources needed to satisfy expectations for equal distribution of income, rising living standards and greater leisure, and to renovate the damaged natural environment.

The second disagreement coincides in part with the Marxist/neosyndicalist difference and relates to the question of the possibility of combining socialism with democracy. Among Marxists, the communists reject this possibility in practice despite the euphemistic use of the term democracy in the Soviet Union and the East European countries and the recently professed commitment of some West European communist parties to certain democratic principles. Most noncommunist Marxian socialists and the neosyndicalists sincerely believe that their own particular conceptions of a socialist society can be realized without fundamental

---

1   For a survey of the origins and historical development of these and related utopian ideas, see Theodore Geiger, *The Fortunes of the West: The Future of the Atlantic Nations* (Bloomington: Indiana University Press, 1973), Chapter II and pp. 234–239.

impairment of democracy. They have in mind not simply the preservation of free elections, representative political institutions and civil liberties. They also believe that socialism would entail little, if any, limitation of economic democracy, that is, of the freedom of blue- and white-collar workers to bargain individually and collectively regarding their wages, benefits and working conditions; to spend their incomes on the goods and services they choose; to determine how much they want to save and in what forms; to take their vacations when and where they please; and to change jobs and occupations as they wish.

The question of the compatibility of socialism—either in Marxist or neosyndicalist forms—and political and economic democracy has been debated since the early 19th century. At the *theoretical level*, no new arguments on either side have been added in the 20th century to the debate as to whether human beings are inherently selfish or are made so by "bad social conditions" which, once corrected, would obviate the need for coercive measures to restrict freedom of choice. What the 20th century has provided, however, is increasing *empirical evidence* that actual socialist systems do involve very substantial narrowing of economic democracy. No predominantly nonmarket economy on the planet today permits its workers anywhere near the degree of freedom to determine their own incomes, work and leisure, and consumption and saving that exists in the OECD market economies even for people living on welfare benefits. And, as the analysis in the foregoing chapters indicates, those OECD economies that have gone furthest in implementing distributional socialism have already significantly reduced their workers' freedom of choice and action by taking away from them in direct and indirect taxes between a third and a half of their earned incomes and giving a greater or lesser portion back to them in the form of welfare benefits whose nature, magnitude and conditions are fixed by command decisions of the government.

The question of the rate of economic growth is also relevant to that of the compatibility of socialism and economic democracy. Those socialists who advocate low or no growth will perforce have to control not only the division between welfare income and wage income and the size and nature of the former but also how the latter is spent on goods and services by blue- and white-collar workers. Under a socialist regime committed to low or no growth, the government would have to limit workers' expenditures on goods and on those services requiring substantial construction and equipment. It would have to assure that workers realized their income gains in the forms of increased *unpaid* leisure and of services with relatively small material inputs. Such a drastic shift in consumption patterns—although imposed by well-meaning politicians and civil servants for "the workers' own good" and the improvement of the natural and social environments—could only be effectuated by means of controls over wages, the use of administered price differentials to regulate material consumption and, at the extreme, rationing. Western societies are still far from a future in which the majority of their people will voluntarily embrace "plain living and high thinking"—as Wordsworth once nostalgically characterized a past that had never existed. Nor would a socialist regime committed to achieving high economic growth rates be much more able to refrain from impairing economic democracy. Given the need to assure the rate and pattern of investment necessary for maintaining high growth while meeting rising consumption expectations and protecting the balance of payments, the government would have to control the increase of disposable income and the labor and other costs of enterprises regardless of whether they were owned by the state or managed by the trade unions in the name of the workers, as envisaged in the worker asset-formation schemes.

The position of the trade unions would become increasingly difficult in a socialist society committed to either high or low growth and regardless of whether socialism was achieved predominantly through government ownership or by neosyndicalist means. For, as explained in Chapter 3, the "natural harmony" that socialists believe would exist by definition in a socialist society is not only unsupported by empirical evidence but rests on very weak theoretical reasoning. No government in a socialist economy could permit free collective bargaining without disrupting its investment, production, consumption, and foreign-trade plans even under the most favorable international economic conditions—which, in any case, are unlikely to prevail in the foreseeable future. Conversely, to the extent to which the unions voluntarily or perforce conformed to the government's plans, they would more and more be regarded by the workers as instruments of the state and as not very different from their former employers. Free-trade unionism as it exists today in Western Europe and North America is unknown not only in the communist countries of Eastern Europe and Asia but also in the professedly socialist nations of the developing world. Nor is its absence in the communist states simply a Leninist aberration of true Marxist doctrine: *free collective bargaining and directive central planning are essentially incompatible*.

Thus, the kinds of socialist regimes for which the noncommunist Marxists and the neosyndicalists are pressing in Western Europe today would sooner or later be compelled to resort to controls over wages and consumption patterns regardless of the sincerity of their devotion to economic democracy. And, the need for internal controls would be strengthened by the likely external pressures and exigencies of the years ahead—the possibility of even higher real energy costs, the increasingly competitive export capabilities of developing nations and the more intense competition among the OECD countries themselves, the uncertainties of exchange-rate fluctuations, and other adverse international developments.

Whether political democracy, too, could long survive the demise of economic democracy is questionable. Time and again in interviews with younger socialists in politics, the unions, the universities, and the communications media, they implied or stated outright that they knew best what was good for the people and were prepared to enforce their prescriptions. Emotionally as well as intellectually committed to socialism and convinced of the benevolence of their intentions, such regimes would be increasingly unwilling to allow themselves to be voted out of office by nonsocialist parties which, they would fear, would undo their "good work." Nor could they permit any substantial revision of their investment, production and consumption plans by freely determined acts of the legislatures. In the end, such regimes could only be replaced by essentially undemocratic means—e.g., prolonged mass unrest, a military coup.

There are signs in Western Europe today that these considerations are beginning to be recognized by some opinion leaders in the postwar generation. One is the emergence of the "new philosophers" in France. Participants in *"les événements de mai"* in 1968, they have more recently broken with Marxism both on philosophical grounds and with respect to socioeconomic prescriptions. The powerful influence exercised by Marxist faculty and students in many German universities has recently been diminishing, while in the United Kingdom moderate leaders have been gaining ground in the trade unions and the Labour Party. The older generation of socialists, although it has certainly yielded to pressure from the younger radicals, has by no means accepted all of the latter's objectives and timing and will undoubtedly continue to moderate their efforts to achieve them. And, the increasing resistance to higher direct and indirect taxes of workers generally—as shown, for example, in the significant element of worker support for the Glistrup movement in Denmark—may indicate the gradual recognition of the inexorable interdependences among welfare benefits, taxes and wages.

However, even if for these and other reasons fully socialist societies with nonmarket economic systems do not emerge in Western Europe in the foreseeable future, the possibility cannot be discounted that a considerable movement in that direction could occur. And, to the extent that such a development goes beyond the existing forms of industrial democracy, the countries involved would be impelled to institute correspondingly more extensive controls not only over their domestic economies but over their external economic relations as well. Directive investment planning to eliminate unemployment, the adverse effects on inflation and international competitiveness likely to arise from full worker parity on company boards, the flight of capital that would be generated by the establishment of shareholding funds dominated by the trade unions, the disincentives resulting from greater equalization of incomes, and the consequences of other proximate steps toward an eventual socialist society would constrain governments to adopt increasingly neomercantilist policies to protect employment and the balance of payments.

Steps beyond the existing forms of industrial democracy would also accelerate the process of cartelization and concerted restrictionism in the European Community as a whole. As the trade unions become more influential in corporate policy making, they would be likely to seek agreements with their counterpart unions in the other countries regarding the allocation of investment, production, employment, and research and development among the branches and subsidiaries of multinational companies. Such pressures would be especially strong if growth rates were in the lower range and would reinforce the inclinations of the management members of European company boards to resort to market-sharing arrangements and other kinds of cartel-like measures whenever marketing difficulties arose. Thus, the scope of competitive market forces within the European Community would be more and more reduced.

If the West European countries involved were all experiencing the same adverse effects of negative-sum welfare/efficiency interactions on the productivity of their economies and the efficiency of their enterprises, there would not be any significant change in their competitive positions vis-à-vis one another. This possibility is recognized by European socialists and is one of the reasons for their frequent transnational contacts, their efforts to bring about coordination of national investment plans and welfare programs in the European Community, and their wide dissemination of new ideas about industrial democracy. However, the probability that these countries would move toward socialism at compatible rates is not very great. More important, they would have to cope in any event with increasingly severe competition from Japan, the United States, the more advanced

Asian and Latin American nations, and probably from the communist states as well, that would be sufficient to impel them into neomercantilist reactions.

Somewhat inconsistently with their foregoing view, European socialists also claim that, whether owned by the government or by union-controlled shareholding funds, enterprises would remain competitive because they would be directed to operate as though they were parts of a market-determined economy, just as many nationalized manufacturing companies do in these countries today. That may well be the intention but realities are likely to dictate otherwise. Many nationalized enterprises in Western Europe are even now able to operate under competitive conditions, domestically and internationally, only because they receive government subsidies to cover their capital and current deficits and they are usually given preferential treatment in obtaining government orders, credit, exemption from antimonopoly rules, and other aids. Yugoslavian enterprises under worker management need to be protected against foreign competition in the domestic market and are subsidized in various direct and indirect ways to enable them to sell many of their products in competitive international markets.

Therefore, if and as the steps toward socialism noted above adversely affect the productivity and competitiveness of existing and newly nationalized enterprises and of those controlled by the trade unions, the pressures to provide them with even greater assistance would inevitably grow. Those producing wholly or mainly for the domestic economy would be protected to the extent necessary against import competition, as in Yugoslavia. Those exporting a significant portion of their output would have to be subsidized in one way or another to continue to sell abroad. In turn, these measures would constrain other countries to take similar steps to protect and assist their own producers. Once started, such interactions tend to become self-reinforcing. At best, this process would lead to intergovernmental concerting of neomercantilist policies through discriminatory bilateral trade arrangements, agreements to share third-country markets, price-fixing cartels, and other devices that would make the favored enterprises in effect, if not in name, state-trading agencies. However, a worst-case outcome would also be possible. If the interests at stake could not be reconciled through such agreements to share the benefits and costs of international trade, the result could be a trade war.

West European socialists are misled by their faith in the essential goodness and rationality of human nature and in the "natural harmony" of socialist societies into believing that economic relations among socialist states would always be conducted cooperatively to their mutual benefit and, therefore, that no significant differences of interest—let alone serious conflicts—could arise among them. Conversely, they insist that, owing to their self-interested motivation, market economies must always compete with one another and, hence, must continually generate conflicts of interest that periodically become so irreconcilable as to lead to wars. Again, neither the empirical evidence nor the theoretical considerations support these beliefs. For example, the state-trading organizations of the East European countries compete as well as cooperate with one another in markets outside Soviet control and would probably do so in their direct economic relations if permitted by the Soviet Union. In the absence of such hegemonic control, West European socialist states would be just as susceptible as the existing market economies to the breakdown of international cooperation and the deterioration of competition into economic combat. The reasons were explained in the mid-1940s—when socialism also seemed a likely prospect in Western Europe—by Jacob Viner in a prescient article in the *American Economic Review*. He concluded:

> I have tried to establish the propositions that the substitution of state control for private enterprise in the field of international economic relations would, with a certain degree of inevitability, have a series of undesirable consequences, to wit: the injection of a political element into all major international economic transactions; the conversion of international trade from a predominantly competitive to a predominantly monopolistic basis; a marked increase in the potentiality of [economic] disputes to generate international frictions; the transfer of trade transactions from a status under which settlement of disputes by routine judicial process is readily feasible and in fact is already well-established to a status where such procedure is not now routine, where a logical, administrable, and generally acceptable code does not seem to be available, where, therefore, *ad hoc* diplomacy is the best substitute available for the nonexistent law or mores, where diplomacy will by inherent necessity be such that the possibility of resort to force in case of an unsatisfactory outcome of the diplomatic negotiations will be a trump card in the hands of the powerful countries, and where weak countries will have to rely for their economic security primarily on their ability to acquire powerful friends, who will probably be acquirable, if at all, only at a heavy political or economic price.[2]

The analysis in this section of the interrelationships of socialism, democracy and neomercantilism is not intended to imply that market economies do not have serious shortcomings and injustices. Indeed, they do have such deficiencies, which is precisely why mixed economies—i.e., predominantly market economies with substantial nonmarket sectors—are both inevitable and desirable in the OECD countries now and for the foreseeable future. Rather, it is hoped that two other conclusions would be drawn.

> *First*, deficient as mixed economies may be, they are nevertheless much more conducive to realization of the very objectives that socialists seek to attain—rising living standards, improving quality of life, and growing scope for individual fulfillment for all members of the society—than are nonmarket economies. They have this advantage because decision making is not concentrated solely or mainly in the government but much of it is decentralized among different kinds of private institutions and individuals. These interacting processes of government and private decision making enable mixed economies to achieve desired social goals by admittedly imperfect *reconciliations*, or tradeoffs, among the incompatible values of personal freedom, social equality and economic well-being. In contrast, nonmarket economies, which perforce must operate through command decisions, are thereby compelled to sacrifice at least one of these fundamental human values to the others—generally freedom and often also economic well-being to equality—however benevolent the intentions and rational the decision-making methods of those in power.

---

2   Jacob Viner, "International Relations Between State-Controlled National Economies," *American Economic Review*, Vol. 34, Supplement (March 1944), p. 320.

Second, the advantage of mixed economies in this basic respect essentially depends not only on having an adequate nonmarket sector but also on assuring that its size and the kinds of benefits it provides leave in the market sector both the resources and the incentives necessary to maintain the latter's efficiency and dynamism. The essence of this requirement is distinguishing between positive-sum and negative-sum welfare/efficiency interactions at macro and micro levels.

IMPLICATIONS FOR U.S. POLICY

The courses of development at macro and micro levels sketched in the preceding sections are all within the limits of the possible but their relative probabilities vary. They are projections of the main ways in which the factors affecting welfare/efficiency interactions that have emerged during the 1970s could work themselves out over the next decade or so depending on the relative importance of the different elements of which they are composed. None of these possible courses of development is inevitable. Their varying probabilities reflect not only the extent to which the factors conducive to each of these projections are inherent in basic socioeconomic processes but also how they might be affected in the years to come by the political choices, explicit and implicit, of the society and the decisions of its policy makers.

Whether and how one of these possible courses of development, or some variant or combination of them, actually occurs in Western Europe over the next decade or so would be of determinative importance for the future of the OECD region. For, except perhaps in France where communism plays an important role, the prospective development of welfare/efficiency interactions—as they are broadly defined in this study—will largely determine (a) whether the North European nations will continue to have mixed economies with efficient and dynamic market sectors that interact with one another and with the rest of the world predominantly in accordance with market forces or (b) whether they will increasingly become nonmarket economies whose external economic relations will be conducted mainly in accordance with unilateral government decisions and intergovernmental agreements. In turn, whichever course prevails will have a major influence on the future development of the rest of the OECD region, including the United States, and hence of the international economic system as a whole. Including France, the North European nations as a group are the richest and most productive in Western Europe, they collectively conduct the largest share of world trade, and they comprise most of the biggest trading partners of the United States and, except for Japan, its main competitors in the markets of other countries. Therefore, if the North European nations are constrained by their own internal changes and resulting external difficulties to resort to increasingly neomercantilist policies, their actions will inevitably impel other countries to adopt similar measures in direct proportion to the importance of the latter's economic relations with the former. The United States, too, would feel such external pressures and would be compelled to react accordingly.

Conversely, the choices and actions of the United States over the next 5 to 10 years will importantly affect the course of development in Western Europe. True, the United States no longer has the power or the will to intervene in the internal affairs of the West European nations, as it could and did during the late 1940s and '50s. Nor, as they did then, would the Europeans be likely today to solicit and welcome such intervention. Rather, the U.S. capacity to influence their development is much like theirs to influence the United States. That is, if the United States were impelled by its own internal changes and needs to resort to increasingly neomercantilist policies in its external economic relations, such actions would strengthen the tendencies that have already been pushing its European trading partners and competitors in that direction. In addition, however, the United States retains a significant degree of leadership influence in Western Europe as the guarantor of the region's security and by virture of its continuing, albeit relatively diminished, status as a superpower. The questions are: (1) how can the United States exercise this remaining leadership influence to help contain the pressures for neomercantilist measures to cope with the problems generated by negative-sum welfare/efficiency interactions in the OECD region and (2) in the event that U.S. efforts are unsuccessful, how can it act unilaterally to protect its own employment and income in an increasingly neomercantilist international economic system?

Before endeavoring to answer these questions, two essential points need to be reiterated.

One is that the solution to welfare/efficiency problems does not lie in efforts to cut back substantially, let alone to abolish, national welfare systems. Chapter 1 has explained that the values and expectations they express are among the most deeply rooted historically and the most strongly felt psychologically in Western societies. At bottom, they are intrinsic parts of the same basic complex of values and motivations that has also helped to produce the technoscientific achievements and the economic dynamism of Western societies. The very cultural and psychological factors that have impelled the restless Western drive to understand and control the forces of nature and society have also generated the expectation that, sooner or later, this knowledge would be applied to improving the conditions of life for all, and not only for a favored few. The problem is not that the enhancement of human welfare in the here and now is an impossible or an undesirable goal. It is that many who sincerely desire to improve the conditions of human living are under the illusion that this goal can be achieved without regard to the economic and psychological requirements for maintaining the productivity of complex interdependent industrialized economies and the efficiency of the individual enterprises of which they are composed.

The second point is that meeting the latter conditions is becoming increasingly difficult not simply because of the illusions of the well-intentioned—let alone the fanaticism of the ideologues and the ambitions of the power seekers—within Western societies. More important, the difficulty arises from the major changes that have been occurring in the international system. In consequence, Western societies can no longer seek to resolve their problems and achieve their aspirations on the assumption that the rest of the world could neither threaten their security nor refuse to provide them with the resources they require on more or less their own terms. On the one hand, the ambitions of the Soviet Union and, on the other, the efforts of many old and new nations in Asia, Africa and Latin America to acquire the freedom of action and the resources to pursue their own interests have combined to increase the political insecurity and to reduce the economic calculability of the planetary system within which Western societies must operate. Nor can the West Europeans rely upon the hegemonic power of the United States to maintain the economic integration of the international system to anywhere near the extent that it was willing and able to do during the postwar period.

These, then, are the realities of the current period of global nationalism within which the United States has to exercise its remaining leadership influence. To be effective, U.S. efforts must be responsive to the tightening limits on the freedom of action of OECD governments imposed both by changes in the international system and by political and social developments within their own societies. Thus, the United States has to recognize the resulting reduced adjustment capabilities of their economies. Such external and domestic constraints operate equally on the U.S. government and consequently must also be taken into account in formulating U.S. policies for coping with neomercantilist trends. The following suggestions are made with these requirements in mind.

(1) If the OECD countries, including the United States, are to deal effectively with the internal and external problems generated wholly or in part by welfare/ efficiency interactions, they will need to know a great deal more than they now do about the nature and magnitudes of the factors and relationships involved. The conceptual framework presented in Appendix A provides a set of initial hypotheses regarding some of the most important of these relationships at the macro level. This provisional model needs to be tested empirically for each country. New data series will be required on the composition and size of market and nonmarket sectors, of government revenues and expenditures, and of national welfare systems, as well as series on rates of return and of investment in the market sector, on the shares of traded-goods production sold in domestic and foreign markets, on basic and marginal tax rates at various levels of family income, and on the other relevant variables noted in Chapter 1. More comprehensive and detailed analyses are needed of the positive and negative effects of various kinds of welfare benefits on labor availability and productivity, including absenteeism; of the relationships among taxes, welfare income and earned disposable income as they affect at-titudes toward work and leisure; and of the other factors involved. The secretariats of the OECD and the EC can play very useful roles in formulating the statistical requirements for the new data series and in coordinating and processing the results, just as they did in the 1950s and '60s with respect to the national income accounts and other statistics needed for demand-management purposes. They should also undertake in-depth empirical studies of actual welfare programs to determine how the various kinds of benefits produce positive or negative effi-ciency effects and how the latter could be eliminated or reduced.

(2) These new data are necessary to enable policy makers in the OECD countries to cope with welfare/efficiency problems. They are also essential for improving popular understanding of the nature of welfare/efficiency interactions and for increasing popular support of measures to prevent or correct negative-sum outcomes. Well-conceived efforts have to be made to educate opinion leaders and the public generally in the OECD countries, including the United States, on the following points:

> ▶ The relationship between welfare and efficiency need not be a tradeoff, let alone a negative-sum game, but can and should be a positive-sum outcome.

▶ The real tradeoff in recent years has been between welfare benefits and earned disposable income and, given the high levels of taxation already imposed on the middle- and upper-income groups, the cost of this tradeoff has increasingly been borne in Europe by blue- and white-collar workers in the forms of rising taxes and high inflation and unemployment.

▶ The only way in which welfare benefits and real earned income can both be increased in market economies without risking a negative-sum welfare/efficiency outcome is through a high enough rate of economic growth. This means that market-sector enterprises must have adequate resources and incentives to innovate and invest and that the availability of the requisite amounts and kinds of labor must be assured by providing sufficient incentives to work and to improve labor skills.

▶ If economic growth rates continue in the lower range, it is all the more necessary that, in negotiations over wages, hours and other collective-bargaining issues, both businessmen and trade-union leaders take adequate account (a) of the need to assure sufficient incentives and resources for investment and exports and (b) of blue- and white-collar workers' own preferences as to how their real income gains should be divided between improved welfare benefits and increased aftertax earnings.

(3) In the course of the 1970s, wage, inventory, investment, and other kinds of subsidies designed to maintain or increase production have become the most important means by which the North European governments have been endeavoring to mitigate the adverse effects on employment and income of the loss of competitiveness in domestic and foreign markets due wholly or partly to negative-sum welfare/efficiency interactions. And, as the analysis in this study indicates, governments are likely to continue to rely in greater or lesser degree upon such production subsidies over the foreseeable future not only for these purposes but also to achieve other social goals—e.g., regional and urban redevelopment, environmental improvement. To prevent competitive escalation of subsidies and other palliatives by the OECD countries, including the United States, it would be desirable for them to agree upon the ways in which and the extent to which these measures could be used. A code of conduct could spell out in as much detail as would be practicable the circumstances in which production subsidies—of all kinds and for all purposes—could be adopted; the forms, magnitudes and duration of such measures; the improved conditions under which they would have to be reduced and eventually eliminated; the procedures whereby countries adversely affected by the subsidies of their trading partners or competitors could institute complaints; and the sanctions that could be imposed, individually and collectively, against countries violating the provisions of the agreement. In theory, such a code could be incorporated into the GATT. However, the large and heterogeneous membership of the GATT and its cumbersome and time-consuming procedures make it an impractical institutional context in which to deal with a problem that is largely a concern of the OECD nations. For these reasons, the OECD would appear to be the most effective institution to administer a code governing the use of production subsidies. The OECD—or rather its predecessor, the OEEC—had somewhat similar responsibilities during the 1950s in connection with the agreement to reduce and eliminate quantitative restrictions on trade among the West European countries. Moreover, the development by the OECD

secretariat of the new data series suggested in (1) above would enable it to provide the member governments with much of the information needed by them collectively to enforce an agreement on the use of production subsidies.

(4) As a safeguard against future contingencies, the United States should consider the desirability and practicability of steps it might take to prevent or mitigate the adverse effects on U.S. multinational corporations if the North European nations were to adopt the more extreme forms of industrial democracy. One possibility would be the prior negotiation of bilateral agreements between the United States and the countries in which such actions are likely to occur that would exempt the existing European subsidiaries of U.S. corporations from future mandatory requirements for full parity of workers' directors on company boards and for participation in worker asset-formation schemes involving the eventual loss of voting control to union-dominated shareholding funds.

(5) Finally, the United States should take account of the possibility that joint efforts like those suggested in the foregoing numbered paragraphs would not be adopted or would prove to be ineffective and that the trends toward neomercantilism and socialism in the OECD region would continue. Against such a contingency, the United States should begin now to explore the kinds of unilateral measures it would need to protect its own employment and income. Whatever unilateral steps are decided upon, however, care should be taken to avoid or to minimize the use of those measures for regulating the external economic relations of the United States that would so increase governmental control over the domestic economy as to impair the effective functioning of its market sector. For, there would be a growing danger that, as the other OECD nations moved toward predominantly nonmarket economies, the United States would be impelled in the same direction by the actions it would take to prevent unacceptable increases in unemployment and declines in real income. At bottom, it is the fundamental commitment of the great majority of the American people—business, labor, farmers, consumers generally—to a predominantly market economic system that generates the U.S. concern about negative-sum welfare/efficiency interactions in Western Europe and their possible role in strengthening the trends toward neomercantilism and socialism. If the major trading partners and competitors of the United States were to become predominantly nonmarket economies, it would be difficult—although not impossible—for the United States to avoid a similar development.

In sum, the task in the OECD countries is to assure that national welfare systems and the future improvements in them generate positive-sum interactions between welfare and efficiency to the maximum feasible extent. The experience of the past 100 years proves that this is possible, the experience of the past 10 years proves that it is crucial. Given the rationality that has been an essential element in the unprecedented social and cultural accomplishments of Western society, there are good grounds for confidence that continuing success can be achieved in the future in improving welfare without adversely affecting efficiency.

Appendix A: Conceptualizing Welfare/Efficiency Relationships

by Neil J. McMullen

Although incomplete, the data presented in this study provide enough empirical evidence for tentatively concluding that welfare/efficiency interactions yield negative-sum outcomes in certain circumstances. These occur when the expansion of the national welfare system and the size of and conditions for obtaining welfare benefits are such as to leave insufficient income and incentives in the market sector for its enterprises and their workers to generate the necessary productive investment, innovation and work effort. The results are not only to impair the efficiency and international competitiveness of the economy, but also, if these effects persist, to undermine its ability to sustain the levels of welfare already achieved, let alone to improve them in the future.

To strengthen the validity of these conclusions, it would be desirable to expand the relevant data and to formulate and test some more specific hypotheses regarding the nature of and conditions for various kinds of welfare/efficiency interactions. Further research along these lines can most effectively be conducted with the aid of a conceptual model or framework that depicts the possible interactions of the key variables involved. Based on the data and analysis so far undertaken for this study, this appendix describes such a conceptual framework and explains the theoretical justifications for its constituent relationships.

OUTPUT/TAXATION RELATIONSHIPS

As explained in the study, the growth of the nonmarket sectors of the OECD countries has mainly resulted from the expansion of their national welfare systems since the early 1960s. During their initial stages of growth in the 1960s, the increasing taxes required to support these welfare systems did not reduce output or incentives to a significant degree, except in the United Kingdom. Indeed, in most countries during the 1960s, the improvement of national welfare systems helped to generate growing output through the positive-sum effects explained in Chapter 2. Increased government expenditures caused greater employment, investment and output while taxes and transfer payments, even though rising, were not yet large enough to impact adversely on incentives. And, even when they did, the stimulus of increasing expenditure on the demand side was probably more than sufficient to offset any drag resulting from higher taxation or other disincentives on the supply side.

In the course of the 1970s, however, these generally positive-sum relation-ships have been changing in most OECD countries. In the mid-1970s, the increase of output slowed substantially due in part to the impact of the OPEC price rise and other developments in the world economy. It also resulted in part from the adverse effect on capital formation and productivity growth of the continuing large rises in tax rates needed to support the rapidly expanding welfare systems and the negative influence of bigger transfer payments on incentives.

Both the positive-sum and the negative-sum relationships between tax rates, on the one hand, and tax revenues and output levels, on the other hand, can be graphically presented as in Figure A–1. At zero levels of taxation, tax revenues are nil and output is low because essential public services are not being adequately provided. As tax rates rise, essential public services, such as justice, security and defense, are provided and economic activity expands rapidly from 0 up toward B. With further increases in tax rates, the government can go beyond essential services and begin to supply other desired public goods and to meet basic welfare needs. As tax rates increase for these purposes, output levels will inevitably peak and then begin to decline because rising taxes and transfer payments reduce the incentives to invest, innovate and work. The point of taxation at which output peaks and the shape of the output/tax curve will vary depending upon a number of factors, including the size of the economy, the uses to which the tax revenues are put, the extent of the commitment to welfare objectives, the intensity of the work and savings ethics in the society, and the time frame over which the output/tax relationships are considered. These factors are all discussed in some detail when alternative curves are examined.

Although the location of the output peak and the shape of the curve will vary among countries and within countries over time, tax rates become sufficiently high and transfer income becomes sufficiently attractive at some point to cause factors of production to withdraw from the producing sector. This occurs at point B in Figure A–1. From this position, the reduction in the supply of productive factors has an increasingly negative impact on productive capacity. In theory, high taxation will eventually lead to a complete withdrawal of labor and a termination of saving. At the extreme, therefore, an effective taxation rate of 100 percent results in no production at all at point C. Such a condition is somewhat akin to a forced-labor camp where all output is taken out by the state and the bare essentials of life are "transferred" in to the workers.

The level of tax revenues generated, relating tax revenues to tax rates, can be constructed from the output/tax curve. This is done along curve OFDC.[1] Tax revenues reach their peak (D) at a higher tax rate than does national output—a result that is generally true for output/tax relationships.

A third concept, the total tax-related cost, is also presented in Figure A–1. This curve (AEFG) represents the difference between the possible output peak (B) and the aftertax income actually received. This is a measure of the total cost of the government's tax program to the society and includes both output taxed away and

---

1   Curve OFDC is derived by multiplying the tax rate times output to yield the tax revenues generated at each tax rate.

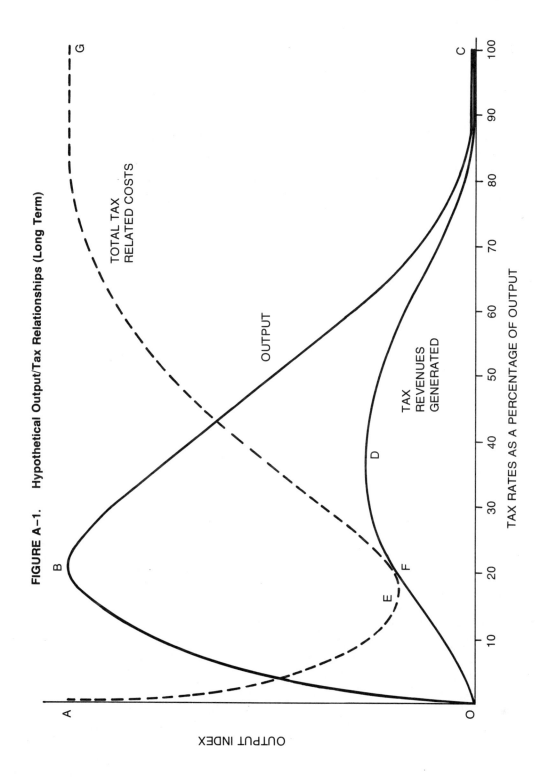

FIGURE A–1. Hypothetical Output/Tax Relationships (Long Term)

output lost to inefficiency. At low rates of taxation, the cost to the society is very high because of the inadequate provision of essential public services. The loss of output to tax revenues is very low, but the loss of output due to inefficiency is overwhelming. As tax revenues and the government's provision of essential and desirable public services rise, efficiency improves dramatically and the total tax-related cost falls sharply. Total tax-related cost reaches a minimum before output reaches its peak because, at that point, tax revenue begins rising faster than output. Beyond the output peak, the total tax-related cost continues to rise as tax rates increase up to 100 percent.

Thus, the extreme points of the tax schedule are identified with anarchy at the low end and totalitarianism at the upper end. The optimum is in between, but people will disagree as to just where the society ought to be, depending upon how they, and the groups with which they identify, benefit or lose from increased taxation and government expenditure. Groups that gain from taxes and transfers would probably prefer to maximize tax revenues at point D and accept a lower level of total output for the society as a whole. Groups that do not benefit from taxes and transfers would probably prefer to minimize total tax-related costs at point E. Tax rates below point E do not make economic sense and would be advocated only by those who opposed taxation or government services on ideological grounds. Similarly, proponents of tax rates in excess of the rate at point D would have to base their positions on a desire to reduce output and/or achieve more equal shares of income with much less total income available to share. The curve shown in Figure A-1 is hypothetical in the sense that it is not now known for any country exactly what tax rate will maximize output at point B, maximize total tax revenues at point D, or minimize total tax-related costs. The results of the regressions reported later in this appendix and other evidence indicate that most of the countries examined in the study may be to the right of point B, with tax rates in excess of the rate which induces maximum output.

Although the shape of the output/tax curve is not yet known for any of the countries studied here, a number of observations about the likely shape of this curve can be made. It would be expected that small and/or high-consensus societies would be more likely to agree on the nature and level of the public goods to be provided and thus would opt for more taxation and more collective consumption than would large and/or highly particularistic societies. Similarly, societies that have a strong propensity for work and saving (perhaps Germany) might be expected to have a higher rate of taxation at peak output than societies with weaker work and savings ethics.

The key issue in determining the shape of the output/tax curve is the elasticity of supply of the factors of production with respect to changes in taxation. In the short run, these elasticities are probably quite low and may even be negative. Families habituated to a particular level of disposable-income expenditures may respond to increased taxes by increasing their supply of labor in the short run. In the longer run, however, rising taxes on factors will likely reduce the supply of these factors. Capital, in particular, would be sensitive to aftertax rates of return. In the long term, high rates of taxation on capital earnings would undoubtedly reduce savings and investment even though, in the short term, high taxation may not have a significant effect on the capital stock already in place. Over a number of years,

FIGURE A–2.   Hypothetical Output/Tax Relationships (Short Term)

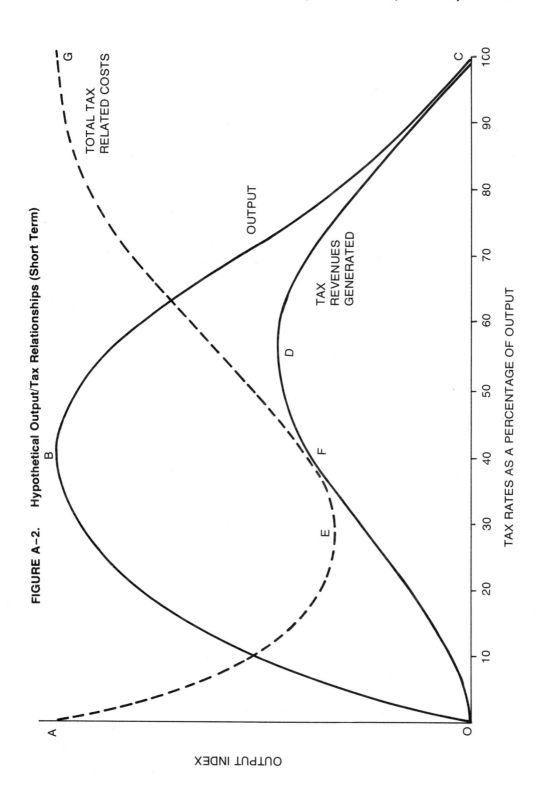

investment will decline, growth in the capital stock will slow, and output will be reduced due to high taxation.

It is the time frame of the response of factor supplies to increased taxes that affects the shape of the output/tax-rate curve. If the hypothetical relationships shown in Figure A–1 are viewed as long term (i.e., the present value of the long-run income stream related to the tax rate), then the hypothetical relationships shown in Figure A–2 would be more representative of the short term. In the short run, the output level of the economy is much less sensitive to the tax rate and income will probably peak at a higher rate of taxation, as will also the level of tax revenues. This is due to the fact that, in the short term, changes in tax rates do not greatly affect output. It is only after workers and investors have accustomed themselves to the changes in taxes that their behavior changes and the output level of the economy is affected. Thus, a society with strong work and savings ethics might experience very little short-run change in output over a wide range of tax rates.

The types of expenditures undertaken by the government affect the shape and position of the output/tax curve. The output/tax relationships in Figures A–1 and A–2 show the real output that will be supplied at various rates of taxation given the government's spending pattern and the society's preferences for public and private goods and for leisure. If the country were to become engaged in a large-scale conflict with overwhelming public support, as the United States did in World War II, then the curves would shift to the right and more output would be forthcoming at higher tax rates. After the war, the curve would shift back to the left to, or at least toward, its prewar position. In normal periods, the curves are unlikely to shift significantly from year to year but may move over time.

If a government were to use its revenues to augment production through large-scale public investment—as opposed to public consumption or transfers for private consumption—then the output/tax curve would shift to the right, with more output forthcoming at high rates. The Soviet Union imposes high taxes on consumption and utilizes the available resources for public capital formation. In effect, the Soviet output/tax curve is moved to the right through the enforcement of relatively fast growth despite high rates of taxation. Conversely, if the Soviets were to decide at some point to transfer these resources to consumers, investment could drop and growth would likely be reduced as the output/tax curve shifted to the left.

POLICY IMPLICATIONS OF THE OUTPUT/TAX CURVE

The implications of these curves for economic policy are quite interesting in that they reveal a supply-side macro relationship not hitherto considered. Figure A–3 presents a representation of the supply-side output/tax-rate relationship combined with the relationship between income and taxes. The aggregate tax schedule (OJNI) represents a hypothetical legislated tax schedule indicating the average tax rates that prevail at each level of national income. Tax rates are set such that, if national income were equal to OM, the prevailing tax rate would be directly below point J (25 percent in this hypothetical case). The tax revenues demanded by the government are shown as curve OLDK. When income is equal to OM, the tax

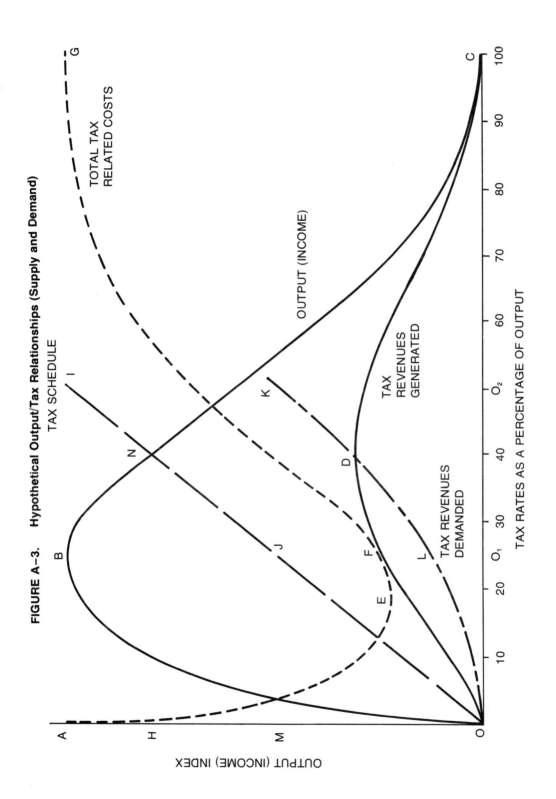

FIGURE A–3.   Hypothetical Output/Tax Relationships (Supply and Demand)

revenues demanded are O_1L, which corresponds to one-quarter of income OM. If national income were equal to OA, the relevant point on the tax schedule is I, resulting in a hypothetical tax rate of 50 percent. The relevant point on the tax revenues-demanded curve is K, and taxes demanded are one-half of OA or O_2K.

The interaction between the output/tax relationship (OBNC) and the aggregate tax schedule (OJNI) will tend to move the economy toward the equilibrium point at N. At N, taxpayers are producing OH of output and paying taxes at point D. This is the level of output that producers choose to produce at the prevailing tax rate (40 percent in this hypothetical example) and the taxes generated equal taxes demanded at the income level OH. If output were initially equal to OM, producers (taxpayers) would find themselves paying lower taxes than expected and would be willing to save and invest more and to work harder to obtain greater available returns, and hence produce additional output. Thus, output and income will tend to rise. However, rising income in a progressive tax structure also raises tax revenues demanded and the proportion of income absorbed by taxes. Until output and income rise to H, producers find themselves paying less in tax revenues than they are willing to generate. If output were initially at A, then producers would find themselves paying more taxes than they are willing to generate, with the result that they would work less and save and invest less, bringing the level of output down to H. Thus, given the aggregate tax schedule in effect, and given the society's willingness to produce goods and services at various tax rates, the hypothetical economy shown here will tend toward a level of output equal to H and an average tax rate equal to 40 percent.

Tax schedules, however, are important policy tools and can be shifted to achieve goals, such as increased output, if the society so desires. A tax reduction would be represented by a shift of the aggregate tax schedule counterclockwise and to the left. After a tax reduction, the aggregate tax schedule would intersect the output curve closer to point B and output would rise. The curve representing tax revenues demanded (OLDK) would also shift to the left and would intersect tax revenues generated closer to point F. The result would be notably higher income with slightly lower tax revenues. A reduction in taxes can result in higher income whenever the intersection of the aggregate tax schedule is to the right of point B. If the intersection is to the left of point B, then output can be increased by raising taxes and using the revenues to provide public goods. In the hypothetical case exhibited in Figure A–3, tax rates and government expenditures have positive-sum effects on efficiency and productivity as they increase up to point B; beyond B, the net impact of rising tax rates and government expenditures has a negative-sum effect on efficiency and productivity.

The evidence presented in this study would tend to indicate that most of the countries considered are to the left of point B on their respective output/tax curves. The regressions explained below also support the conclusion that, as a group, the North European nations have been on the downward-sloping section of the output/tax curve. Clearly, any such conclusion has to be very tentative and a great deal more work needs to be done in estimating the relationships between tax rates and output over time and among countries. It may never be possible to know the exact shape and position of the relationship for a given country at a given time, but it should be possible to estimate whether current tax rates are to the left or right of the income-maximizing rate at point B and to the left or right of the tax revenue-maximizing rate at point D. Furthermore, a "typical" curve for a collection of countries at similar levels of development could be estimated. Such a collective curve would provide an approximation as to the shape and position of a particular country's curve. This would help policy makers to ascertain their own country's output/tax-rate curve and to clarify the true costs of increasing or reducing taxation.

TAXATION AND PUBLIC EXPENDITURES

The discussion thus far has assumed a balanced budget with government expenditures equal to taxes. As a general rule, such an assumption has not been far wrong because government surpluses or deficits have not been a large proportion of national income until the last few years. If expenditures were to differ from taxes in a consistent manner, then the effect would be to shift the output/tax curve. By running a deficit, for example, a country can achieve a higher level of income and/or a higher rate of growth—if the additional resources available to the public sector are not used counterproductively. A deficit, or for that matter foreign assistance, reparations or windfall gains of any sort, can be used either to reduce taxes or to shift the output/tax-rate curve. In any event, short-term income will be higher. The longer-term effect of a deficit, or other injection of resources, depends on when, how and if repayment is made and on how productively the resources are utilized. Funds borrowed at commercial rates of interest and normal terms of repayment should increase long-term income if they are used wisely. Funds which do not have to be repaid will have a greater long-term impact if utilized equally well. As explained in Chapter 4, the Netherlands has enjoyed such an injection over the past few years in the form of taxes collected from foreigners in the sale of natural-gas resources. This has allowed the Netherlands to enjoy public expenditure in excess of tax revenues generated by domestic factors of production and shifted the output/tax-rate curve to the right.

The contrary situation is facing other nations because of the rapid and highly visible rise in energy prices. Higher prices for imported oil have had an impact similar to an excise tax whose revenues are not spent on additional public goods, thus reducing expenditures and incentives. Higher energy prices have an effect similar to shifting the aggregate tax schedule counterclockwise and to the right, resulting in lower incomes at high levels of taxation. As with domestic taxation, this will tend to reduce output as savings and investment decline and workers adjust to the reduction in their purchasing power. If such a price rise were fully justified by market realities, then the effect would be more correctly represented by a downward shift in the output/tax curve. A genuine scarcity of energy would have the effect of reducing the productivity and output of all other factors of production. Whether the phenomenon is represented as a shift in the output/tax curve or in the aggregate tax schedule, the result in terms of output is the same for the energy-importing societies.

Thus, the relationships considered above best depict a situation in which tax revenues rather closely represent government expenditures and there are no windfall gains from or losses to the outside world. Departures from these conditions can be handled but they add complication, manifesting the increased complexity of economic policy in the final quarter of the 20th century.

RELATIONSHIP TO AGGREGATE DEMAND

The concepts discussed relate real output and income (i.e., output and income at constant prices) with effective real rates of taxation. The analysis indicates that real output will tend to move toward that level at which tax revenues generated equal tax revenues demanded. If output is below this level, then revenues demanded are less than the revenues that producers are willing to generate. Realizing higher aftertax income and profits, producers increase their economic activities until tax revenues demanded increase to absorb fully the tax revenues generated. These relationships focus on the impact of tax policy on the total amount of output produced, that is, on the aggregate supply effects of tax policy.

The level of aggregate demand is determined by other, principally Keynesian, relationships which are well known and have been investigated by economists over the last 40 years. There is no point in reviewing the existing state of knowledge on the determinants of aggregate demand; suffice it to say that fiscal policy, the relationship between government expenditures and tax revenues, is generally regarded as one of the factors which determine aggregate demand in the short run. Until the past few years, national income determination, or macroeconomics, was almost entirely demand-oriented. Supply constraints were not considered to be serious obstacles to the expansion of national income so long as the proportion of unutilized industrial capacity did not become too low. The concept of potential GNP was developed to bring the supply side into the picture, but this concept only incorporated labor and historic trends in labor productivity into the analysis. Capital, technology and innovation, industrial raw materials, agricultural products, and labor skills were all assumed to be readily forthcoming at prevailing prices. Through the 1950s and early 1960s, for example, U.S. national income was generally less than potential GNP and the various components of production were available at relatively stable prices.

Then, during the period of the late 1960s and early 1970s, the supply assumptions implicit in the macroeconomists' approach to national income determination were violated one by one. The end of the era of demand-determined national income came with the sharp rise in agricultural prices and the threefold increase in the real price of energy in 1973 and 1974. Macroeconomic policy makers have had to incorporate a number of supply considerations into their analysis, but it is not at all clear that all of the important supply considerations have been correctly integrated into their macroeconomic models. In particular, the impact of public expenditure and taxation policy on the supply of goods and services has been generally ignored. Policy makers are just beginning to be aware of the effect of high taxes and extensive transfers of income on the supply of labor, particularly skilled labor, the formation of capital, and the development of innovations.

The output/tax relationships described earlier provide some of the missing pieces on the supply side of macroeconomic analysis. They indicate links between the tax system and the types of government expenditures, on the one hand, and the supply of goods and services, on the other. The nature of government expenditures, the incidence of taxation, along with the other factors described, influence the shape and position of the output curve. Transfers and other subsidies for nonproducers, a high incidence of taxation on producers, as well as extensive regulation of the production process, tend to reduce output and increase unemployment, while subsidies for production and taxation of consumption, rather than production, would tend to increase output and reduce unemployment. The level and aggregate progressivity of the tax system directly determine the tax schedule. Together, the output curve and the tax schedule determine the level of national output at which factors of production are willing to generate the tax revenues demanded by the public sector.

For an economy to be in equilibrium, the level of real output supplied by factors of production must be equal to the level of real output demanded by purchasers. If output demanded does not equal the output producers desire to supply at current tax rates, then adjustments will take place in prices, employment, inventories, and/or the trade balance.

If aggregate demand—as determined by monetary and fiscal policies, savings and import propensities, and investment and export demand—exceeds the level of output producers are willing to supply, then prices will rise, inventories will fall, and unemployment may decline. In the short run, output may increase and exceed the equilibrium level for some time because producers do not adjust instantaneously to disequilibrium conditions. Rising prices may encourage some workers and investors to supply more factors of production, but higher prices—through progressive taxes—also increase the real burden of taxation, which will tend to reduce the supply of labor and capital provided by other producers. The net effect on output depends on what the government does with the increased real revenues. During the late 1960s and the 1970s, it seems that most additional revenues went to finance transfers and entitlement income, which tended to reduce output supplied at each tax rate. As well, inflation tended to raise real taxes, shifting the tax schedule to the right. The outcome has been higher taxes and lower output than would have resulted from lower taxes or the use of government revenues for production-oriented purposes.

When aggregate demand is less than the level of output that producers are willing to supply, then unemployment will rise, inventories will rise, and the rate of price increase should moderate (falling prices could result if demand were significantly less than supply for a sustained period). Insufficient aggregate demand would undoubtedly increase unemployment in the short run, and the positive effect of the moderation of inflation would only occur slowly.

The relationships discussed above and diagrammed in Figure A–3 are a part of the supply side of macroeconomics. The output/tax-rate issue and the aggregate tax schedule represent the impact of government tax policies and government expenditure programs on the supply of goods and services. It is important to emphasize that these relationships are part of a large and complex system that determines national income, employment, price levels, and tax revenues. Much additional research is clearly needed before the output/tax-rate issue and the aggregate tax schedule can be accurately estimated and correctly integrated into macroeconomic analysis. These relationships should enrich macroeconomic analysis and improve policy making but they should not be looked upon as a replacement for existing theory or a panacea for policy makers.

RESULTS OF REGRESSION ANALYSIS

To illustrate quantitatively the relationships described, some regressions were prepared involving variables for which the relevant data were readily available for five countries—France, Germany, the Netherlands, Sweden, and the United Kingdom—for the period 1965–75. The variables for which data were available are:
> ▶ the rate of change of output per manhour as an indicator of productivity growth;
> ▶ the share of GNP utilized for investment, excluding public investment;
> ▶ the share of GNP allocated to government consumption and investment; and
> ▶ the rate of inflation of the GNP deflator.

These are, at best, only partially representative of some of the welfare/efficiency indicators listed in Chapter 1. The share of private investment in GNP is probably not a bad surrogate for investment in the market sector. The share of government spending is probably representative of the nonmarket sector, but this is only a conjecture until more basic statistical work can be done. The inflation rate is a useful indicator of economic imbalances, bottlenecks and disequilibria in national economies. And, the rate of change of output per manhour is a good indicator of efficiency gains. Total factor productivity growth should also be looked at but, again, the data are not available for enough countries over enough years to do any systematic statistical analysis.

The most straightforward measures gave the best results and attempts to experiment with alternatives did not improve the explanatory powers of the analyses. A particularly disappointing alternative was the failure of a "discomfort index" (the rate of inflation plus the rate of unemployment) to explain variations in efficiency. Unemployment should be a good indicator of disequilibrium and low efficiency growth in an economy, but this has not proven to be the case in the analysis carried out to date. Public civilian expenditure was separated from defense expenditure, but this did not help in explaining variations in productivity. Finally, a number of alternative measures of productivity were used, including growth in output per capita and growth in output per person in the labor force. The results were generally similar to those reported below.

Using pooled data from the five countries, the muliple correlation analysis indicates that, over the period 1965–75, increased productivity was positively correlated with investment as a proportion of GNP and negatively correlated with high rates of inflation and high levels of government expenditures relative to GNP. More specifically, a 10 percent rise in investment relative to GNP (e.g., from 20 percent to 22 percent of GNP) is associated with a 10.7 percent rise in the rate of productivity increase (e.g., from 3.30 percent to 3.65 percent); a 10 percent increase in government expenditures is associated with an 11.9 percent fall in the rate of productivity growth; and a 10 percent rise in the rate of inflation is associated with a 4 percent decline in the rate of productivity increase. The detailed results of the multiple correlation analysis are given in a note to this appendix.

This attempt at systematic quantification must be considered tentative and preliminary. For now, the most that can be concluded is that the available data tend to support, rather than rebut, the concepts advanced in this study. Clearly, much more research needs to be done before hypotheses can be rigorously formulated and tested.

CONCLUSIONS

The various output/tax relationships and the other interactions explained here need to be integrated into macroeconomic analysis where they can contribute importantly to policy making in the OECD countries. Recognition of the supply impacts of government expenditure and taxation policy is long overdue. An improved understanding of the supply relationships of national income determination is essential if macroeconomics is to progress and continue to provide useful analysis for policy makers.

The output/tax relationships shown in Figure A–1 present a simplified overview of the welfare/efficiency phenomena that are documented in this study. The region to the left of point B is generally associated with positive-sum welfare/efficiency interactions where benefits far outweigh costs. In the region near point B, a zero-sum relationship occurs as welfare gains begin to be offset by efficiency losses. To the right of point B, efficiency costs accumulate while welfare gains diminish, resulting in an increasingly negative outcome. Shifts in the output/tax curve, as well as movements along the curve, can be positive-sum, zero-sum or negative-sum in their outcome. The evidence at hand argues that, except probably for Germany, the North European countries analyzed in this study are more or less to the right of the maximum point of their output/tax relationship. Thus, they are paying a high price, in terms of output, in order to increase the nonmarket-sector's control of resources. To continue to increase the nonmarket-sector's share of national income, without a dramatic shift in public expenditure patterns, will likely result in prohibitively high costs in terms of stagnating output and rising unemployment. Signs of such a shift in government expenditure are already evident as producers' subsidies become more common in these countries, although a reduction in taxes would probably be a more efficient long-term method of encouraging production.

In sum, the questions raised in this study are central to the economic and political future of all the industrial nations. The next step in a serious quantitative examination of welfare/efficiency relationships has to center on improving the data base available for statistical analyses. Time series for the size of the market and nonmarket sectors of the OECD countries are an essential first step. Information on beforetax and aftertax returns to factors of production are also needed. In addition to the necessary empirical analysis, a good deal of theoretical work needs to be done to specify better the crucial relationships which determine aggregate supply. The relationships discussed in this appendix and the evidence presented in the study should help to bring a new richness and relevance to macroeconomic policy in the years ahead.

NOTE TO APPENDIX A

The results of the multiple correlation analysis summarized in this appendix relate increases in output per manhour to private investment as a share of GNP, public consumption and investment as a share of GNP, and the rate of change in the GNP deflator. The private investment and public consumption and investment variables were lagged two years to enhance their effect on the structure of the economy and the resulting productivity gains, and to reduce the spurious cyclical correlation with productivity growth that is known to exist.[2] The inflation variable was for the current period. The period covered was 1965 to 1975 for the dependent variables and the data were pooled time series for France, Germany, the Netherlands, Sweden, and the United Kingdom. The correlation coefficients are not unreasonable given the fact that most of the annual variation in growth rates of output per manhour is associated with cyclical movements in national income and not structural factors, such as past investment levels.

The results are shown below in tabular form.

Variable	Output per Manhour Coefficient	T–Statistic	Mean = 0.0336 Mean	Elasticity
Constant	0.0509	1.9194	1.0000	
$(Pvt. I/Y)_{-2}$	0.1539	1.9699	0.2332	1.0680
$(Govt./Y)_{-2}$	−0.2417	−3.0866	0.1647	−1.1851
Inflation	−0.2112	−4.0127	0.0632	−0.3971
$\bar{R}^2$ = 0.464			SE = 0.0144	DW = 1.612

Lagging the inflation variable two periods reduces the correlation coefficient and the significance of the inflation variable, but does not materially affect the elasticity picture.

Variable	Output per Manhour Coefficient	T–Statistic	Mean = 0.0336 Mean	Elasticity
Constant	0.0368	1.2575	1.0000	
$(Pvt. I/Y)_{-2}$	0.2003	2.3292	0.2332	1.3900
$(Govt./Y)_{-2}$	−0.2487	−2.8107	0.1647	−1.2197
$(Inflation)_{-2}$	−0.1854	−1.7091	0.0479	−0.2646
$\bar{R}^2$ = 0.332			SE = 0.0161	DW = 1.687

2   It is widely observed that gains in productivity are procyclical, occurring in the upswing and at the peak, while reduced productivity growth occurs on the downside. Investment and government shares also vary over the cycle, with investment being procyclical and government spending countercyclical.

Appendix B:
The Meaning of Efficiency

by Harold van B. Cleveland

The common sense meaning of "efficiency" is the amount of output per unit of input. In the simplest case, that of a mechanical or a chemical process, in which one wants to know how many units of a single homogeneous input it takes to yield a given amount of homogeneous output, the problem of definition and measurement is also simple. Thus, a steam locomotive converts 8 percent of the energy burned, measured in BTUs, into mechanical energy (momentum) measured in foot-pounds per second, which can also be expressed by means of a standard conversion factor in BTU equivalents.

The problem of definition and measurement ceases to be simple as soon as the inputs and/or outputs are not homogeneous. This is, of course, the case of all economic production processes, which always involve inputs of various kinds of labor, materials, land, and capital and may also yield more than one kind of product. (Sometimes it is convenient to consider technical knowledge or human capital as a distinct input.) Thus, efficiency in an economic sense requires some common unit or standard of measurement so that inputs can be added up and compared with output, and the result compared with that produced by a different combination of inputs. That unit is, of course, money—the price (cost) of the various inputs and outputs. So, one is pushed back from the question of efficiency to the question of what determines the prices (costs) in terms of which efficiencies are to be measured and compared.

In a centrally planned command (nonmarket) economy, the planning body predetermines the prices of all inputs and outputs. Enterprises are efficient or inefficient depending on how much the money value of their output exceeds the money value of the inputs. Direct comparison of the efficiency of an enterprise in one planned economy with an enterprise in another planned economy, or with an enterprise in a market economy, can be done only in rather crude, physical terms. Thus, one can show that it takes more or less direct labor, or total labor, to produce a ton of steel. But, without common or comparable prices, such comparisons can yield only the grossest results. The same is, of course, true for comparisons of the efficiency or productivity of national economies. Thus, international comparisons of the productivity of labor logically presuppose a measure of total output (GNP) in which the components of output are all valued at the same prices, or at prices that are presumed to be the same because they are determined in the same international market. In principle, the common prices could also be determined by a supranational socialist planning agency.

However, the concept of efficiency as it has traditionally been used in economic analysis presupposes that the prices at which inputs and outputs are reckoned are not arbitrarily established but have a determinate relationship to economic "value." The theory of value that prevails today among Western economists has its philosophic roots in 18th-century utilitarianism. The utilitarians started from the premise that value is wholly subjective. What has positive value (utility) or negative value (disutility) is entirely a matter of individual choice and taste. Thus, the utilitarians used the term "satisfaction" and "value" more or less synonymously. All that can be said objectively is that utility/disutility will diminish/ increase with the amount of the good/labor involved; hence the principle of diminishing marginal utility/increasing marginal disutility. Together, these principles—that economic value is subjective, that it diminishes with the quantity of the goods consumed, and that the disutility of labor increases with the quantity the individual supplies—lead logically to the proposition that a free, competitive exchange of goods in a market will maximize the sum total of satisfactions (the excess of utility over disutility in the community). Since no one knows better than the individual what kinds and amounts of goods and services will most satisfy him and how much of what kind of labor he is willing to give in return, it is only by a free interaction involving (potentially and in principle) the whole community that these decisions can be optimally made.

In making this argument for free markets, the utilitarians and classical economists emphasized the subjectivity of utility or, as it was often put, the noncomparability and noncommensurability of individuals' utilities. Given the subjectivity of value in utilitarian theory, there are no objective criteria for the distribution of social benefits, so the free market must "decide." While the utilitarians emphasized the value or utility side of the argument for free markets, later theorists, such as Hayek, emphasized the cost or disutility side. Writing in an age when the economy had become much more complex and was under the threat of central planning, they emphasized the problem of information—the impossibility of knowing centrally enough about subjective wants and preferences, and about the objective conditions of demand and supply in a myriad of markets, to do as good a job as the market in allocating resources and determining the composition of output to the end of maximizing individual satisfactions. If planning substitutes for markets, serious mistakes will be made. Resources will yield less utility than if free markets made the "decisions."

Thus, there is implicit in the idea of economic efficiency a standard of comparison: namely, that composition of output, pattern of resource allocation, and structure of relative prices and wages which would exist at equilibrium in an economy in which markets were private, free and competitive. *In short, the notion of economic efficiency includes not only an end (maximizing economic value or utility) but also a necessary means, a freely competitive market.*

From the beginning, the classical economists recognized exceptions to this generalization for public goods, which have been elaborated by latter-day welfare economics to include many new kinds of public goods and "bads" (negative externalities such as congestion and pollution). The public-goods exception may seem inconsistent with the central utilitarian principle that values, including economic utility, are subjective, since the government, in deciding what is a public good or "bad," must decide for the whole community, without allowing individuals the choice of buying it or not in a free market. Theoretically speaking, this is correct. As Unger puts it, "In both the private and the public spheres, subjective value means exchange value, and its hegemony is the hegemony of the market."[1] But, in practice, there are some public goods that are so universally desired, or whose existence is so fundamental to the existence of a community, such as military security, public order, suppression of crime, and public sanitation, that virtual unanimity on their value can be assumed, even though that consensus cannot conveniently be put to a market test.

Another important exception is that economic organizations—particularly the large organizations characteristic of an advanced industrial economy—are themselves exceptions to the principle that free-market interchange among individuals maximizes economic satisfactions (efficiency). Indeed, any economic organization exists because, in its internal relations, it is a more efficient—less costly—way of combining productive factors than the unorganized market provides. As the seminal article on this point puts it, "The operation of a market costs something, and by forming an organization and allowing some authority (an 'entrepreneur') to direct the resources, certain marketing costs are saved. The entrepreneur has to carry out his function at less cost, taking into account the fact that he may get factors of production at a lower price than the market transactions which he supersedes, because it is always possible to revert to the market if he fails to do this."[2] However, there is an optimal size of any economic organization beyond which it ceases to contribute to efficiency. Then, it becomes a public good to prevent its further enlargement, as by antitrust laws, for example.

The conflict between "welfare" (in the sense used in this study) and "efficiency" arises when the government insists on creating public goods (or suppressing public "bads") that are *not* so universally desired—that involve conflicting values and interests, such as major redistributions of income or wealth. Here, the community is clearly imposing objective values rather than accepting existing subjective values revealed through the market, or by a nearly universal consensus. Thus, the sum total of individual satisfactions will be diminished. For, the subjectivity or noncomparability of individuals' utilities means that giving some people more income and others less, as compared with what would happen as a result of market forces, cannot increase the net total of utility.

Taking from Peter to pay Paul does not increase the *sum* of Peter's and Paul's "satisfaction,"[3] unless one introduces an *objective* standard of judgment: that it is better for both of them to reduce their economic inequality. If Peter and Paul agree that it would be better to do so, then we have a case analogous to the consensus that it is good to raise taxes to pay for external and internal security—the case of a public good that is (almost) universally desired. Some minimal income and wealth redistribution may be in this category—for example, a guarantee of "social

---

1   Roberto M. Unger, *Knowledge and Politics* (New York: Macmillan Publishing Co., 1975), p. 186.

2   R. H. Coase, "The Nature of the Firm," in American Economic Association, *Readings in Price Theory* (Chicago: R.D. Irwin, 1952), p. 338.

3   The principle of diminishing marginal utility does not apply to an individual's income or wealth. It applies only to his ownership or consumption of particular goods and services.

minima." But, in principle, utilitarianism (classical economics) takes the preexisting distribution of income and wealth as given. Any change in it by public fiat is, therefore, *ipso facto* "inefficient."

This is a static model. If one recognizes that income distribution affects incentives and the ability to save and to invest in physical and human capital, then any official intervention to redistribute income or wealth will also affect adversely the growth of productivity and income—efficiency in a dynamic sense. It will do so by *definition*, since it will yield a different level of saving and a different level and pattern of investment than that which a free market would yield.

The utilitarian premise that economic values are subjective and can be revealed only through the market (or by a nearly universal consensus) is rejected by the contemporary world. We have now moved almost to the opposite extreme of insisting that the only legitimate economic values are the objective ones that are politically sanctioned and imposed by the state. The extent of the change is often hidden by claims that much official economic intervention is designed to correct "market failures." On closer examination, it usually turns out that this term is given so broad a meaning as to justify almost any intervention that some interest group favors, regardless of the impact on efficiency in the utilitarian or market sense. The contemporary socialist view that market economies are inherently unstable, prone to unemployment, inflation, "structural imbalances," and so forth unless carefully steered and extensively controlled by governments, is an example of this ideological tendency.

While it is clearly true that, in our times, governments cannot avoid imposing many objective standards on markets that are bound to impair efficiency in this strict sense, it is crucially important to understand that a tradeoff is involved. The besetting sin of contemporary economic ideologies is to assume that both efficiency and "welfare" (politically imposed) can be achieved by means of economic interventionism or economic planning. For this reason, it is important, for those who wish to resist and reverse this tendency, to grasp clearly that *the concept of economic efficiency is inseparable from the concept of a freely adjusting market*. There is no other means to economic efficiency. While considerations of economic justice (or welfare) may well justify some sacrifice of efficiency, unless this basic point is understood, the danger is that efficiency will be impaired to the point where neither efficiency nor justice is politically possible, because the community itself breaks down. Then the community will face the Hobbesian alternatives of anarchy or tyranny. *Fiat justitia pereat mundus*.

Index

absenteeism, 16, 18, 27, 32, 45, 67–68

adverse effects of increased welfare. *See* negative-sum welfare/efficiency interactions

aggregate demand, 8; and taxation, 136–138

antitax movements, 21, 99–100, 119

asset-formation. *See* worker asset-formation

autogestion, 47n, 59n

Bacon, Robert, 16, 33, 73

balance of payments, 19; Denmark's, 96–97; Germany's, 88; Netherlands', 91, 94; Norway's, 101, 104; Sweden's, 68; United Kingdom's, 74, 81, 82

Belgium, 6

beneficial effects of increased welfare. *See* positive-sum welfare/efficiency interactions

Blanc, Louis, 59n, 116

boards of directors, workers on, 46–53; *see also* individual countries

"brain drain," 32, 77–78

Bullock report, 48–49, 51

Calvinism, 11–12

Cambridge University Department of Applied Economics, 84

Canada, 6

capital: returns on, 17, 30, 33, 68, 73, 88, 93, 102; welfare effects on, 30–32

capital-broadening investment, 35, 73, 86–87, 91, 109–110; *see also* investment

capital-deepening investment, 33, 35, 73, 110; *see also* investment

cartelization, 113, 119

Cleveland, Harold van B., 6, 141–144

Coase, R.H., 143n

code on production subsidies, 125–126

codetermination, 38n; *see also* industrial democracy

collective bargaining, 40, 45, 57, 118

Confederation of British Industry (CBI), 48, 79, 81

corporate income tax, 32; *see also* individual countries

corporate state, 60

correlation analyses on welfare/efficiency interactions, 138–140

curve of output/tax relationship, 127–135

data base for economic analyses, 19, 124, 139

definitions of terms used in this book, 14–16

Delouvrier, Paul, 48

democracy: economic, 117–118; enterprise, 104; industrial, 38–61; interrelationship with socialism and neomercantilism, 113–122

Denmark: Glistrup antitax movement, 99–100; hourly compensation in manufacturing, 99, 106; international competitiveness, 96–97; nonmarket sector as percent of GDP, 17, 97; personal-income tax rates, 97; prospective developments, 111–112; taxation, 97–98; unemployment, 99; unit labor costs, 99, 107; vicious circle in, 37; welfare/efficiency interactions in, 96–100; workers' relations with trade-union leaders, 99–100; workers on boards of directors, 48, 49

"discomfort index," 138

distributive justice, 9–10; influence on trade unions, 41

distribution of income. *See* income distribution

Dutch economy. *See* Netherlands

EC. *See* European Community

economic growth rates, 21–22, 109, 111, 114, 117, 125

efficiency: concept of, 141–144; criteria, 10–12; defined, 15; interrelationship with welfare, *see* welfare/efficiency interactions

egalitarianism, 10, 41, 67, 79, 92, 95, 102, 115

Eltis, Walter, 16, 33, 73

employment, 2, 18, 20–23, 35–37; by nonmarket sector, 20–21, 63, 65, 73, 76, 85, 97

entrepreneurship, 32, 78, 80

environmental measures, 31, 103–104

European Community: cartels in, 113; Commission's views on workers' directors, 49–50; economic integration in, 4; investment planning by, 59–60; future restrictions on competition within, 119

executive remuneration, intercountry comparisons, 32–33

expenditures, public. *See* government expenditures

exports. *See* individual countries (international competitiveness)

France, 6, 110, 115, 118, 122; industrial democracy in, 47–48
future economic developments, 3–4, 108–113;
business concern over, 110–111; German business concern over, 88–91

General Agreement on Tariffs and Trade (GATT),
3, 125
Germany: concern over economic future,
88–91; executive compensation, 33; hourly
compensation in manufacturing, 87, 106; international competitiveness, 88–89; investment in industry, 86–87; nonmarket sector as
percent of GDP, 17, 86; personal-income tax
rates, 28, 86; prospective developments, 111;
rising costs of welfare system, 85–86; taxation, 85, 86; trade-union attitudes regarding
investment and productivity, 35, 51, 88,
89–91; unemployment, 85, 88, 89; unit labor
costs, 87, 107; welfare/efficiency interactions
in, 84–91; workers on boards of directors,
46–47, 49, 50–52; works councils, 42–43, 57
Glistrup. See antitax movements
government expenditures, 8, 15, 17, 18, 35–37,
108–109; as percent of GDP, 17; correlation
analyses on, 138–140; data lacking on, 19, 124;
in Denmark, 97; in Germany, 85–86, 89; in the
Netherlands, 92; in Norway, 103; in Sweden,
64, 70–71; in the United Kingdom, 72–73,
75–76, 81, 83
Great Britain. See United Kingdom

"hidden economy," 29, 93–94
hourly compensation, 106; see also individual
countries
"humanization of work," 31–33, 103–104

ID. See industrial democracy
import penetration. See individual countries
(international competitiveness)
income distribution, 8, 28–29, 40–41, 64, 92, 95,
101–102; historical background on, 9–10
income tax, 18, 27–28, 32–33; see also individual countries
incomes policy, 29, 36, 59, 98
indexing of welfare benefits, 25, 29, 70, 76, 85,
92, 97
indicators of negative-sum outcomes, 16–20
individual countries. See Denmark, Germany,
Netherlands, Norway, Sweden, United Kingdom
industrial democracy, 20, 38–61; background
on, 39–42; at boardroom level, 46–53; as enterprise democracy in Norway, 104; at shop-
floor level, 42–46 (see also works councils);
and socialist goal, 113–114; at stockholder
level, 53–57; as transforming West European

economies, 57–61
inflation, 18, 21, 66, 81, 82, 84, 88, 99; and public
expenditure, 137, 138–140
international competitiveness. See individual
countries
international economic system, 1–5, 23, 110,
120–123, 126
International Monetary Fund (IMF), 81
investment, 13, 17, 18, 21–23, 30–31, 32–33,
34–35, 36–37, 109–110; correlation analyses
on, 138–140; directive planning of, 41, 59–61,
117–120; in Denmark, 98; in Germany, 86–87,
91; in the Netherlands, 93; in Norway, 102; in
Sweden, 68; in the United Kingdom, 73
Italy, 6

job-security laws, 30–31, 110

labor: confederations, 39–40; costs in OECD
countries compared, 106–107; increased welfare's effect on, 27–30; movement in the
United States and Europe compared, 39–40;
see also individual countries, workers
laissez-faire concept, 11–12
leisure: managers' preference for, 32, 80; paid,
17, 22, 27; unpaid, 22, 61, 117; workers'
preference for, 18, 27; see also absenteeism
Lindbeck, Assar, 33

macroeconomic policy, 16–20, 26, 35–37, 108–
113, 117–118, 125, 132–139; in Denmark, 96,
98–100; in Germany, 88–91; in the Netherlands, 94–96; in Norway, 101, 104–105; in
Sweden, 65, 69–72; in the United Kingdom,
75, 81–84
management: in Britain, and class consciousness, 80; in Germany, 86; worker participation in (industrial democracy), 38–61; see also
"brain drain," entrepreneurship
marginal tax rates, 28–29, 32–33; see also individual countries
market sector: defined, 15; efficiency in, 142–
144; ID movement in, 38–61; relationship
with nonmarket sector in OECD countries,
16–19; see also subsidies
market-sector income, defined, 15
Marx, Karl, 59
Marxism, 59, 60, 115–117; diminishing power in
Europe today, 118–119
McMullen, Neil J., 6, 16, 17, 127–140
Meidner Plan, 53–56, 58, 71
mercantilism, 11; see also neomercantilism
mixed economies: advantages of, 121–122; possible transformation into socialist systems,
57–61, 113–122
model of welfare/efficiency interactions, conceptual, 124, 127–140

welfare/efficiency interactions (cont.)

background on, 8–10; income-related benefits, 14, 25, 30; indicators of adverse effects,
16–20; industrial democracy effects on,
38–61; and labor, 27–30; negative-sum,
12–23; and neomercantilism, 3–4; in the
Netherlands, 91–96; in Norway, 100–105;
positive-sum, 12–14; problem of, 8–28; prospective developments of, 108–122; in Sweden, 62–72; and technological development,
32–33; types of interactions, 24–37; in the
United Kingdom, 72–84; U.S. policy as affected by, 122–126; welfare criteria, 10–12;
and worker ownership, 56–57; of workers on
company boards, 51–53; and workers' interest in productivity, 34–35; *see also*
negative-sum and positive-sum welfare/
efficiency interactions

West Germany. *See* Germany

worker asset-formation, 53–58, 90; *see also*
profit-sharing plans

workers: adverse effects of welfare on, 27–30;
beneficial effects of welfare on, 26–27; on
boards of directors, 46–53; interest in productivity, 34–35; ownership of stock, 53–58, 90;
preference for leisure, 18, 27; *see also* industrial democracy, labor, trade unions

works councils, 38, 42–46, 53, 58

Yugoslavia, 47n, 116, 120

National Planning Association

NPA is an independent, private, nonprofit, nonpolitical organization that carries on research and policy formulation in the public interest. NPA was founded during the great depression of the 1930s when conflicts among the major economic groups—business, farmers, labor—threatened to paralyze national decision making on the critical issues confronting American society. It was dedicated, in the words of its statement of purpose, to the task "of getting [these] diverse groups to work together . . . to narrow areas of controversy and broaden areas of agreement . . . [and] to provide on specific problems concrete programs for action planned in the best traditions of a functioning democracy." Such democratic planning, NPA believes, involves the development of effective governmental and private policies and programs not only by official agencies but also through the independent initiative and cooperation of the main private-sector groups concerned. And, to preserve and strengthen American political and economic democracy, the necessary government actions have to be consistent with, and stimulate the support of, a dynamic private sector.

NPA brings together influential and knowledgeable leaders from business, labor, agriculture, and the applied and academic professions to serve on policy committees. These committees identify emerging problems confronting the nation at home and abroad and seek to develop and agree upon policies and programs for coping with them. The research and writing for these committees are provided by NPA's professional staff and, as required, by outside experts.

In addition, NPA's professional staff undertakes research designed to provide data and ideas for policy makers and planners in government and the private sector. These activities include the preparation on a regular basis of economic and demographic projections for the national economy, regions, states, and metropolitan areas; the development of program planning and evaluation techniques; research on national goals and priorities; planning studies for welfare and dependency problems, employment and manpower needs, education, medical care, environmental protection, energy, and other economic and social problems confronting American society; and analyses and forecasts of changing national and international realities and their implications for U.S. policies. In developing its staff capabilities, NPA has increasingly emphasized two related qualifications—the interdisciplinary knowledge required to understand the complex nature of many real-life problems, and the ability to bridge the gap between the theoretical or highly technical research of the universities and other professional institutions and the practical needs of policy makers and planners in government and the private sector.

All NPA reports have been authorized for publication in accordance with procedures laid down by the Board of Trustees. Such action does not imply agreement by NPA Board or committee members with all that is contained therein unless such endorsement is specifically stated.